TO THE HANDS OF THE POOR
Water and Trees

TO THE HANDS OF THE POOR

Water and Trees

Robert Chambers
N.C. Saxena
Tushaar Shah

INTERMEDIATE TECHNOLOGY PUBLICATIONS

Published by Intermediate Technology Publications
103/105 Southampton Row, London WCIB 4HH, UK.

© 1989 Robert Chambers, N.C. Saxena and Tushaar Shah

Reprint 1991

ISBN 1 85339 047 X

Printed in India at Rekha Printers Pvt. Ltd.,
A-102/1, Okhla Industrial Area Phase II, New Delhi 110 020.

Dedicated to

Jenny, Naomi and Rama

Contents

PART FOUR: PRACTICAL STRATEGY

Chapter Ten: Analysis and Action   229

Preface

We have written this book for all those concerned with rural poverty and resources: policy-makers, including political leaders, planners, technical specialists and administrators, at both Union and State level; the headquarters and field staff of Government Departments and NGOs; academics, scholars and consultants; aid agency staff; and the many journalists, lawyers and other concerned professionals and citizens who are engaged in the struggle to see what best to do.

For this book is part of that struggle. It has its origins in a seminar at the Institute of Economic Growth in Delhi. The subject was the cruel paradox of mass poverty coexisting with vast resource potentials in much of rural India. These potentials were seen to lie in changing resource access and use, and included canal irrigation, lift irrigation, land reform, wastelands development, forests, and agroforestry. Ideas were sought about approaches which would be politically and administratively feasible. Realism demanded that while the poorer would gain, the less poor would not directly lose, or could be induced to accept their loss. This helped to narrow the focus to lift irrigation and trees. Both presented large-scale potentials which had not yet been exploited. We found evidence that key aspects of both had been neglected and that the scope for benefits to the poorer were greater than commonly supposed. Evidence and argument led us logically to new policies.

Some of these policies are being adopted; some are, in the run-up to the Eighth Plan, being debated; and some are not yet on the agenda. All, we believe, are feasible and desirable. Resolutely implemented, the impact on many millions of the poorer could be dramatic.

We have been driven to conclude that official and professional misperceptions of the priorities of poor people have hindered seeing how to help them; that the efforts of NGOs are often good but overperceived, with wide indirect effects but direct impacts which are often minuscule; that a portfolio of programmes of the middle range is promising; but that, in contrast with all these, crores of the poorer could gain at once and on a vast scale by abolishing restrictions, changing regulations, and clarifying rights, supporting these reforms with multiple channel communication to inform the poor of their entitlements.

We have organised the text to make the argument and conclusions quick to grasp. The table of contents gives a full listing of headings. Each chapter starts with an abstract. Reading these gives an overview in a few minutes. Chapters 1, 2 and 3 set the framework. Chapters 4, 5 and 6 deal with lift irrigation, and chapters 7, 8 and 9 with trees. Of these, chapters 4 and 7 are about group and community initiatives, 5 and 8 about private rights and markets, and 6 and 9 about policy implications. The final chapter summarises the analytical and practical conclusions.

As co-equal authors, we have written the text and drawn these conclusions as joint efforts, at the same time dividing work by specialisation: Shah has concentrated on lift irrigation, Saxena on trees, and Chambers on the framework. To the general chapters we have all contributed. It is not in the nature of a book like this that each author can fully and finally endorse every sentence, especially those which are technical; but on matters of major importance we are in very substantial agreement.

Responsibility for the views expressed rests with us as individuals, and not with any organisation. We have tried to be careful in analysis, use of evidence, and interpretations, and have read, revised and debated the text through several revisions. All the same, errors and omissions must surely remain. We hope that readers will treat these, and points of disagreement, not as reasons for rejecting the whole, but as challenges to do better.

*   *   *   *

Many have contributed to this book. We thank the rural people who have given us their time, information and insights. They are many, and here nameless, but their contributions have been generous and fundamental. Headquarters and field staff in Government organisations and in NGOs have helped in many ways, with information, arrangements and ideas. Those who have commented on drafts or made other critical inputs, include William Bentley, Anthoney Bottrall, Kamla Chowdhry, M.L. Dantwala, G.N. Kathpalia, D.T. Lakdawala, Gilbert Levine, Niranjan Pant, S.P. Sanghal, Madhu Sarin, Anil Shah, and William Stewart; participants in workshops at the University of Roorkee, the Narendra Dev University of Science and Technology at Faizabad, and the Institute of Development Studies, Sussex; and others who will recognise their evidence and ideas. While differences of opinion remain, there is a sense in which this has been a collective effort, and to all those, named and not named, who have helped in this we express our gratitude.

Our investigations, discussions and writing have been possible through financial and administrative backing from several organisations. Institutional bases and support have been provided for us severally by the Council for Social Development, New Delhi, the Indian Council for Social Science Research, New Delhi, the Institute of Rural Management, Anand and the Institute of Development Studies at the University of Sussex. The Ford and Rockefeller Foundations made a grant to the Institute of Development Studies for the writing of the book which enabled us to meet and collaborate, and which ensured publication at a low price to make it more accessible to those for whom it is written. We also acknowledge with gratitude assistance received from other organisations including the Department of Rural Development, GOI, and the National Wastelands Development Board.

Last but not least we wish to thank those who have struggled with successive drafts of the text – Helen McLaren at IDS, Balbir Misra and Asha Thapa at CSD, and Vasantha Radhakrishnan at IRMA.

*   *   *   *

In the course of our fieldwork, reading and debate, we have changed some of our views; and we recognise that events and policies move on, and will generate new needs, new insights, and new agendas. There can be nothing finished or final, no last word, about problems as complex and intractable as rural poverty and resources. All the same, we do have a sense of having arrived at conclusions which for the present fit together and are feasible.

The test that matters, though, is action and impact. That now depends on those to whom the book is addressed. The true test is whether what we have written helps others make things better for the poorer. That we can only hope, not know. It is readers who will give the answer.

The authors

List of Figures

List of Tables

PART ONE

The Paradox of Poverty

CHAPTER ONE

Poverty and Priorities

ABSTRACT

India has the greatest concentration of rural poverty of any country in the world. Despite many development achievements, the performance of programmes directly targeted to the rural poor has been disappointing. Part of the problem is normal professional views of poverty, influenced by urban employment rather than rural livelihood, and by the need to measure poverty. Deprivation is complex, and can be understood as interlocked poverty, physical weakness, isolation, vulnerability and powerlessness. Besides income, poor people's evident priorities can be expressed as survival based on stable subsistence; security based on assets and rights; and self-respect based on independence and choice. For many poor people, security and self-respect seem to have risen in importance.

Lift irrigation and trees fit the livelihood priorities of the poor. For both resource-poor farmers and labourers, reliable and adequate irrigation raises incomes, spreads earnings to lean months of the year, reduces risk, and often removes the need for seasonal outmigration. For their part, trees provide subsistence and income through minor forest products, firewood, fodder and seasonal crops. Where they can be cut and sold freely, trees owned by poor people can enhance their security, as savings banks cashable to meet contingencies and avoid debt.

Professionals have undervalued the potentials of lift irrigation and trees for the poor. In this book we ask how it can be the poorer who benefit and gain more from their exploitation.

1.1 The Challenge

The challenge is the scale and awfulness of rural poverty in India. There are other countries where suffering is immense and prospects grim: those which have been racked by war, like Afghanistan, Angola, Eritrea, Ethiopia, Kampuchea, Mozambique, Sudan, and Uganda, and much of the vast region of Sub-Saharan Africa which is locked in debt and economic crisis. And there is China with a rural population even greater than India's. But India has one-sixth of humankind, and nowhere outside India is there such a concentration of so many rural people who are so poor. In 1988, perhaps more than 200 million rural people were below the poverty line.

The manifestations of this poverty are many and well known. The press,

and activists in voluntary agencies, repeatedly expose exploitation and violence against the poor. To landless labourers minimum wages are rarely paid.
The deprivation of women is reflected in their low life expectancy relative to
men, compared with most other countries. Bonded labour in its several forms
persists on a large scale. Every year millions of households migrate in distress
to urban areas, or more commonly to other rural areas, in their struggle to
survive. The misery of life in urban slums itself reflects the pressure of
migration, of people driven from rural areas in desperation. Successive
governments and successive Five Year Plans have confronted the task of
reducing and eliminating rural poverty and exploitation of the poor. No
other democratic government has ever had to face such a challenge.

It is all too easy to take a negative view of what has been achieved. Negative
social scientists are adept at showing what has gone wrong. But there have
been many achievements. Comparing 1985 levels with 1950, and in spite of
population more than doubling, per capita GNP still rose in real terms by 69
per cent (TSL 1986:1). Both irrigated area and foodgrain production were
roughly trebled in the same period. In the quarter century 1960 to 1985, infant
mortality was brought down from 165 to 105 (UNICEF 1987:90), and life
expectancy for women rose from 42 to 55, and that for men from 43 to 56
(WDR 1984:262 and 1986:232). Major advances were made in industrial
development, power generation, rural road construction, rural electrification, safe water supplies, education and many other aspects of development. Perhaps most important of all, as Sen has pointed out (1983), India
since Independence in 1947 has been able to intervene to prevent mass starva-
tion in famine, in contrast with China's record of many millions of deaths in
the famines of 1959 to 1961.

Of many anti-poverty policies and programmes, those which have had the
highest profile have been officially administered and targeted directly to the
rural poor. They have included three main types: for land reforms; for asset
provision; and for income and consumption support.

Land reform has again and again been identified as the change best able to
reduce poverty, and legislation has been passed in the States. In some, notably
West Bengal, Kerala and Karnataka, where there has been organised grass-
roots political support, the gains by the poor have not been negligible.
Elsewhere it is true that some redistribution has taken place to the extent that
ceiling legislation has been implemented. Land reform legislation and
threats of enforcement have also sometimes brought indirect benefits where
large landowners have sold land to smaller buyers while they can. But about
the general record there is no dispute. Those who would have lost from
effective implementation of land reforms were the less poor and more powerful, and they subverted reform at the local level. Achievements have fallen far,
far short of hopes: those with large landholdings have usually managed to
hold on to them; and in most places the landless and near-landless have
gained rather little, or nothing.

Of other anti-poverty policies and programmes, those with highest profile have been for asset provision and for income and consumption support. India is alone in the world in the scale and persistence of attempts to administer benefits direct to target groups. Programmes such as the Composite Programme for Women and Pre-school Children (1969), the Small Farmers Development Agency (SFDA) (1971), Training Rural Youth for Self-employment (TRYSEM) (1979), the Integrated Rural Development Programme (IRDP) (1979), the National Rural Employment Programme (NREP) (1980), the Development of Women and Children in Rural Areas (DWCRA) (1983), and the Rural Landless Employment Guarantee Programme (RLEGP) (1983), have sought to target and benefit the poorer in rural areas. Other special programmes have been directed to groups such as Scheduled Castes and Scheduled Tribes. The priority of these programmes is indicated by the resources dedicated to them: in the Seventh Five Year Plan (1985–90), of the order of Rs 10,000 crores (excluding bank credit) was allocated to direct targeted anti-poverty programmes of this sort. Probably in the whole of human history, no nation has so determinedly attempted positive discrimination to individual beneficiaries on such a scale.

Reviews of programmes for asset provision present a contradictory picture. To evaluate the evaluations would itself take a book. For our purposes, the question is whether such programmes as designed and implemented can achieve their objectives on a large scale and massively reduce rural deprivation.

To answer that question requires a critical look at the evidence. Most attention has been given to the largest programme, the Integrated Rural Development Programme (IRDP), for which an allocation of Rs 2,400 crores from government funds and bank credit of Rs 3,800 crores was made for the Seventh Plan period 1985-90. During the first three years of the Seventh Plan some Rs 4,400 crores were expended on the programme (GOI 1988d:17). The objective of the IRDP is to identify households below the poverty line (PL) and provide them with a productive asset through a subsidised loan so that they can rise above the PL. The assets have included animals such as milch buffaloes, milch cattle, goats, sheep and poultry; equipment such as sewing machines, camel carts, hand carts, rickshaws or bicycles for hiring out; or working capital for petty trading, tea or *pan* shops and the like.

The programme has been subject to much penetrating criticism (see e.g. Rath 1985). In-depth micro-level studies in the social anthropological mode (e.g. Hirway 1986 a and b; Copestake 1987; Kurien 1987; Dreze 1988) have presented consistently adverse findings. Wrong selection of beneficiaries, "leakages", failures of enterprises, loss of assets, saturation of small markets for produce, and the loan which puts poor people in debt so making them more vulnerable, are among the factors reported responsible. Large-scale evaluation surveys have been less unfavourable, but analysis of questionnaires and of likely responses in the interview situation suggest favourable biases in the findings, generating and sustaining what has been called "the IRDP delusion" (Dreze 1988:80–85). There is a credible case that selective perception of success cases and systemic biases in survey data have combined to mislead. The conclusions are that the very poorest rarely participate; that many of the beneficiaries have been above the poverty line; that corruption has been routine; and that a substantial proportion of the poorer beneficiaries have been made worse off by the programme. There are surely exceptions, especially where local political conditions favour the poor, as to some extent in West Bengal. But for most of the country, while current micro-level political and administrative realities persist, and contrary to some appearances and statistics, we doubt whether the IRDP can achieve its objective of massive improvement in the economic status of the poorer rural people. For a detailed critique of the IRDP, examining carefully the apparent contrast between anthropological studies and large-scale surveys see Dreze (1989).

There are dangers of negative generalising from land reform and asset provision programmes to those for direct income and consumption support. The record with famine relief is, by international standards, impressive. The major programmes which subsidise consumption by the poor such as the fair price shops and ration books, Tamil Nadu's midday meals, and Andhra Pradesh's rice at 2 rupees a kilogramme, though sometimes very costly and badly targeted, do help many of the poorest. For their part, wage and food programmes like the Maharashtra Employment Guarantee Scheme, the NREP, the RLEGP, and food-for-work programmes can provide critical support for the able-bodied poor in bad years and at bad times of the year. Some scholars, such as Rath (1985) and Hirway (1986 a and b), disenchanted with the IRDP, have argued for greater stress on such employment programmes. Whatever their benefits and potentials, however, they are vulnerable to leakages and abuses similar to those of the IRDP. However necessary and desirable they are, their main function is to provide a safety net or floor under some of the poorer and more vulnerable. They cannot and do not directly provide lasting and self-sustaining solutions.

Our conclusion is that even if all existing anti-poverty programmes were universal successes, the scale and depth of poverty are such that the case for seeking and trying other policies and measures would be strong; but that given the high costs and severe shortcomings of so many programmes, the case is overwhelming.

1.2 Starting Points

To see how best to reduce poverty, there are many starting points. Many policy-makers, analysts and development practitioners start with clear ideas of what should be done. Some of these spring from ideological principles— Marxist, socialist, Gandhian, humanist, or neo-classical, among others. These principles affirm and indicate the primacy of certain objectives and certain means of achieving them. Others start from specialised professional stances, whether those of administrators, agricultural engineers, agronomists, animal scientists, doctors, economists, educationalists, engineers, extensionists, foresters, health workers, lawyers, plant pathologists, seed breeders, soils scientists, veterinarians, or others. Trained in specialised disciplines, they bring their skills to bear on the sectors of their competence, and give priority to those problems and solutions which their training has taught them to identify. Yet others, mainly academic social scientists, take a negative view of anti-poverty programmes and of "development", and see obstacles in social relations and exploitation more readily than solutions. Others again, mainly practitioners and physical and biological scientists, take a more positive view, and see practical physical solutions more readily than obstacles. Many of these outsiders to rural life are confident that they are right and that they know both the problem and the solutions.

The failure in practice of so many normal professional solutions points towards two other, less familiar and less comfortable, starting points. One is to examine the perceptions and priorities of professionals—those normal, non-poor, urban-based and numerate members of elites who define poverty and what should be done about it. The other is to examine the perceptions and priorities of the poor themselves. Neither has received much attention in anti-poverty discussions. Most professionals—politicians, bureaucrats, scientists, academics and others, and including ourselves—have plunged into debate and action in the middle, without questioning what has brought us there, what we are conditioned to see and to believe, or what others see and believe. We have had neither time nor incentive to examine ourselves and our predispositions, nor the poor and theirs. In contrast with normal professional practice, our starting point here is different: it is to stand back and analyse the divergent views of deprivation and priorities held by these two groups—professionals and poor people themselves.

1.3 The Professional Poverty Trap

Professionals' views of poverty can be seen as part of the problem. Many underperceive rural poverty. "Rural development tourism", the phenomenon of brief, rural visits, has anti-poverty biases (Chambers 1983:10-27) which are spatial (tarmac, roadside, accessible), project (to places where there are special projects), personal (meeting those who are more influential and better off, and men rather than women), seasonal (concentrated in the cool, dry seasons after harvest when people are less poor, better fed and healthier), diplomatic (courtesy to the less poor impeding contact with the poorer), and professional (limited to narrow concerns of professional interest, not the holism of deprivation). In consequence, much rural poverty remains unperceived.

The biases of rural development tourism are compounded by the life cycles of many professionals, whether officials, academics, or even sometimes those who work in voluntary agencies. When young and inexperienced, they may work near the grass roots, in less accessible areas, and based in villages or small urban centres. But as they grow older, seniority and promotion draw them inwards to larger and larger urban and administrative centres, and upwards higher and higher in organisational hierarchies. As they become more influential, so they become more remote from field realities, their field visits become more vulnerable to anti-poverty biases, and their own direct experience grows more out-of-date. Many ties and pressures hold them in the city: one Secretary for Agriculture was even forbidden by his Minister to make any rural visit on a week day. Perversely, then, those responsible for rural and agricultural policy are precisely those who are most tied down in urban areas, and least able to gain new unbiased and up-to-date field experience.

The biases of rural visits and of life cycles are, though, only some of the more obvious parts of the problem. Less obvious, but at least as serious for policy and practice, are the structures of professional thinking. Two deserve special attention—the urban concept of employment as contrasted with rural livelihood, and effects of the need to measure poverty.

EMPLOYMENT THINKING AND LIVELIHOOD THINKING

The first defect of normal professional analysis is "employment thinking". Employment, in its common and commonsense meaning, is a concept of the urban, industrial, formal sector economy where people have jobs. It implies employers, employees, and cash remuneration. Transferred to rural and subsistence conditions, it often does not fit. Rural people are often members of small or marginal farm families, or landless labourer families, and often piece together a living through many different activities and enterprises.

For them, the concept of livelihood fits better than employment. Livelihood is used here to describe an adequate and secure stock and flow of cash and food for the household and its members throughout the year, and the means to meet contingencies. The Greek proverb "the fox knows many things, but the hedgehog knows one big thing" can apply here. Employees in formal urban and industrial situations tend to be "hedgehogs", with one job, one employer, and one source of income, while many (though not all) poorer rural people are "foxes", seeking livelihoods by exploiting a repertoire of varied activities at different seasons. To help a hedgehog usually requires organisation and political action. To help a fox also entails strengthening the repertoire and adding to it.

MEASUREMENT BIAS

The word "poverty" is itself a problem. It is used in two different senses. In its first, broader and popular sense, it is a synonym for deprivation, and covers many aspects of hardship. In its second, narrower and technical sense, it refers to what professionals measure in assessments of poverty. Problems arise when these two meanings are confused.

Planners and policy makers need measurements of deprivation in order to identify priorities and to know what progress is being made in reducing it. Poverty lines which measure flows—either of income or of consumption—

have a long history, originating in urban conditions where workers have regular wages. In India, the National Sample Survey (NSS) provides a national coverage for planning and policy purposes, and measures not income, on which good data are difficult to obtain, but consumption. NSS consumption data are therefore used to assess changes in poverty throughout the country, and we ourselves use them for assessing relative poverty in different regions. But they indicate not deprivation, in its many aspects, but only reported measurements of one aspect, consumption.

The professional problem here is that the narrower technical meaning of poverty subsumes the broader popular sense of the word. Phrases are used like "time trend in poverty", "the percentage of the population in poverty", and "variation in the extent of poverty" referring not to deprivation, nor even to wealth and income, but to NSS records of consumption. This obvious point is recognised by thoughtful analysts (see for example, Thakur 1985; Ahluwalia 1986), but also often overlooked. Deprivation is then seen as poverty, and poverty is seen as what has been measured and is available for analysis. Deprivation and poverty are then defined, not by the wants and needs of the poor, but by the wants and needs of professionals.

1.4 The Nature of Deprivation

Recognising the limitations of the normal professional view of poverty raises anew questions about the nature of deprivation and how to reduce it.

Deprivation has many dimensions and definitions. It can be seen as ascribed: people are born into groups, such as Scheduled Castes and Scheduled Tribes, with inescapable social disadvantages, and women are born into an underprivileged gender. Solutions are then sought in programmes targeted to those groups and that gender. Or deprivation can be seen as locational. Poorer people are concentrated in certain zones and districts. Solutions are then sought in special regional or district programmes such as the Drought-Prone Areas Programme (1970), the Tribal Area Development Programme (1972), the Hill Areas Development Programme (1975) and the Desert Development Programme (1977). Or deprivation can be seen as lack of access to services and resources, such as education, health, transport, convenient clean water, fuel and so on. Solutions are then sought in the spread of schools, clinics and health workers, roads and buses, water supplies, community woodlots, and the like. These normal approaches through special programmes for disadvantaged groups and areas, and for spreading services, have their strengths but have rarely in practice been based on or drawn from the analysis and priorities of deprived people themselves. Two further approaches can serve as correctives: the first is to use "outsiders'" categories to separate out dimensions of deprivation, and the second is to enquire into the priorities of the poor themselves.

Outsiders' categories will always be open to question and to modification in the light of what poor people themselves want and need. Many sets of categories are possible. One with some explanatory and prescriptive power is to separate deprivation into five clusters of disadvantage: physical weakness, isolation, poverty, vulnerability and powerlessness. Physical weakness refers to lack of strength, undernutrition, poor health, physical disability and a high ratio of dependents to active adults; isolation refers to physical remoteness, ignorance and lack of education, and lack of access to services and information; poverty refers to lack of income (flows of food and cash) and of wealth (stocks of assets); vulnerability to exposure to contingencies and the danger of becoming poorer and more deprived; and powerlessness to inability to adapt, cope and choose, and weakness in the face of exploitation and demands by the powerful.

These five clusters of disadvantage interlock and reinforce each other to form a deprivation trap (figure 1.1).

They also present alternative points of direct attack: physical weakness through feeding programmes, health services, inoculations, and other preventive health programmes; isolation through roads, communications, education and extension; poverty through redistribution of assets and works programmes; vulnerability through social insurance; and finally, powerlessness

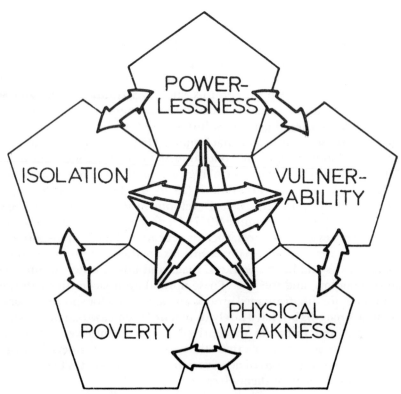

Figure 1.1: The deprivation trap
Source: Chambers 1983: 112

through organisation of and by the poor and legal aid. The easiest and often most successful programmes have been directed against physical weakness and isolation. Direct targeted programmes against poverty, like the IRDP, have as we have seen, at best a mixed record, while programmes to reduce vulnerability and powerlessness have mostly been less prominent and less successful. Programmes which are directed against one aspect of deprivation may also aggravate another: the IRDP can increase vulnerability and even powerlessness, by entailing indebtedness and new obligations to patrons who arrange the loan and the transfer of the asset. In contrast, any programme which effectively reduces vulnerability and powerlessness will enable poor people to stand more on their own feet, adapt to changing conditions, and have greater freedom to make their own decisions and choices.

1.5 The Priorities of the Poor

Up to this point, the argument has been conducted in terms of outsiders' categories and ideas of priority. But the dangers of such outsiders' analysis, and the importance of eliciting and meeting the priorities of poor rural people themselves, have more and more been recognised. Writing about definitions of deprivation can be yet another form of professional projection and arrogance. If the poor are to define their condition, and their priorities for alleviating it, then they should speak for themselves. This requires professionals to make careful, sensitive and sustained efforts to enable poor people to articulate their needs and priorities. But to wait and wait until much more is understood in "our" knowledge system could be as harmful as to assert dogmatically that we know what the poor want. The best approach seems, with what evidence we have, to put forward working categories and hypotheses, expecting and welcoming their modification for different places, peoples, and periods as more is learnt and understood from the poor themselves. In doing this, we have found especially useful work by Gulati (1981), Jodha (1985), Breman (1985), and Hirway (1986b). Gulati studied the lives of five poor working women in Kerala with care and described them in detail. Jodha, in villages in Rajasthan, used anecdotal material and discussions with villagers to identify variables which villagers themselves considered indicators of change in their economic status. Breman, in South Gujarat, spent much time with very poor people, including rural migrants. Hirway conducted field research in Gujarat involving a survey and long discussions with participants and non-participants in government anti-poverty programmes. What follows here is not limited to these sources, but does, often without direct acknowledgement, draw substantially on them.

The most basic point is made by Jodha. His study compares households in two villages in Rajasthan. He first surveyed them in 1964–66, and then again some twenty years later in 1982–84. During the second period, he elicited from villagers their own criteria and indicators of economic status. He then separated out those households—35 of the total of 95—whose per capita incomes at constant prices had fallen during the twenty years by 5 per cent or more.

Astonishingly, he then found that these households were on average better off according to 37 of the 38 criteria of economic status given by the villagers. (The one exception was milk consumption reduced by the emergence of an external milk market.) The significance of this finding is not to suggest that income is unimportant: to the contrary, some of the criteria were linked with income, for example, indicators of consumption, and non-reliance on low pay-off activities such as food gathering and badly paid part-time petty jobs. It is, rather, to suggest that poor people's priorities include much more than just those two—income and consumption—which are given primacy by outsider professionals in poverty line thinking and in anti-poverty programmes.

Three other qualifications apply to any generalisations. First, people's wants, needs and priorities change over time. Whole societies and their citizens shift in their aspirations. There is nothing static about what people want, or their relative priorities. Second, the criteria and priorities of poor people vary—by person, gender, age, ethnic group and social custom, caste, occupation, experience, local conditions, seasons, and degree of deprivation. To allocate relative significance between these is not easy, and will itself vary, but two of widespread importance are gender and degree of deprivation. Third, professionals and poor people may have a tendency, when they interact, to concentrate on physical and economic aspects of deprivation, to the neglect of those which are social, psychological and spiritual. But as Appadurai has pointed out (1985:6), measures of standard of living in the aggregate lose:

> the critical qualitative dimension which must belong to any robust conception of the standard of living. Components of this qualitative dimension include: the perception of security in livelihood, the sense of freedom from harassment and abuse at home and at work, the feeling of dignity in day-to-day transactions, the belief in the reliability of officialdom, the expectation (or lack of it) that life will improve for one's offspring and so forth.

Starting with the physical, there may be widespread agreement among poor adults in giving priority to health. This includes freedom from sickness and disability, adequate food, long life, low infant and child mortality, and healthy children. These are obvious and near universal human aspirations, but can be overlooked in any narrowly economic analysis. That said, a second, and linked, priority can be captured in the concept of a secure, adequate and sustainable livelihood. However, evidence from poor people themselves suggests that their priorities include much more than health and livelihood, and that putting their priorities first means also including their social and psychological needs.

On the basis of the evidence we have been able to study, we postulate that for many people there is a hierarchy of three objectives or priorities. These have links with income, but are additional to and different from it. All three can overlap and coexist, but as the lower ones are more and more met, so the higher ones become more significant. The three are:

survival	based on stable subsistence
security	based on assets and rights
self-respect	based on independence and choice

SURVIVAL

For the desperate poor, basic incomes and consumption for survival are the prime preoccupation. In the dimensions of deprivation, they link with physical weakness and poverty. They also fit the normal focus of professional attention to wage rates, numbers of days worked, seasonal slack periods, and subsistence and cash flows. Professionals tend to see the poor as "living-from-hand-to-mouth", which is indeed the case for the very severely deprived. Their strategies include stinting, begging, borrowing, casual labour, craft work, collecting common property resources, micro-cultivation, seasonal migration, family-splitting, reciprocity with poor relatives and neighbours, seeking patrons, theft, and any number of petty occupations.

The priority of subsistence for survival is reflected in the intent and design of government anti-poverty programmes and policies like the NREP, the RLEGP, the IRDP itself with its aims of raising beneficiary households above the poverty line, the programmes for ration books and fair price shops, and controlled low prices for basic consumption goods.

One dimension of survival and subsistence is adequate and stable flows of income and consumption round the whole year. At certain seasons many of the poorest rural households are driven to activities with very low returns. One of the criteria of wellbeing in Jodha's villages was reduced dependence on activities which were low pay-off or socially damaging such as gathering food, fuel or fodder, undertaking part-time petty jobs (for example fencing to get one meal as a wage), withdrawing children from school during the crop season to work and earn, and migrating seasonally for work. The grave suffering endured by rural migrant workers has been observed and recounted by Breman (1985). The vast majority of rural migrants would probably prefer not to move if they could only contrive adequate year-round livelihoods in their places of normal residence. The personal and social costs of migration are high—in family splitting, physical and psychological stress, vulnerability, prevention of children's education, and insecurity of possessions left behind. Women left behind by male migrants suffer increased work burdens and more difficulty in basic survival (Jetley 1987). Adequate and stable incomes in one place are likely to be high in the priorities of the very poor.

SECURITY

Security is more easily overlooked. In the dimensions of deprivation, it links with vulnerability. It concerns the ability to meet contingencies without further impoverishment, and depends on rights, assets and access to money whether through savings, sale of assets or loans.

The value of security to poor people has been underperceived partly through employment thinking, measurement bias, and the obvious priority of subsistence for survival for the desperate poor. These have diverted attention from the importance to poor people of their net asset position and their ability to meet contingencies. Security for a formal sector urban employee can be sought through improved terms of service, medical insurance and sickness benefits, pension funds, and the like. Security for a poor rural household has in the past come more from patron-client and mutual sharing and borrowing arrangements, but these, worldwide as well as in India, have weakened and have also become less acceptable to poor people themselves. Poor rural people have a horror of debt. Yet they still need cash to meet contingencies such as sickness, accidents, food shortages, bribes, legal fees, ceremonies, dowry, bridewealth, funerals, theft, damage by fire, flood, or storm, the death of an animal, and so on. Moreover, the costs of some contingencies, notably health treatment and dowries, have risen. These trends have left many poor people more exposed than before, deprived of loans from their traditional patrons, and subject now to heavier demands for large lumpsum payments. Urban-based professionals have been slow to recognise this new need.

The policy implication is to enable poor households to own and command assets and reserves which they can cash or use to meet contingencies without having to sacrifice their independence, security and peace of mind by getting into debt.

SELF-RESPECT

Self-respect, and the independence it usually implies, are terms which may not exactly capture the reality of aspiration, but there is evidence that something like self-respect and independence are increasingly desired by poor rural people. In the dimensions of deprivation, this links with powerlessness. There is a danger here of imputing to and imagining for people values which they may not hold, and of using words and concepts they do not use. All the same, self-respect and independence, including freedom from humiliating subservience, seem to matter to them more and more. Hirway emphasises the the distaste her informants felt for debts, not just because of high interest rates, or forced labour for family members, but also because what followed from them included "abuses and insults", "helplessness, insults and pain", and "touching the feet of the lenders and swallowing insults and abuses" (1986b: 147, 142, 144). They said "We always have to touch the feet of the rich to get a loan" (ibid: 155). Perhaps too this is some of the significance of the first category listed by Jodha, in reporting the ways villagers perceived change in their own economic status—"reduced indispensibility of support/mercy and resources of traditional patrons, landlords and resourceful people . . .". Jodha reports possible manifestations of this as indicated by villagers to be changes in:

— the extent household members engage as attached or semi-attached labourers
— households having their shelter on landlords'/moneylenders' land
— extent of off-season food borrowing from patrons
— extent of seed loan in kind from patrons
— extent of marketing of produce through patrons only and diversification of sources of periodical borrowing (1985:6)

There would seem to have been major social change in the value given to self-respect and independence. A typical observation, which we can confirm from much of our own experience, is that of Etienne (1985:98) on a revisit to long-term informants, whom he found had lost their "cowed demeanour" and were more decisive.

The priority and balance between survival, security and self-respect varies. To all generalisations there are exceptions. There are many of desperate poor for whom immediate income and consumption, through paid work for those who can work, and through direct support for those who can not, is the first priority. Nor do we neglect income and consumption above the level of survival. Higher and stable incomes are a major underpinning for security and self-respect, enabling poor people to choose and have more of what they want and need. Incomes underlie all three priorities and shift the balance up the scale: as incomes rise, so security and self-respect become more prominent. It is not just the social changes described, but also the improvements in economic status of many of the poor, in some areas at least, which have given security and self-respect a higher priority now than in the past.

1.6 Water, Trees and Livelihoods: The Fit

For the poor to gain better livelihoods through access to and command over natural resources, the most obvious resource is land. The greatest opportunity lies in land reform, with changes in tenure and redistribution of land to the landless and land-poor. Most of the more productive land is in private hands, and its equitable redistribution presents the greatest, most obvious and most direct means for providing sustainable livelihoods for the poorer. But in the short and perhaps medium term we do not see much prospect in most States of the major political change necessary as a precondition for effective land redistribution.

In the meantime, the poorer in rural areas remain either landless or resource-poor farm families. For them, support for better livelihoods can be sought in several other ways. These include non-farm activities, generating labour shortages, providing better paid work on more days of the year for those who need it, cheap food through public distribution systems, and more productive and less risk-prone farming for RPFs.

Nothing in this book should be taken as weakening the case for land reform or for other programmes which effectively help the poorer. But beyond and in addition to these better known approaches, the question is how well the other two great resource potentials, for lift irrigation and for trees, fit or can be made to fit the livelihood needs of the poorer. To our knowledge, neither has been adequately analysed from this livelihood perspective. We will describe the livelihood potentials of each from the points of view of subsistence and income, seasonality and migration, and security and self-respect.

WATER FROM LIFT IRRIGATION

Change from rainfed to lift irrigation agriculture usually leads to increased intensities of cultivation, reduced risks of crop failure, higher inputs, and higher and more stable production, incomes and employment, with corresponding effects for the rural poorer.

i) *Subsistence and income*

The subsistence and income effects of new irrigation for RPFs and for landless labourers are usually strongly positive, but they differ in form.

For RPFs the most obvious effects are from increased production, whether for subsistence or for sale, leading to higher incomes (unless prices for produce fall so much as to offset gains). For RPFs irrigation means more productive work on their land, and the increased intensities associated with irrigation give them productive work on more days of the year. With irrigation, an RPF family which under rainfed conditions worked part-time for others, may cease to do so, and be able to give more timely and adequate attention to its own crops. Production and income are thus usually higher and more stable.

For labourers the most obvious subsistence and income gains from new irrigation come from work on more days of the year, especially where a second or third cultivation season is added. Reliable and adequate irrigation raises employment. A study by Silliman and Lenton (1987) reviewed evidence from 45 micro-studies, 25 of them from India, and found that with few exceptions they confirmed a positive relationship between irrigation and employment, especially from increased cropping intensity. One study (Mehra 1976) which disaggregated the employment effects of irrigation and of high-yielding varieties (HYVs) found the contribution of irrigation to employment to be greater than that of HYVs.

The sharp contrast for male labourers between irrigated and unirrigated conditions is illustrated by two West Bengal villages studied by Ghosh (1984, 1985), and represented in figure 1.2. In the irrigated village there was virtually no dead season, but work all round the year, with additional immigration of seasonal labourers at the peak periods. In the unirrigated village there were two severe gaps with almost no work, implying that labourers must either seek other low paid local work, or migrate, or suffer serious deprivation. Few can have had adequate livelihoods. In contrast, high intensities of irrigation appear livelihood-intensive for labourers, filling in the slacks and providing for a continuous flow of cash and food to the household.

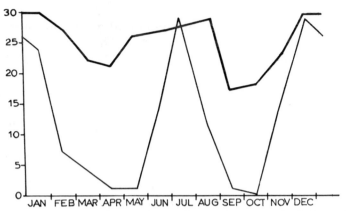

Figure 1.2: Average number of days of employment of adult male casual labourers in two West Bengal villages
— an irrigated village in Burdwan District
— an unirrigated village in Bankura District
Source: Ghosh cited in Chambers 1988:12

Other common benefits of irrigation to labourers are often, though not always, a rise in daily wage rates; more reliable employment and income; and where labourers have to buy food, lower food prices when higher production from irrigation brings prices down.

ii) *Seasonality and migration*

The countermigration benefits of irrigation have not received the attention they deserve. When two or three cultivations a year replace one, the need of labourers and RPFs to migrate diminishes and may disappear. Effects on the quality of life can be sharp. Permanent migration to urban slums has its own forms of misery, as so painfully presented in *City of Joy*, the well-researched novel of Lapierre (1986). Rural seasonal migration is perhaps usually worse, as Breman (1985) has described for landless labourers in Gujarat. Family splitting may take place, with the old and infirm left behind with perhaps a young girl of school age to look after them. The uncertainties and deprivations of walking, camping and seeking work can be harrowing. The rewards are low and often leave little or nothing saved. Seasonal labour migration is often forced migration, a risky strategy of the desperate in their struggle to survive.

In contrast, when irrigation ends the need to migrate, families can stay together. It is less difficult to send children to school. As in one part of Maharashtra, girls may for the first time be sent to school (IFAD 1984:29). House improvements are easier to undertake. Possessions are less vulnerable to theft. Moreover there are indirect gains to other poor people in the areas to which the outmigrants formerly went, since competition for work is reduced and wages may even rise.

iii) *Security and self-respect*

Irrigation also protects against the impoverishment of having to dispose of assets or take debts. It is not just that work and incomes rise. It is also that they are more reliable. In a bad monsoon, rainfed crops may fail, but crops irrigated from groundwater usually yield well, even if the groundwater table falls. Groundwater is thus a cushion or buffer against bad years, and the deprivation and indebtedness they otherwise entail. The dangers of having to dispose of assets, as when RPFs have to mortgage or sell land to buy food or meet debts, are diminished. For Bangladesh, Howes (1985:114) has described how irrigation by poor families with handpumps has arrested their slide into landlessness.

Irrigation can also liberate from demeaning social relations. With a reliable supply of irrigation water to a small or marginal farm, or with reliable employment where demand for labour exceeds supply, the need to maintain good relations with moneylenders and employers is less. There is a danger, for the poor, that employers will seek to reduce their labour needs by growing labour-sparing crops or mechanising. In India, though, it seems more common for irrigation to bring a sharp net increase in labour demand. This means that labourers' hassle finding work diminishes and labour relations may be transformed, with a shift in the balance of power towards labourers. With irrigation, they need to go less far looking for work, and to spend less time and suffer less stress travelling, searching and supplicating for work. For RPFs and landless labourers alike, it ceases to be so necessary to "touch the shoes of the rich" as insurance against those dreaded bad seasons or bad times of a year when food runs out and loans are needed to survive. Irrigation thus supports self-respecting independence.

TREES

The livelihood effects of trees have not been a focus for comparative study. Like irrigation, they have a counterseasonal quality and role in livelihoods. Their deep roots tap soil moisture or groundwater long after rainfed surface crops dry up, and they can photosynthesise and be productive and useful in various ways for much more of the year. They are less vulnerable than ground crops to bad years of rainfall. Trees are perennials but some produce seasonal crops, and all trees accumulate biomass year by year until they die. They are thus partly drought-proofed, and many can provide both crops and assets. Their livelihood effects can be examined under the same headings as for lift irrigation.

i) *Subsistence and income*

Trees can be on forest, revenue or other public land, or on private land. Rights and access to trees and their products vary widely. Where poor people have rights of usufruct, whether in forests or on common or private land, trees can provide for subsistence and income in many ways. The rich litany of non-timber forest and tree products includes edible fruits, nuts, roots and condiments; wild animals, insects and honey; waxes, resins, gums and dyes; medicaments and drugs; leaves, bamboos, and canes; and much else. But fodder and firewood are perhaps the most widespread in their collection and use. Tree fodders, grasses and browse for animals are of enormous importance, and in the Himalayan foothills are the major sources of nitrogen which maintains soil fertility on farms. For many of the poor, especially women headloaders, collecting, transporting and selling firewood from forests is basic to their subsistence strategy. For others, it is picking, stacking and selling leaves for plates or for *bidis*. For many millions of tribals, forest products are their main means of subsistence and source of income. For many RPFs, too, trees on their land are key components in their farming systems, and stabilise and supplement their subsistence and income.

ii) *Seasonality and migration*

In many livelihood strategies of the poor, trees are a counterseasonal element (Chambers and Longhurst 1986). Tree-related activities can be season-bound, as with collecting fruits, nuts and leaves, and the seasons when they become available may or may not coincide with agricultural labour peaks. Where they come at other times of the year, they can fill in the troughs in labour demand. The picking of tendu leaves (sec 7.2) is an example, occurring as it does in the lean, dry season. Other tree-related activities, like collecting and selling firewood, or making charcoal, are less time- and season-bound than crop-related activities, and can be saved up for the slack season. Moreover, in bad years, sale of trees can provide a means of getting by: during the drought of 1987 some water supplies failed in the lift irrigation projects of the Sadguru Foundation in Panchmahals District in Gujarat, but some farmers avoided distress migration by selling trees they had grown on their land as part of a social forestry programme (Jagawat 1988). Tree fodders, too, support year-round livestock strategies in which animals can remain in the same place instead of having to migrate, with all the loss of condition and risk of disease which that can mean. Grasses usually dry up and become less palatable and less nutritious as dry seasons progress, but many tree fodders are flush and green at those times, and can be cut and fed to animals, bridging the fodder gap of the late dry season before the monsoon.

For both people and livestock, thus, trees support counterseasonal strategies, filling in the slack seasons, and reducing the need to migrate.

iii) *Security and self-respect*

Perhaps even more important than subsistence and anti-migration effects are the actual and potential contributions of trees to security and self-respect. Worldwide, evidence has accumulated of the use by poor people of trees as savings banks and as means to meet contingencies (Chambers and Leach 1987).

Trees as savings banks and cashable assets for poor people have striking advantages—cheap establishment, often high rates of appreciation where water supply is adequate and trees survive, divisibility on sale, and sometimes the ability to regenerate through coppicing when cut. Their main disadvantages can be insecure rights, prohibitions on cutting and selling, a long gestation period, problems of marketing and price, and risks of loss. But in general, trees come out well compared with other assets. Jewellery, livestock, land and bank deposits grow in value more slowly, and none of them coppice when cashed.

Trees can thus provide security through means to meet contingencies. These may be occasions when wood itself is needed, as for marriage feasts or funeral pyres (Vidyarthi 1984:829). More significantly, they are used to deal with other big needs and emergencies. In Tamil Nadu it has long been a practice to grow casuarina trees as savings towards a daughter's dowry or for a child's education. Slater wrote in 1918 that

> a plot of barren land planted with casuarina is a splendid savings bank for a ryot who can foresee a period of heavy expense in six or seven years' time: as, the marriage of a daughter, or the education of a·son at the University (Slater 1918:5)

Trees can also be used to deal with sudden emergencies which are not foreseen, through cutting and selling them to meet a major health expenditure, a bribe, a fine or a legal expense.

The value of trees in strategies for savings and security is enhanced by their use to obtain credit and liquidate debt. Concerning credit, Hill reports from her field research in Karnataka that:

> the possibility of letting out small plots for wood planting provides impoverished men with a reliable type of credit, since the lumpsum granted them at the outset is automatically liquidated by the landowner's share of the net value of the wood when it is sold, which usually agreed as one half (Hill 1982:159)

An example of liquidating a debt is provided by a farmer, Kalji Chaatra of Thala Village in Panchmahals District, Gujarat, who planted 200 eucalyptus on a small plot of land, and later sold them to redeem an acre of land he had pledged to raise money to marry his son. As these cases illustrate, tree-growing can be a strategy for avoiding or escaping debt. In the Karnataka practice, not only is credit obtained and indebtedness avoided, but at the end of the lease the lessor receives half of the net value of the wood as a further lumpsum; nor is there any interest on the credit to be paid in the interval. In the Panchmahals example, it is noteworthy that it did not take long to repay. In good growing and market conditions, the appreciation in value of trees can be like a high interest rate in a savings bank. Poor people with suitable small plots of land can then accumulate wealth in trees fast enough to pay off debts even when interest rates on those debts are high.

Trees have, thus, a potential for liberating poor people from debt and dependence. In the right conditions, trees as poor people's savings banks, reduce vulnerability and provide cashable assets which can replace and substitute for demeaning and dependent relations with moneylenders and patrons.

1.7 **Professional Neglect**

Despite the excellent fit between lift irrigation and trees on the one hand, and poor people's priorities—for subsistence and incomes, slack season support to avoid migration, and security and self-respect—on the other, these connections have received little attention from professionals. They have not fitted dominant professional and bureaucratic specialisations.

Groundwater and lift irrigation have been "minor" irrigation, compared with the more prestigious "major" irrigation by large canals. Groundwater and lift irrigation have been mainly in the private sector and dispersed in small units, not in the public sector and manifest in large physical works like dams and canals. Even within departments of government charged with Minor Irrigation, lift irrigation has been a poor relation to irrigation by surface flow from minor irrigation dams, defined to include those with command areas up to 2,000 hectares. Nor has it been in the interests of Irrigation Departments wishing to construct large canal irrigation systems to emphasise the competing potentials of groundwater and lift irrigation. For their part, until recently, most economists have concerned themselves with macro-statistics and with power supply to the agricultural sector rather than with field-level economics, overlooking the significance of the sale of pumped water and of water markets. Moreover, the perspectives of livelihoods, employment, wages, counterseasonality and migration, and security and self-respect, have not been part of the normal professional or bureaucratic concerns of those involved with lift irrigation. Rather, attention has often concentrated on the much perceived and emphasised dangers of overexploitation of groundwater.

Similarly, Forest Departments have been mainly concerned with protection and production forestry on forest land, especially for timber. Subsistence from forest trees is part of "minor" forest products, a parallel with "minor" irrigation. The growing of trees outside forests—on revenue wastelands, and more so on private lands, have not been traditional concerns of foresters. The perspective of livelihoods has had low priority, and until recently tree fodders and minor forest produce did not receive anything like the attention given to timber. Nor has it been in the interests of those concerned with the protection of trees in forests, and their publicly and privately profitable exploitation, to consider or promote tree planting for the poor. Indeed the idea of poor people having secure access of trees within forest boundaries has been anathema. Although changes are taking place, the attitude has been conservationist and custodial, with those whose livelihoods depended on forest products regarded more as a danger and nuisance than as collaborating managers.

Paradoxically, the low professional attention to minor irrigation, minor forest products, trees outside forests, and the priorities of the poor for livelihoods, has preserved potential which is still unappropriated and undeveloped, and so still available for the poor. Lift irrigation and trees fit well with the needs and priorities of the poor—for subsistence and income, for stable year-round livelihoods, and for security and self-respect—and present untapped potentials and opportunities for them. In the normal processes of development, most of the gains go to the rich and less poor. The question we confront in this book is how the poorer can capture more of these potentials and gain more from these opportunities.

CHAPTER TWO

The Poor and the Potentials

ABSTRACT

Rural deprivation can be described as of two types: the core poverty of the landless or near landless in accessible areas with flat, fertile, and often irrigated lands; and the peripheral poverty of those in remoter hinterlands, usually with undulating and less fertile lands and rainfed agriculture. Core poverty is concentrated especially in the Eastern Gangetic basin and peripheral poverty especially in Madhya Pradesh and neighbouring regions. Together these comprise a "poverty square", with at least two-thirds of the national total for rural population below the poverty line and with massive untapped potentials for lift irrigation and for trees.

Nationally, potential benefits from lift irrigation have been understated both absolutely and relative to canal irrigation. Estimates of groundwater potential have risen and continue to rise, in our assessment from the old estimate of 40 m ha gross area irrigable to 80 m ha. Lift irrigation water is better controlled, more productively used, and more valuable, than that from canals, and with new agricultural technology its value has risen.

With good soil moisture, trees can be poor people's pumps, growing by lifting their own water. On degraded lands, estimated at 84 m ha (36 forest, 12 revenue, 21 uncultivated private, 13 cultivated and 2 strips), the biological potential is often in the range of 5 to 50 times current production for biomass and for minor or non-wood forest products. For most tree and forest products past demand has exceeded supply and real prices have risen. Future demand prospects are good, especially for minor forest products, fuelwood and timber.

Each of 12 States which account for 94 per cent of the rural poor, has substantial groundwater potential and/or reclaimable wastelands per poor family, indicating vast scope for generating and diversifying livelihoods for the poor.

2.1 Poverty of Core and Periphery

In this book we are mainly concerned with direct benefits to poor people through their command over, and access to, resources. It is true that there can be indirect gains for them from the development of natural resources, through multiplier effects and trickle-down; and there is a large and learned literature on the indirect benefits to poorer people that flow, or do not flow, from agricultural growth (Griffin 1974; Bell et al. 1982; Mellor and Desai 1986; Hazell and Ramasami 1988). But for livelihoods with security and self-respect, it is usually better for the poor if they themselves command rights to assets, if it is they themselves who appropriate, own and exploit the resources. This they can best do if they live close to these resources. There are possibilities of in-migration to areas where unused or underused resources present opportunities, but this has two shortcomings: first, those who already live there either have exclusive rights to their local resources, or are strongly placed to exclude outsiders; and second, those who are able to migrate and settle, except as labourers, tend to be the less poor, with strong families and some resources in cash and kind. For the poorer, the opportunity lies more in undeveloped and unappropriated resources close to where they live, especially, as we shall explore below, those from water for lift irrigation, and those from trees.

Despite the diversity of rural deprivation and resources in India, two patterns can be seen: deprivation within the cores or economic heartlands, core poverty; and deprivation of the peripheries or economic hinterlands, peripheral poverty.

This distinction is supported by Dasgupta's (1975) comparative analysis of 126 villages studied by five Agro-Economic Research Centres in the fifties and early sixties. Dasgupta found that villages polarised into those ("A" villages) which were more accessible to towns, larger, more irrigated, with greater concentration of landholdings and more landlessness, and those ("B" villages) which were remoter, smaller, with less or no irrigation, more equal landholdings and less landlessness. While much has changed in the three decades since the surveys were conducted, the features noted are a matter of common observation including our own. They are also associated with different endowments of ground and surface water, public land, and potential for trees. Core (or heartland) and periphery (or hinterland) conditions are contrasted in table 2.1. In sum, in core areas, groundwater tends to be the more important resource, although trees and agroforestry can be very significant for core area RPFs. In peripheral areas, in contrast, degraded land—forest revenue and private—is more abundant, and usually has potential for trees and the ratio of surface lift irrigation potential to groundwater lift potential tends to be higher.

Core and peripheral poverty often share insecure tenure of land, but in other ways differ. In core poverty there is more landlessness; non-agricultural activities tend to be more significant in poor people's strategies, and dependence and exploitation are more mediated by social relations, within village society. RPFs in core areas are poor because they have little land and often unreliable or non-existent access to irrigation water. Peripheral poverty, in contrast, is linked more with water scarcity, resource degradation, lack of infrastructure, and distance from markets; and dependence and exploitation are more commercial and bureaucratic in relations with contractors and officials. RPFs in peripheries have more land but most of their agriculture is rainfed and most of their soils infertile.

Core and peripheral conditions can be found in the same taluka, block,

Table 2.1: Tendencies in poverty and resources of cores and peripheries

			Core	Periphery
p h y s i c a l		Access to towns	High	Low
		Topography	Flat	Undulating
l i v e l i h o o d s		Self-employed in agriculture	Fewer	More
		Landless	More	Fewer
		Employment days/year	Higher	Lower
		Tenancy	Higher	Lower
r e s o u r c e s	*Water*	Dominant agriculture	Irrigated	Rainfed
		Groundwater potential	Higher	Lower
		Ratio of surface water lift to groundwater lift potentials	Lower	Higher
		Soil fertility	Higher	Lower
	Land	Public land		
		Revenue land per family	Lower	Higher
		Encroachment or allotment of revenue land	Higher	Lower
		Forest land to family ratio	Low or nil	High
		Private land		
		concentration of land ownership	High	Low
		RPFs have	Very small holdings	Larger holdings but rainfed, and with poor soils

district, region or state. To map them except on a large-scale, is difficult. At a macro level, most core heartlands have flat land including the Gangetic plain, the Mahanadi, Godavari, Krishna and Kaveri deltas, and other areas of intensive irrigation development as are found in the lowlands of Gujarat, Maharashtra, and Tamil Nadu. Peripheral hinterlands include the Himalayan foothills, other mountains and hills, the Chotanagpur plateau in south Bihar, much of the Deccan plateau, and almost all tribal and heavily forested districts of central India.

In contrasting core and peripheral areas and poverty, we are not asserting that all dimensions always vary together. There are exceptions: Kerala, as so often, is anomalous, with heartland features but undulating terrain. Rather we are saying that covariance is common enough between the physical, livelihood and resource conditions for core and periphery poverty to be useful and usable categories for description, analysis and policy.

2.2 Where the Rural Poor Are

Rural deprivation has many aspects, and can be measured by many indicators. All have limitations. We have taken four. Rural infant mortality rates and rural female literacy rates are good indicators of the wellbeing of children and women. Numbers and proportions of the population below the poverty line, for all their shortcomings (sec 1.3) do capture an important dimension. Per capita net domestic product has the weakness of including urban as well as rural income, with distortions from the wealth of large cities like Bombay for Maharashtra and Calcutta for West Bengal, but still shows up orders of magnitude which are significant.

These four indicators reveal a striking concentration of rural deprivation in what has been called the "poverty square", including most of Uttar Pradesh, Bihar, West Bengal, Orissa, and Madhya Pradesh. In 1984, these five States alone were estimated to contain 125 million below the poverty line, or 56 per cent of the national total. The poverty square also includes neighbouring hinterland and tribal areas of Andhra Pradesh, Maharashtra, Gujarat and Rajasthan. The "square" as a whole then accounts for at least two-thirds of the rural population below the poverty line.

For the three central States of the square—Uttar Pradesh, Bihar and Madhya Pradesh—the other indicators confirm deep deprivation, as indicated in table 2.2, all lying along the bottom five out of 17 States for each indicator. Moreover, all three were well below the national average for reported improvement in the poverty ratio (the proportion of the population below the poverty line) over the seven-year period from 1977–78 to 1984–85.

National priority has been given to agricultural development in these regions. A substantial percentage improvement in the poverty square as a whole would mean that large numbers of the very deprived would be better off. In pointing this out, however, we do not mean to divert attention from other areas. Deprivation is found everywhere, and our analysis applies to all States.

Any strategy of resource-based livelihoods for and by poor rural people supported by lift irrigation and trees depends not just on where the people are and their rights and access, but also initially on the scale, value and location of the resources—ground- and surface water, and land for trees, which will now be examined.

2.3 Lift Irrigation and Groundwater Potential

Water is lifted for irrigation from two types of source: surface water, such as

Table 2.2: Deprivation in Bihar, Madhya Pradesh and Uttar Pradesh

	Total rural population below PL 1984–85 millions	Percentage of rural population below PL 1984–85 (per centage)	Per caput State net domestic product 1985–86 (Rs)	Percentage improvement in poverty ratio 1977/8 to 1984/5	Female literacy rates 1981 rural	Rural infant mortality rate 1986
Bihar	32.3 (16)	51 (17)	1548 (17)	13	11 (14)	111 (13)
MP	21.7 (15)	50 (16)	1988 (15)	16	9 (16)	124 (14)
UP	42.4 (17)	46 (15)	1988 (14)	8	10 (15)	156 (17)
All-India	222	40	2,355	21	18	105

Notes. Figures in parentheses are rank positions among 17 States. Rajasthan had the lowest rural female literacy, at 7 per cent.

Sources

1. Sample Registration Bulletin 1988, Registrar General, Ministry of Home Affairs, New Delhi

2. Statistical Outline of India 1988–89, Tata Services Limited, Bombay, page 22. The figure for Orissa, Rs 1,534, was for 1984–85. Assuming a modest improvement in 1985–86, Orissa has been placed in 16th position, as it was in 1984–85.

3. GOI 1985a; GOI 1988e

lakes and ponds, dam reservoirs and tanks, rivers and streams, and canals and drains; and groundwater. Depending on local conditions, and to varying degrees, both are usually forms of common property or open access resource, although appropriation is sometimes subject to government regulation. Both types are important, but nationally groundwater has the larger potential and is given more attention here.

In normal official statistics, irrigation is divided into the following categories:
minor

a. groundwater

b. minor surface, comprising lift irrigation from surface water and gravity irrigation with commands up to 2,000 ha

major

c. canal irrigation with commands above 2,000 ha (technically 2,000–10,000 ha = medium and above 10,000 ha = major)

We will consider these in turn.

GROUNDWATER

Ability to extract and appropriate groundwater depends on rights and access to the land above it, but it is not a restricted private resource like land because it flows in the ground and is not alienable. It is appropriated by lift irrigation systems (LISs) and by crops and trees which draw it up through transpiration.

In the absence of a clear law defining and enforcing ownership and use rights, groundwater is appropriated by those who command the land over it and who have the means to lift it.

The nature of groundwater makes its potential difficult to estimate. Groundwater is replenished from rivers, dams, canal seepage, lateral flows, and return flows by percolation down again from irrigation itself. It is in motion, and is depleted by outflows into streams and rivers, as well as by evapotranspiration. The penetration of rainfall depends on slope, soil type, soil condition, vegetative cover, and rainfall regime. Aquifer potentials also vary according to whether they are confined, semiconfined, or unconfined. Finally, being below the ground and sometimes far below, groundwater assessment is especially problematical. As a result of these and other factors, estimates of groundwater potential in India are fraught with technical difficulties.

Further complications arise from the links between groundwater and surface flows. Surface flows replenish groundwater, so that groundwater and lift irrigation often gain from canal irrigation. Conversely, groundwater extraction which lowers the water table increases return flows from reservoirs, rivers and streams into the ground. Adverse effect can occur in both cases: oversupply of canal irrigation water leads to waterlogging, as with Sharda Sahayak in Uttar Pradesh, and groundwater extraction can diminish dry season flows, affecting users downstream. Case by case the balance between these two effects will vary; for our purposes we assume that they balance out, with oversupply and waterlogging augmenting dry season flows to compensate for the effects of groundwater extraction.

Groundwater potential in India has been expressed in two ways. The first is as an *area*, the gross area irrigable on a sustained basis; gross area here refers to the area cropped, with two crop seasons in one year on the same land counting as two. The second is as a *volume*, the utilisable potential of water; this has traditionally been taken to be 70 per cent of the net renewable recharge, less 15 per cent for industrial and domestic uses. These two methods of calculation have given rise to wildly different estimates of the ultimate potential utilised. As Sangal (1987: II 151) has noted, estimates of groundwater irrigation by area show that by 1985 about 70 per cent of the ultimate potential had been achieved, while in terms of volume only about 27 per cent of the annual recharge was being utilised as of June 1986.

Part of the explanation for this remarkable discrepancy is that estimates of the volume of utilisable potential have risen steadily but also dramatically over two decades, from 17.7 m ha m in 1969 to 45.7 m ha m in 1988, an increase of nearly 160 per cent. There are three main reasons for this rise:

i) *Increase in groundwater*

As new canal irrigation has been installed, so seepage and recharge of groundwater have increased. The gross storage capacity of dams rose 14-fold in the 32 years from 1951 to 1983 (Sinha 1983:1–21) and the gross area reported irrigated by canals rose from 1.3 m ha in 1951 to 19.5 m ha in 1985. Seepage has consequently increased from reservoirs, canals, water courses, field channels, fields and drains. Moreover, such seepage has far exceeded the rates projected. Figures available for seven large canal systems in India show transmission losses actually measured of the order of four times those assumed in planning (Chambers 1988:113–14). Just how significant a factor canal recharge of groundwater can be is indicated by the experience of the Punjab. In 1934 rain water contributed 80 per cent of total recharge. By about 1980, the percentage contribution of rainfall had dropped to 51, with no less than 39 per cent from return seepage from canal irrigation and 10 per cent from return flows from irrigation by groundwater (Sangal 1980:8). Elsewhere, a rise in groundwater tables has been widespread. Dhawan's investigations in Mula command have stressed the impact of canals on groundwater availability (Dhawan 1987). The Mahi-Kadana Project in Gujarat is another example, with reported rises of almost a metre a year in parts of the command in the latter seventies (Sarma et al. 1983:199; Michael 1983:210). There, as elsewhere, the rapid spread of canal irrigation has led to a rapid rise in groundwater potential.

ii) Changing parameters for estimating

For a long time, groundwater recharge estimates were made by using highly approximate estimates of coefficients of recharge from rainfall, canal seepage, irrigation return flows and specific yields of soils in different areas. A major nationwide programme of hydrological surveys undertaken by the Central Groundwater Board and State Groundwater Organisations has generated more reliable and accurate estimates of these coefficients which are substantially higher than those assumed earlier. More reliable recent estimates using the water balance equation method have shown groundwater recharge to be greater than earlier supposed (MWR 1986:4).

iii) Discovery and inclusion of new groundwater

Earlier estimates were evidently based on known groundwater. As with oil reserves elsewhere, so with hard rock groundwater and with deep aquifers, exploratory surveys discover more. Such surveys have been conducted on a continuous basis by State Groundwater Boards and lead to higher estimates of the potential.

There are also two reasons to believe that the actual potential from groundwater is larger even than these higher estimates.

The first is that known or assessable resources have not necessarily been included in estimates. As late as 1983 (Sinha 1983:K-20), water in the deeper confined aquifers did not find any place in the currently available district or State groundwater estimates. The Chief Hydrologist of the Central Groundwater Board in 1983 considered that "Groundwater flow through the confined aquifers in the unconsolidated and semi-consolidated sediments have tremendous developmental potential," also pointing out that confined aquifers represent low cost water transmission systems from areas of recharge to the areas of discharge (ibid: K-21).

The second is the dynamic nature of groundwater. The concept of groundwater potential is based on measures of mean annual recharge which can be drawn upon without depleting the aquifer. Groundwater has been built up over thousands of years and may be several or many times larger than the mean annual recharge. It is then easy to think of it as a stock which should not be "mined", but constantly replenished by flows from rainfall and other seepage. "Mining", in the sense of extracting more than can be replaced, does occur. But this has tended to impede recognition of quite common conditions where the optimal rate of withdrawal will be higher than the *current* mean annual recharge. The space available for recharge depends on the depth of the groundwater table. A detailed analysis of water table fluctuations in the Mahi Command in Gujarat, found that the monsoonal recharge was substantially lower in areas of high water table than in areas of low water table; in other words, failing to run down the water table sufficiently before the monsoon reduces the capacity of the region to harvest as much rainfall as it otherwise could (Shah 1988:20). Moreover, unless the groundwater table is lowered in normal years, space will not be created to capture the rainfall of the years of exceptionally good and well-distributed rainfall. In such conditions, quite common on canal irrigation commands, it is difficult to estimate ground-water potential, and easy to underestimate it.

Increases in the actual and estimated groundwater potential, have passed largely unnoticed except among the professions closely concerned. This has allowed the relative significance of canal irrigation to be exaggerated. Much of this can be attributed to the static view normally taken of the estimates of the National Commission of Agriculture, 1976. This calculated ultimate irrigation potential in terms of gross million hectares irrigable. In 1976 these were given as 70 million from surface water, and 40 million from ground-water (GOI 1976:43) later refined to 58.5 million for major and medium canals, 15 million from minor surface sources, and 40 million from ground-water to give a total ultimate potential of 113.5 million hectares. These estimates were a useful and significant step forward at the time of the NCA, but they became sanctified through repetition, and even 12 years later were still being used in the Planning Commission and donor agency reports. Yet, as we will argue, they now overstate the potential from canal irrigation and understate that from groundwater.

The Commission began with the rule of thumb that to irrigate a cropped hectare it took 0.90 ha m of canal water or 0.65 ha m of groundwater. The difference was accounted for by the transmission losses of canal irrigation. However, the Commission considered that with "more scientific and economical use of water" the average from canal water could improve to about 0.72 metres. No similar improvement was allowed for with groundwater. It was on the basis of 0.70 metres that the ultimate potential from canal water was evidently calculated. This procedure can be questioned on three grounds:

1) Conveyance losses on canals have been found to be of the order of four times those planned for (see table 2.3), and are also difficult and costly to reduce.

2) The efficiency of application of groundwater is in practice far higher than that of canal water.

3) It is reasonable to suppose that efficiencies of groundwater use would not remain static but improve.

Table 2.3: Some reported transmission losses

Project	Canal/ System	Lined (L)/ unlined (U)	Losses assumed in planning (in cusec/msf except Dantiwada)	Losses measured or observed (in cusec/msf except Dantiwada)
1. Dantiwada	Left canal	U	10%	40%
(Gujarat)	Left canal	L	2%	6%
2. (a) Nagarjunasagar (Andhra Pradesh)	Left canal	U	8	86
2. (b) Nagarjunasagar (Andhra Pradesh)	Left canal	U	8	21.2
3. Mahanadi Canal System (Madhya Pradesh)		na	2–8	39.7
4. Mula (Maharashtra)	Right bank	na	2–8	24.25
5. Tawa (Madhya Pradesh)		na	2–8	22.9
6. Nagarjunasagar	Right bank	na	2–8	16.7
7. Chambal	Right main canal	na	2–8	15

Sources: Chambers 1988: 114 citing Murthy 1980: 142 for 1 and 2a, PAC 1983: 100 for the remainder.
Notes:
1. Cusec/msf = cubic feet per second per million square feet of wetted perimeter.
2. Losses assumed in planning cited by the Public Accounts Committee were 2 cusecs/msf for lined canals and 8 cusecs/msf for unlined canals. The figure 2-8 cusecs/msf is given in the table since the PAC source does not indicate whether the canals were lined or not.

Despite these factors and trends the NCA's 1976 figures have been reproduced without modification in numerous official and planning documents together with time series data on progress with irrigation development. Even the Seventh Five Year Plan 1985-90, repeats them (GOI 1985e :72). Over time, these figures have progressively created the impression that most of the groundwater potential had already been exploited, and that the main opportunities for future new irrigation lay with major and medium canals. This then appeared to justify high continued investment in new canal irrigation projects.

Recent estimates of available annual groundwater range from 39 to 42 m ha m; Sangal (1987:II-155) put it at 39.4 m ha m; the Ministry of Water

Resources at 41.9 m ha m (MWR 1986). In 1988 these were revised upwards, following statewise reassessments, to 45.66 m ha m, with downward revision for Uttar Pradesh, Haryana and Himachal Pradesh far outweighed by substantial rises in Andhra Pradesh, Assam, Bihar, Jammu and Kashmir, Maharashtra, Orissa, Tamil Nadu and West Bengal (Padmanabhan 1988).

At 0.65 metres per ha, the available recharge would irrigate a gross area of 70 m ha, some 75 per cent more than the earlier estimate of 40 m ha. Even this new estimate is probably low, for improvements in water use efficiency are more likely in groundwater irrigation than in canals. Indications are that even at present the national average of (irrigation) water use per gross ha irrigated by groundwater is substantially lower than 0.65 metres. Official estimates place actual groundwater draft at 10.7 m ha m per year (Sangal 1987:135). The area irrigated by groundwater is about 28 m ha (Sinha 1988:135). Taken together these figures imply an average of 0.38 metres of water drawn per gross ha irrigated. This may appear low, but much groundwater irrigation is fine-pointed, protective and supplementary, for example in kharif, in contrast with much canal irrigation which tends to be supplied regardless of need relative to rainfall. The actual figure for groundwater drawn per gross ha irrigated may lie somewhere between tbe two estimates of 0.38 and 0.65 m respectively. A revised estimate of ultimate potential based on volume, taking the renewable recharge at 46 m ha m per annum, would then lie between 70 m ha (which in the light of the discussion above seems low) and 120 m ha (which seems unrealistically high). To err on the side of caution, we still postulate for working purposes of comparison a low figure of 80 m ha as ultimate potential from groundwater.

For a sounder perspective, revised estimates of other ultimate potentials are also required. These concern the other two categories used by the NCA—minor irrigation from surface sources, and major and medium canal irrigation.

MINOR IRRIGATION FROM SURFACE WATER

Minor irrigation from surface water includes surface gravity irrigation from reservoirs and anicuts with command areas of less than 2,000 ha, and lift irrigation from rivers, streams, reservoirs and other bodies of water. No estimate is available of the relative significance of gravity and lift. Official figures give 9 m ha of potential created from these sources against an ultimate potential of 15 m ha. It is difficult to know whether lift irrigation from surface water has been rising or falling as a proportion of the total. Sangal (1987:II:152) has recently shown that the rate of growth of surface water-based gravity and lift irrigation has been far slower, at only just over 1 per cent per year, than for groundwater based irrigation, at 9.5 per cent per year. Whereas in 1950 the former accounted for half the area under minor irrigation, its share has fallen to less than 25 per cent while the share of groundwater-based irrigation has soared to 75 per cent.

Surface lift irrigation potential is difficult to assess. Lift irrigation from reservoirs could become an extensive practice, especially since water is usually more productive with lift than with gravity irrigation. Lift from canals is already practised in some places, for example in Gujarat where it is permitted to get water to high patches (pers. comm. Sangal). There is also a band across northern India, from Gujarat to Orissa, where many streams present lift irrigation potential, and which the NCA can be presumed to have taken into account. In sum, the potential from surface lift may have been underestimated, but for present purposes we accept the estimates of the NCA.

Table 2.4: Growth of lift irrigation : Surface and groundwater

Source	Ultimate potential (m ha)	Cumulative potential created (m ha)		Rate of growth
		1950	1985	1950–85
Surface	15	6.4	9.0	1.17
Groundwater	40	6.5	28.0	9.5
Total	55	12.9	37	

Source: Sangal (1987: II-152)

CANAL IRRIGATION

For canal irrigation a distinction is needed between potential which appears technically feasible and that which is economically and politically feasible. Technical, economic and political factors taken together suggest that the ultimate feasible potential from major and medium canal irrigation will be much less than 58.5 m ha. Some of these factors are:

— the optimistic estimate of 0.70 ha m of water per ha irrigated
— the low performance and inherent difficulties of canal irrigation systems (Chambers 1988)
— the increasing capital costs of canal irrigation, especially because most of the better sites have already been used, which will make many proposed further investments very expensive
— the failure of canal irrigation to cover its recurrent, let alone its capital, costs
— public resistance to, and the social and economic costs of, the displacement of populations by reservoirs and canal irrigation works
— environmental costs including the loss of forests
— high reservoir siltation rates, foundby Singhal and Singhal (1981:424) for eleven Indian reservoirs to be on average four times the rate predicted
— effects of flooding, waterlogging, and salinity

These considerations lead us to a downward revision of the estimated ultimate potential of 58.5 million ha for the area that will prove technically economically and politically feasible, for major and medium canal irrigation. As a working figure, we postulate 40 million ha. The NCA's figure has been so often repeated that this new estimate will appear iconoclastic. It may be proved low, but we present it without apology as our best guess in the hope that it will lead others who are better informed to raise or lower it as necessary.

Table 2.5: Standard and revised estimates of irrigation potential

	Potential utilised	Estimates of ultimate potential		Estimates of potential remaining for exploitation	
	I 1985/86 target	II Standard	III Revised	IV Standard II-I	V Revised III-I
Major and medium canal	26(24)	58.5(52)	40(30)	32.5(63)	14(19)
Minor surface	9(14.5)	15 (13)	15(11)	6 (12)	6(8)
Minor ground-water	27(13.5)	40 (35)	80(59)	13 (25)	53(73)
Total	62(100)	113.5(100)	135(100)	51.5(100)	73(100)

Figures are in million hectares.
Figures in brackets are percentage.
  Sources: I NIRD 1986
           II Standard estimates of ultimate potential:
               National Commission on Agriculture 1976
          III See text
Revised estimates are for technical, economic and political feasibility.

The broadly indicative estimates in table 2.5 present radically different proportions for the remaining irrigation potential from those current as late as in 1988. Minor surface irrigation declines only from 12 to 8 per cent, but major and medium canal irrigation drops from 63 to 19 per cent while groundwater rises from 25 to 73 per cent. The reader who is shocked by these working estimates may wish to conduct a personal exercise with different assumptions. If our main arguments are correct, the outcome, even if different from ours, will still mean a sharp rise in the relative importance of untapped potential from groundwater to that of canal irrigation, still reversing their positions to place groundwater decisively in the first place.

2.4 The Rising Value of Lift Irrigation Water

The productive value of irrigation water has risen sharply over the years, especially in the last three decades; and so has the value of its ownership and use by rural people, especially the poor. This can be understood in an historical perspective.

Canal and well irrigation have had a long history in India; however, intensive irrigation for high productivity per ha was rather limited until the 1960s. The canal systems of northern India were built and managed by the Raj to cover large areas under protective irrigation which served to reduce the risk of uncertain monsoons. Likewise, the dependence on the use of human and animal power for lifting water from open wells and surface water bodies resulted in low water output per unit of time. Most "desi" varieties of food and cash crops popular amongst Indian farmers before the 1960s exhibited a low response to better moisture management and fertiliser applications. Much of traditional agriculture in pre-1960s India was thus characterised by low inputs and low output per hectare. The bulk of the value added in farming was appropriated as land "rent" and wages, paid out as well as imputed.

Constraints on intensive irrigated farming were progressively removed in many parts of India during the fifties and sixties. The scale of irrigation increased with the construction of many new major canal irrigation projects. Rapid propagation of modern tubewell and waterlifting technologies using diesel or electric pumpsets made it possible to lift large quantities of water per unit of time at lower cost and with less drudgery. In many areas irrigation became more intensive. Most decisively for production, the spread of the HYV-fertiliser technology in the late sixties in the Indus and Gangetic basins and later in other regions removed the "desi" seeds' constraint of low yield response to intensive input and water application. As a result, intensive irrigation led to major increases in gross income per ha through: (a) higher yield per acre through profitable expansion of fertiliser use, (b) superior cropping pattern with more of high value crops, and (c) increased land use intensity. Studies establishing the substantial output and income impact of intensive irrigation are far too numerous to survey here; and the fact of the impact itself is accepted widely. To highlight the orders of magnitude involved, we present a summary table from Dhawan (1985) giving aggregate estimates of the impact of irrigation on value added in farming.

What is not so well researched and understood is the change in input-output relationships in irrigated farming and the share of water in the rapidly rising value added on irrigated farms. Indicative evidence suggests several hypotheses; the most striking of these is that the value added by irrigation (as also the value of gross output per ha) increases dramatically as the "quality" of irrigation service improves. "Quality" here may imply several things; but in the main, it indicates dependability, adequacy, and the degree of control that an irrigation source offers to the user over the timing and quantum of water application.

These vary according to the source. Lift irrigation generally offers a higher quality of irrigation service than gravity flow systems, whether major from canals or minor from tanks. It is more dependable than streams, drains, ponds and other small water bodies with their tendency to go dry.

Studies which compare the productivity of different irrigation sources present useful evidence. Careful analysis by Dhawan indicates that in four Indian States for which data were available, the output impact of groundwater per net irrigated hectare was roughly double that of canals (table 2.7).

Table 2.6: Impact of irrigation on value added/ha

	per rainfed ha (Rs at 1970-71 prices)	Value added per gross irrigated ha (Rs in 1970-71 prices)	Approximate increase in value added/ha due to irrigation		
			Rs in* 1970-71 prices	Rs in 1981-82 prices	(3) — — — (1)
	(1)	(2)	(3)	(4)	(5)
1. Indus Basin: Punjab Haryana	350	1,830	1,725	3,920	4.93
2. Gangetic Basic UP, Bihar	440	2,200	2,000	4,545	4.54
3. Southern Peninsula. TN. AP	530	2,225	1,850	4,204	3.49
4. Deccan Plateau Maharashtra.	260	4,550	4,430	10,068	17.04
5. All India	–	–	2,200	5,000	–

*Since these estimates are obtained by regression analysis, col 3 figures are not equal to the difference between cols 1 and 2.
Source: Dhawan 1985

Table 2.7: Output impact of groundwater, canals and tanks 1977-79

Tonnes of food grain per net irrigated hectare additional to rainfed yield.

	Groundwater	Canals	Tanks
Punjab	4.4	2.1	—
Haryana	5.3(1)	2.0	—
Andhra Pradesh	5.2	2.9	1.5
Tamil Nadu	6.0	2.1	1.8

Note: The groundwater impact for Haryana is higher than for Punjab partly because unirrigated yields were lower. Haryana figures are for 1976-77 and 1978-79.
Source: Dhawan 1985:11 and 13

Amongst lift irrigation systems, own tubewells rank highest in terms of the quality of irrigation service: Kolavalli (1986) aptly calls them "on demand" irrigation systems. Other options such as depending on other private tubewell owners or on State tubewells are inferior. A study by Mellor and Moorty (1975) in Uttar Pradesh concluded that purchased private tubewell irrigation was generally more dependable, and therefore productive, than State tubewells. A new recent body of evidence confirms that farmers in many areas prefer purchasing water from private tubewell owners to depending on State tubewells (Shah 1987c; Asopa and Dholakia 1984). Lowdermilk and colleagues have shown in a study in Pakistan (table 2.8) how wheat and paddy yields rise as lift irrigation sources give farmers better control over supply.

Table 2.8: Average yields per ha under four water supply situations in Pakistan (1978)

Water supply situation	Average yield per ha in kg			
	No of farms	Wheat kg/ha	No of farms	Paddy rice kg/ha
1. No control (no tubewell)	170	1681	75	1308
2. Fair control (public tubewell)	33	1868	13	1775
3. Good control (purchase from private tubewell)	133	1962	35	1962
4. Very good control (tubewell owner)	42	2242	9	2148
5. Total	376		132	

Source: Lowdermilk et al. cited in Tiffin and Toulmin (1987:6).

An illustrative analysis of the economics of irrigation from different sources is presented in figure 2.1. Irrigated farming entails higher cash as well as imputed costs of labour, fertiliser and land rents; but as the quality of irrigation service improves, these costs rise less sharply than does the value of gross output. If all these costs are deducted from gross value of output, we are left with the total surplus generated per ha by irrigation. This is represented by the area enclosed by the top two curves. A user of irrigation service would, in principle, be willing to pay for the service anywhere up to this total surplus per ha which is the true measure of the value of water.

How this surplus is distributed between the user and provider of irrigation service depends on how it is priced. In most canal irrigation projects, the bulk of the surplus accrues to users: in tank irrigation, almost all of it accrues to the users due to the difficulties of extracting service fees from them (Marothia 1986; Von Oppen and Subba Rao 1985). Subsidised prices of State tubewell water play an important part in turning over to users the bulk of the surplus State tubewells help to create. In all these cases, the fixing of service fees administratively understates and conceals the true value of water.

But this is not true of the sale of irrigation by private LIS owners which, as we shall see in chapter 5, is more prevalent than most researchers and policy makers have imagined. With private sales, the price of irrigation service is determined by the interplay of demand and supply and provides insight into the real value that farmers place on irrigation.

The value of irrigation water supply is not reflected in irrigation fees on most public irrigation projects. Many irrigation scholars lament that these are woefully low — usually less than 10 per cent, but often as low as 2-3 per cent, of the value of output per hectare. In contrast, the share of output claimed by private providers of water is much higher, often about a third.

With water share-cropping in North Arcot District, a standard arrangement was for one-third of the crop share to go to water sellers; Shah (1986b) has found similar contracts widely used in Telangana regions in Andhra Pradesh

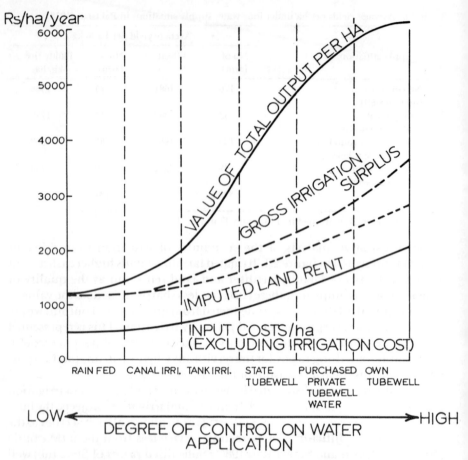

Figure 2.1: Creation and distribution of irrigation surplus

Technical Note: This figure is not based on any one study comparing the economics of various irrigation sources but on several studies (including those reported in the text). Notable amongst these are Dhawan 1985; Brahmbhatt 1986; Kolavalli 1986; Palanisami and Vardharajan 1985; Kartar Singh 1978; Lowdermilk et al. 1978; Von Oppen and Subba Rao 1985; Sarma 1985; Sirohi et al. 1985.

and in many parts of Gujarat where, however, several types of water lease arrangements are in use. One of the more common is that the water seller supplies water and bears half of the fertiliser cost; the land owner supplies land, labour and the other half of the fertiliser cost; and the produce is shared equally between the water seller and the farmer. In effect, the share of water in such an arrangement becomes equal to that of land and labour. However, a one-third share for only water is also widely observed in Gujarat. In Navli village of Kheda district, for example, a tripartite contract is quite common; the tenant supplies labour, fertilisers, seeds and other inputs; the landowner supplies land; the well owner supplies water; and all three share the output equally (Shah 1988).

Cash sales of water by private tubewell owners are similar. A village study of Tamil Nadu in the late seventies (Guhan and Mencher 1983: 1021) found farmers paying cash equivalent to a third of the crop as the share of water to the seller. In Gujarat, where water selling by tubewell owners has a 30-year old history, water prices have risen by tenfold from Rs 2.50-3.00/hour in the mid-sixties (PEO 1968; Patel and Patel 1971) to Rs 25-30/hour in more recent times (Shah 1985). Small farmers all over Gujarat have shown themselves willing to pay Rs 1,200-1,400 (1985 prices) per acre for water to grow irrigated instead of rainfed paddy. With the spread of irrigation and the multiplication of irrigation sources, one might have expected demand for purchased water to have shrunk: but the opposite has occurred: irrigated farming based on purchased water has rapidly expanded.

If we assume that private sellers skim as much of the irrigation surplus as they can, then the prices they charge, especially in water scarce areas, give some indication of the productive value of water. The evidence that we have cited indicates that the irrigation surplus may be as high as a third or more of the gross value of irrigated output. But private water sellers do not necessarily extract the entire surplus generated by irrigation. There are areas where water sellers enjoy limited bargaining power and share irrigation surplus more equitably with users. The cost of irrigation with purchased water from private tubewells for instance, is considerably less in the Gangetic plains in northern India than in some water-scarce areas of south and west. Further, the one-third crop share system of water sales widely used in the latter areas is rarely observed in water-abundant areas of the north and east. In Bangladesh, with conditions comparable to some parts of east India, crop sharing against water is still common but the crop share paid to water sellers has rapidly declined from a third in 1981 first to one-fourth and then to one-fifth and even in a few circumstances, to one-tenth (Palmer-Jones and Mandal 1986). Notably, this steep decline occurred over a period of only five to six years.

The conclusion is that lift irrigation presents opportunities for greater benefits to resource-poor farmers: through the changes in agricultural technology which have raised the productivity and value of water; through the greater dependability and ease of control of lift irrigation compared with canal; and through shifts in the distribution of surplus which give bigger shares to water purchasers. These benefits can be sought both where water resources have yet to be appropriated, and where they have already been exploited. Just how these benefits can be gained by the resource-poor is the central concern of chapters 4, 5 and 6.

POTENTIAL OF TREES ON DEGRADED LANDS

We now examine the potential of trees. Our main focus is on degraded lands, but this must be qualified as follows.

Potential exists in some fertile and well-endowed core areas, where groundwater is close to the surface, for poor people to gain by growing trees on their marginal and small farms and home gardens. Where water tables at their seasonal lowest are within reach of tree roots, the trees can transpire and photosynthesise, and so add biomass and value, through all or much of the year, depending on species. Unlike rainfed annual crops, trees do not have to depend directly and immediately on precipitation for their water. They are thus less riskprone than rainfed ground crops. Through transpiration, they pump the water up and use it without the capital and recurrent costs of lift irrigation. They also need not demand labour at the times when poor farmers have the chance to earn wages by working for others. In favourable conditions, trees planted on small plots can in effect be poor people's pumps as well as savings banks, while freeing them for income-earning work.

In the analysis which follows, both non-degraded and degraded lands will be considered, but with the main focus on those which are degraded, since they present the more evident and widespread potential. As with groundwater and lift irrigation above, we will assess three aspects: scale and ownership of the resource, in this case land, especially degraded land; production potential; and demand, supply and price.

2.5 Land-use Classification

The breakdown by category of India's approximately 329 million hectares of land is given in table 2.9.

Table 2.9: Estimated land resources in India in m ha

Category	Sub-category	Area	
Lands considered fit for vegetation	Cultivated land	142	
	Forest land	67	
	Fallows/culturable wastes/ pastures/groves	55	
	Total area of culturable lands		264
Lands considered unfit for vegetation	Uncultivable wastelands (permanent snow, ice, rock outcrops, desert etc)	20	
	Urban and other non-agricultural lands (towns, roads, rivers etc.)	20	
	Area for which no records are available	25	
	total	65	
	Grand Total		329

(GOI 1986d)

Estimates of land legally declared as forest differ. The Forest Department claims 75 m ha, while the Agriculture Department gives 67 m ha. The difference is accounted for by unclassed forests and land under shifting cultivation. However, area under actual tree cover is much less than either of these figures.

2.6 Estimates of Degraded Land

Land where trees can be planted without adversely affecting agricultural production fall into four categories:

1) CULTIVATED LANDS

The area available for agro-forestry and growing trees on cultivated lands is difficult to estimate. All, or almost all, cultivated land can grow trees, and private tree planting depends on many factors. Degraded lands can give a lower boundary to any estimate, since on degraded lands trees usually have the clearest advantages compared with other land uses. The National Commission for Agriculture's estimate of 85 m ha of net sown land subject to wind and water erosion was found to involve double counting by Bhumbla and Khare (SPWD 1984) whose scaled down estimate of 38 m ha has been accepted by the National Wastelands Development Board (NWDB 1988a). Any figure is bound to be highly speculative, but if we take agroforestry as occupying one-third of the total area, this would give some 13 m ha which should be under trees.

2) STRIP LANDS

These include farm bunds and boundaries, roads, railway lines, canals and drains. The Fuelwood Committee (Planning Commission 1982) estimated the potentials of these as follows: 60 of the 142 m ha of cultivated land presented scope for planting along bunds and boundaries (which, at 2 per cent of the area, would amount to 1.2 m ha); and 12,24,000 km of roads, 60,000 km of railway lines, 1,50,000 km of canals and 20,000 km of drains also provided suitable strips, amounting to 0.9 m ha. The total strip lands available was therefore of the order of 2 m ha.

3) DEGRADED FOREST LANDS

The Forest Survey of India (FSI 1988) has estimated that almost half of the forest area has a crown density of less than 40 per cent. The National Remote Sensing Agency has found (NRSA 1985) that the area under good forests declined from 46 to 36 m ha from 1970-73 to 1980-82. There must have been further denudation of forest lands since 1982, as Social Forestry Projects did not cover forest lands (sec 9.1). Therefore we accept the National Wastelands Development Board's estimate that 36 m ha out of the total of 67 m ha of forest land are degraded (NWDB 1988a: 26).

4) UNCULTIVATED DEGRADED LANDS

Estimates of uncultivated degraded land is a residual category that is difficult to assess. Problems are presented by definitions and by statistics.

The definitions of the Ministry of Agriculture, SPWD and the NWDB conflict. Although far from perfect, we accept that given by the NWDB (1987 a):

> Wastelands mean degraded land which can be brought under vegetative cover, with reasonable effort, and which is currently lying underutilised and land which is deteriorating for lack of appropriate water and soil management or on account of natural causes. Wasteland can result from inherent/imposed disabilities such as by location, environment, chemical and physical properties of the soil or financial or management constraints.

Key words in this definition such as "underutilised", "deteriorating" and "disabilities" are open to subjective interpretation, so that an exact figure cannot be derived from this definition.

The second problem concerns statistics. Land statistics are well developed for cultivated and forest lands, but not for non-forest and non-cultivated lands (Romm 1981). Information needed for assessing their potential, like ownership, extent and type of degradation, and present and possible future uses, has never been collected on a systematic basis for the entire country.

This makes it difficult to estimate how much of the 55 m ha of the non-forest and non-cultivated land is degraded. The National Commission on Agriculture (GOI 1976:126) believed that the entire area of 55 m ha classified under groves (3 m ha), fallows (24 m ha), pastures (12 m ha) and culturable wastelands (16 m ha) was degraded. Had it not been so it would be under the plough! The NWDB has accepted this contention (1985).

Not all this land can be degraded: land classified as "groves" would seem likely to have trees on it; not all fallows are necessarily degraded; and on some of these lands social forestry has been undertaken. In the absence of any other estimates, we make the arbitrary assumption that one-fifth of this land is not degraded, giving a total of 44 ha of uncultivated degraded land. Even this may not be entirely available for tree plantation, as a part may be required for schools, panchayat buildings, cattle resting places, wells and dwellings. A study of 15 eastern Uttar Pradesh districts (Tiwari 1986:45) where pressure on land is acute, found that of 6,21,000 ha of community and private uncultivated land, only 3,93,000 or 65 per cent was available for growing trees. In dry areas, the proportions available were higher. We estimate the area of degraded lands available for tree growing as 75 per cent of 44 m ha, i.e. 33 m ha.

In sum, then, with qualifications and reservations, the orders of magnitude of degraded land available and suitable for growing trees and where trees are not now growing, may be as shown in table 2.10. Table 2.11 compares our estimate with estimates given by others.

Table 2.10: Estimates of land available for tree growing in m ha

Category	Area
Cultivated lands	13
Strips and boundaries	2
Degraded forest land	36
Uncultivated degraded lands	33
Total	84

Table 2.11: Estimates of degraded land in India

Estimated by	Area considered degraded in m ha	Comments
1	2	3
1. National Commission on Agriculture (GOI 1976)	175	This figure includes 85 m ha of agricultural land, considered degraded by the NCA, which has been questioned by Bhumbla and Khare (SPWD 1984)
2. Gadgil et al. (1982:14)	88	Gadgil's breakup is pasture lands 12 m ha, degraded forests 36 m ha, culturable waste 17 m ha, and 23 m ha of fallows. He assumed that the entire area of culturable waste, fallows and pasture lands was degraded. He did not consider cultivated degraded lands in his estimate
3. Bentley (1984)	115	This includes 15 m ha of marginal agricultural lands and recently deforested forest lands
4. Bhumbla and Khare (SPWD 1984)	93	They considered only non-forest wastelands. Adding 36 of degraded forest area the total becomes 129 m ha. NWDB accepts this figure of 129 m ha (1986b)
5. Vohra (1985:34)	103	The breakup is forest land 30 m ha, uncultivated land 33 m ha, and crop land 40 m ha
6. Khan (1987:13)	80	According to Khan, a forester working in the NWDB, this consists mostly of degraded forests and private marginal land, a conclusion similar to ours
7. World Bank (1988:5)	115-130	This includes 32-40 m ha of degraded agriculture land. The rest of the breakup is similar to that given by Gadgil et al. above

Note: In comparing our total of 84 m ha with those of others, it may be noted that of the 38 m ha of degraded cultivated land we have included only 13. If we had taken the figure of 38, our total would become 109 m ha.

OWNERSHIP OF DEGRADED LANDS

Cultivated lands, and farm bunds and boundaries, are almost entirely privately owned, and access to them is predetermined by ownership. Although much of this land is owned by large farmers, resource-poor farmers with some land are very numerous. They include small and marginal farmers generally, some larger but still poor farmers in dry, infertile areas, and the landless poor to whom 5 to 6 m ha of degraded land has been allotted in the past two decades (sec 8.3).

Public wastelands are of three types: forest wastelands, wastes which are owned by the government but used by the community, and grazing lands which are vested in village bodies. The latter two are also referred to as revenue wastelands, as their management is supervised by the revenue departments. One of the authors, in a study for FAO (Saxena 1988), estimated that of the 55 m ha of uncultivated non-forest lands some 35 m ha, consisting of fallows, groves and owned/allotted/encroached land, are now under private control, whereas the rest 20 m ha was still under the control of the revenue departments. Assuming the same ratio the breakup of 33 m ha of degraded uncultivated land available for tree growing, shown in table 2.10, would be 21 m ha private and 12 m ha with the revenue departments. Thus ownership of 84 m ha of land could approximately be as in table 2.12.

Table 2.12 : Ownership of degraded land available for tree growing (m ha)

Category of land	Total area	Available for trees (for new plantation)	Private	Forest dept	Revenue/ other depts.
Cultivated	142	13	13	—	—
Forest	67	36	—	36	—
Uncultivated/ non-forest	55	33	21	—	12
Strips	already included in the above	2	1	—	1
Total	264	84	35	36	13

The State-wise breakup of degraded forest land is available (NWDB 1986b), whereas for private and revenue lands approximate calculations could be attempted, based on other studies (SPWD 1984; Saxena 1988). This would look like as shown in table 2.13.

We would like to sum up this section with the following observations. First, our estimates for availability of land are similar to the estimates given by others. Second, it seems that the major potentials are on private (including

Table 2.13: State-wise ownership of degraded lands

(Figures in m ha)

Name of the State	Reporting area	Area of degraded lands			
		Private	Forests	Revenue & others	Total
A.P.	27.4	3.8	3.7	0.9	8.4
Assam	7.9	0.5	0.8	0.2	1.5
Bihar	17.3	2.5	1.6	0.2	4.3
Gujarat	18.8	2.0	0.7	1.2	3.9
Karnataka	19.1	2.9	2.0	1.1	6.0
M.P.	44.2	4.2	7.2	2.5	13.9
Maharashtra	30.8	3.9	2.8	1.4	8.1
Orissa	15.5	1.2	3.2	0.4	4.8
Rajasthan	34.2	5.7	1.9	3.2	10.8
Tamil Nadu	13.0	2.4	1.0	0.2	3.6
U.P.	29.8	2.9	1.4	0.5	4.8
W.B.	8.9	0.7	0.4	0.1	1.2
Others	37.3	2.6	9.1	1.1	12.8
All India	304.1	35.3	35.8	13.0	84.1
rounded to	304	35	36	13	84

encroached) and forest lands. This is consistent with the experience of field officers about not getting suitable revenue lands for social forestry. Third, all estimates, including ours, are based on the breakup of land resources (table 2.9) given by the Agriculture Statistics Department. This assumes that the total of potentially productive land is 264 m ha, a figure which has remained unchanged for more than a decade (GOI 1988b), and which may now need revision.

2.7 Production Potential

This vast area would be of little significance without production potential. Not enough is known about how much these lands are below their potential productivity (which itself is a function of technology) with reference to the available soil and water nutrients. Nor is it adequately known what kinds of treatment, such as soil, water and nutrient conservation and concentration, tree plantation, and the creation of micro-environments are required to restore their productivity and achieve their potential. While there are many unknowns, assessments of biological potential can be outlined for three categories of land: forest lands, revenue lands, and private degraded lands.

FOREST LANDS

For forest lands, two varying estimates of current productivity are available. On the basis of remote sensing data Warner (1982) estimated current productivity for the entire 67 mh of forests at 0.4 cu m of wood per hectare per year, but the Forest Survey of India (FSI 1988:31) estimated a productivity of 0.7 cu m in 1985. The FSI estimate includes both recorded and unrecorded removals from forests and hence appears more accurate.

These levels are dramatically lower than the potential. One indication is that the world average is 2.1 cu m per ha per year. More directly relevant are evidence and estimates from India. One example is bamboo in Karnataka. The total area under bamboo in Karnataka is 1 m ha, but total yield is only 60,000 tonnes, or 60 kg per ha per year. Taking into account the soil structure, the Principal CCF estimates that the yield should be between 750 and 3750 kg per ha per year (Shyam Sunder and Parameswarappa 1987b:2023), that is 12 to 62 times the present yield. An official report (GOMP 1987:38) lamented the fact that incremental productivity per ha per year of forests in Madhya Pradesh was only 0.30 cu m, whereas potential is quoted as 5 cu m, which is 17 times the actual. A more general estimate of over 30 years ago worked out the potential productivity of the forests as ranging from 1.8 cu m per ha per year in Rajasthan to 10.6 in Andaman and Nicobar, with an average of 6 cu m per ha per year for the country (Paterson 1956 cited in FSI 1988:31). This contrasts with the much lower estimate (FSI 1988) that most of the Indian forests are capable of productivity of at least 2 cu m per ha per year. It is striking that even this lower level is about three times the current productivity, indicating a vast potential.

OTHER UNCULTIVATED LANDS

Biological potential cannot, in practical terms, be considered in isolation from costs. With revenue lands, to increase their productivity would often require investments in irrigation and soil improvements, which will be in addition to normal costs of seedlings, plantation and protection. It may be generally indicative that a study (USAID 1988) found the investments in community plantations in Gujarat to be about Rs 2000 per ha (during 1974-76) with actual yields in 1986 of 1.8 tonnes (2.5 cu m) per ha per year of wood, and 0.26 tonnes of grass, giving a respectable internal rate of return of 15 per cent.

Another study (Narain 1985) observed that bouldery riverbeds belonging to class V to VII of land in the Doon Valley (Uttar Pradesh) were successfully utilised for fuel and fodder plantation of *Dalbergia sissoo, Crysopogon fulvus, Acacia catechu* and *Eulalioposis binata* yielding 5.5 t/ha/yr wood and 3.8 to 4.2 t/ha/yr grass thus giving an income in the range of Rs 1100-2250 per ha per annum. On similar land another study (Singh et al. 1982) reported 3 to 4 t/ha yield from fuel-fodder plantation of *Albizzia lebbek, Grewia optiva, Bauhinia purpurea, Leucaenea leucocephela,* and *Crysopogon fulvus* and *Eulalioposis binata* grass.

Other costs and yields were estimated for revenue and private land by the Agriculture Finance Corporation in 1986. At the request of the NWDB it identified large chunks of wastelands in the country, and prepared model projects for their development. Their recommendations can be summarised as in table 2.14.

Table 2.14: Cost of reclamation of wastelands as estimated by Agriculture Finance Corporation in 1987: costs, species and yield

Name of district	Area of identi-fied waste-land in ha	Cost of recla-mation including overheads in lakh Rs	Cost per hectare Rs	Main species proposed	Av. yield in mt /ha/ year
1. Chittoor (A.P.)	500	50.5	10,100	eucalyptus, subabul, teak, bamboo, mango, and grasses	8
2. Srikakulum (A.P.)	600	57.41	9,600	eucalyptus, subabul, cashew *Casuarina*	6-8
3. Surat (Gujarat)	1251	109.6	8,600	eucalyptus, subabul, teak, bamboo	4-6
4. Sabarkantha (Gujarat)	976	86.72	8,900	same as above plus *Prosopis juliflora*	4-6
5. Hassan (Karnataka)	400	41.2	10,300	Mango, sapota, eucalyptus, *Casuarina*, tamarind	5-7
6. Meerut (U.P.)	625	91.00	15,000	Poplar, euca-lyptus, babul, sheesham, mulberry	4-8
7. Raebareli (U.P.)	434	56.70	13,500	*Prosopis juliflora*	6-7

Source: NWDB 1988c.

Thus an investment of 9 to 15,000 rupees per ha would increase the productivity from almost nil at present to 4 to 8 mt (or 6 to 12 cu m) per ha per year, which is eight to 16 times higher than the present productivity of government forests. The ratio of yields to costs of planting trees on farm bunds, roadsides and canal banks would be much more favourable as they generally have good moisture and are more productive than revenue waste-lands. The cost of planting trees in 1988 in various State social forestry projects, at Rs 4000-8000 per hectare including overheads, have also been lower than the average for the AFC reclamation projects.

Output from tree planting projects depends on many factors with soils, climate and moisture, species, technology and protection among the most important. Not all can be controlled or predicted. Because they vary, especially survival and protection, output from similar lands can vary by a factor of as much as 10. This means that isolated examples can mislead. Some production results are even derived from laboratory conditions, without the field problems of cattle and human pressure.

Protection appears to us the most important factor. On private lands it is usually moderate to good, but on public lands lack of protection is often a major weakness. Improvements (see chapters 7 and 9) are feasible but to be realistic we hesitate to estimate a productivity for public lands of more than 2 tonnes (3 cu m) per ha. This is less than an average of 5 to 6 tonnes for private farmers without irrigation, but about four times the present productivity of government forests.

PRODUCTION POTENTIAL OF MFPS

Conventional calculations measure potential of forest lands in terms of production of wood only. For people living near forests, many non-wood products, like leaves, seeds and fruits are more important. These many "minor" forest products (MFPs) as they are misleadingly known, provide subsistence and income, including during the slack seasons. Of the total wage employment in the forestry sector, MFPs have accounted for more than 70 per cent (Gupta 1982a:2). More important is the opportunities for self-employment that these provide to the forest dwellers, for which no data are available. From palmyrah trees alone over 28,000 families derive sustenance in Tamil Nadu (Jambulingam and Fernandes 1986:23).

Their potential production and employment is several times higher than the present (table 2.15).

Most of these estimates are based on the report of the NCA, and hence reflect the field situation of the late sixties. As the data for some of the MFPs discussed in Chapter 7 show (sec 7.2), production has further fallen, thus increasing the gap between production and potential.

We conclude that the potential production of MFPs has scarcely begun to be tapped. Not least, this is because research has so far neglected most of them. We see no reason to disagree with the recent authoritative estimates, made by the Ministry of Welfare, Government of India (GOI 1987b) which have assessed that though the production potential of tendu was 2.5 times present production, that for most MFPs was at least 10 times higher.

On the basis of all this evidence, and these estimates, we conclude that degraded forest, revenue lands, and private wastes have the biological potential to produce on an average, well over four times as much as biomass as currently, in some cases as much as 10 times more; that some of this potential is to produce more MFPs with a high value to weight ratio; and that the investment costs for this transformation do not appear excessive compared with the results.

Table 2.15: Current and potential production of and employment in collection of non-wood forest products in India (excluding processing)

(Production : Tonnes)
(Employment : Man years)

Description	Production		Employment	
	Current	Potential	Current	Potential
Fibres and flosses	83,600	125,400	58,000	87,000
Grasses	350,000	525,000	1,200,000	1,800,000
Bamboo and canes	2,206,000	4,309,000	92,000	180,000
Essential oils	32,266	102,547	27,220	140,830
Mahua	85,000	490,000	28,600	163,000
Neem	6,000	418,000	1,000	70,000
Karanj	56,000	111,000	19,000	37,000
Kusum	30,000	90,000	6,700	30,000
Sal seeds	240,000	5,504,000	53,000	1,123,000
Tans and dyes	187,400	290,000	21,170	33,200
Gums and resins	107,344	175,500	172,300	258,450
Tendu leaves	320,000	480,000	215,000	322,500
Lac and tasar	41,800	62,700	101,500	152,250
Sarpagandha	600	1,600	16,000	42,670
Kuth	600	1,000	16,000	26,670
Cinchona	1,420	2,000	23,635	33,335
Tamarind	2,50,000	375,000	NA	Na
Edible products like wild fruits	NA	NA	NA	NA
Total	3,998,030	13,052,747	2,051,125	4,499,905

Source: Gupta and Guleria 1982a:133; ISST 1987

2.8 Demand

Much, however, depends upon demand. To be able to grow trees, and make land much more productive biologically, is one thing. For the returns to justify that investment is another. There may be overriding long-term ecological reasons for tree planting; but economic considerations also strongly influence what government, panchayats and private farmers decide to do.

Past changes in demand can provide some pointers to the future. In the past two decades, demand for wood and tree products has grown fast. Demand has two segments: demand from those who collect such products free of charge, and demand from the commercial and industrial sector. There is some overlap of these two segments as several products like wild fruits, oil seeds and even fuelwood, are in part consumed and in part sold by those who gather them.

Past and future demand for tree products can be considered under three headings: the so-called minor or non-wood forest and tree products; fuelwood; and industrial wood.

MINOR OR NON-WOOD TREE PRODUCTS

Non-wood products are harvested and marketed from both private and public land, but those obtained from forests predominate. Demand projections for many of these important MFPs are unfortunately not available. We are giving below projections for some of the MFPs, which are based on the six volumes of study (GOI 1988c) done for the Department of Tribal Development, Government of India.

Marketed production of oilseeds from trees (*Mahua, Neem, Karanj, Kusum* and Sal are the main species) in 1981-82 was 0.5 million tonnes. On the supply side, the Forest Research Institute estimated that it could be increased to 67.71 million tonnes. On the demand side, subject to price factors, oilseeds from forests could perhaps substitute for part at least of the over 1.5 million tonnes of edible oil (equivalent to 12 million tonnes of oil seeds) imported annually. Even if the production of oilseeds were increased from 0.5 to 4.5 million tonnes it could create employment for 2 million people for 100 days in a year, with earnings, at Rs 20 a day, of Rs 400 crores a year. The opportunity to save foreign exchange and help the poor simultaneously is striking.

Tasar silk is a commodity produced mainly by tribals spread over seven States. The host trees are mainly Sal, *Arjun* and oak. India produces 22 per cent of the total world production. Production of tasar in India during 1981-86 increased by 23 per cent a year, and its demand till 1996 is likely to increase by at least 15 per cent a year. This would require additional plantations over 50,000 ha; and could absorb 58,000 new tribal families, besides strengthening the economy of 1 lakh tribals already engaged in its production.

Tamarind is a widely occurring tree in India, especially in the southern States. Every part of the tree has value. Its fruit, collected during December-March, is widely used in preparing curries, sauces and chutneys. In a year, a good tree yields 1.5 quintals of tamarind fruit valued at Rs 300. Annual marketed production of tamarind fruit is about 2,50,000 tonnes. Although estimate of its future demand has not been made, during the period 1981-86 its market price, as well as exports revenue, increased at an annual rate of 20 per cent, or 2.5 times the annual rate of inflation. Prospects for a buoyant future demand would seem good.

Grasses and leaf fodder are other important MFPs obtained from public lands. The Committee on Fodder and Grasses estimated that in 1985 only about 57 per cent of dry fodder and 27 per cent of green fodder requirements were being met (table 2.16).

Table 2.16 indicates orders of magnitude, and confirms the common observation of a big unsatisfied demand for fodder. As human and animal populations increase, and the quality of cattle improve, so too the demand for fodder can be expected to rise further, including the demand for the leaf fodder and grasses provided by forests.

Table 2.16: Supply and demand for fodder

	Dry fodder	Green fodder
	(in million tonnes)	
Requirement	780	932
Total supply	441	250
Of which supply from		
Agriculture crop residues	236	—
Grasses	205	—
Cultivated green fodder	—	208
Leaf fodder, weeds etc.	—	42

Source: NWDB 1987c:35.

FUELWOOD

Estimates for future fuelwood demand are so disparate that a degree of agnosticism is in order. Estimates for the year 2000 A.D. vary from 163 mt by the Planning Commission to 300-330 mt by the Advisory Board on Energy. The Forest Survey of India (FSI 1988:46) estimated that there was a gap of 130 mt in demand and production of firewood in the country in 1987. The confusion arises for two reasons. First, foresters assume that all fuelwood is removed only from the forest areas and as logs. Other sources are conveniently forgotten. This tends to put the blame on forest dwellers for deforestation. Second, it is difficult to be precise about demand for an item which is mostly collected and where substitutions occur: smaller twigs and leaves can substitute for larger sticks and logs; and where fuelwood is easily accessible and opportunity cost of rural labour remains low, fuelwood can substitute for other non-commercial and commercial fuels, leading to higher estimates of demand.

Consumption figures are a safer guide. An earlier estimate (GOI 1962) gave the requirement of fuelwood in 1960-61 as 60 million tonnes. This was being met with 10 mt from recorded forest sources and 50 mt from private and community lands and from unrecorded removal from forests.

We take this as the base figure. A survey in 1981 (table 2.17) gave a figure of 94 mt as fuelwood consumption in 1978-79. Thus the annual rate of growth in fuelwood consumption between 1960-61 and 1978-79 works out to be 2.5 per cent. This is also supported by the Working Group on Energy Policy (GOI 1979), which worked out a growth rate of 2.5 per cent in consumption of fuelwood during the period 1953-54 to 1975-76. We shall assume that consumption after 1979 grew at the rate of 2.0 per cent, because of faster economic growth and increased opportunities for modern fuels. This would mean a projected consumption of 145 mt in 2000-2001.

On sources of fuelwood, table 2.17 indicates orders of magnitude. 73 per cent of fuelwood was collected, and only 27 per cent was purchased. Even if

Table 2.17: Sources of supply of firewood in India in 1978-79

(million tonnes a year)

	Rural			Urban			Grand Total
	Logs	Twigs	Total	Logs	Twigs	Total	
Collected from							
i. own land	5.2	9.1	14.3	—	—	—	14.3
ii. neighbour's land	0.3	3.0	3.3	—	—	—	3.3
iii. forest land	4.6	18.9	23.5	—	—	—	23.5
iv. roadsides etc.	1.3	24.4	25.7	0.4	1.6	2.0	27.7
Total collected	11.4	55.4	66.8	0.4	1.6	2.0	68.8
Purchased	8.7	3.3	12.0	11.1	2.6	13.7	25.7
Total	20.1	58.7	78.8	11.5	4.2	15.7	94.5

Source: Leach 1987:43

Note: As regards collection from private lands, the 28th round of National Sample Survey indicated (NWDB 1986a: 11) that about 30 mt (as against 14.3 + 3.3 = 17.6 mt shown in the above table) of fuelwood is obtained from private houses, gardens and from trees around the houses.

the unreasonable assumption was made that all the logs purchased come from forest land, the total removal of logs from forests would only be 4.6 + 8.7 + 11.1= 24.4 mt. This compares with a recorded production of 15 mt of firewood from logs from forests. Illegal removals from forests do occur; but the assertion of the Forest Survey of India (FSI 1988:46) that the imbalance of 130 mt between demand and production of firewood is one single cause for deforestation does not seem tenable.

Sources of fuelwood change; in the past ten years, more fuelwood has come from *Prosopis juliflora*, considered a weed by foresters, than from social forestry plantations. In Tamil Nadu alone, the total yield of *Prosopis* for fuelwood was 1.8 mt in 1984 (GOTN 1988:20), accounting as a single species for one-fifth of the total fuelwood consumption. But even with the advent of *Prosopis*, fuelwood shortages persist. The Tamil Nadu study found that while farm households used 2500 to 3500 kg of fuelwood annually, agriculture labourers were able to use only 1000 to 2000 kg a year. The study observed (ibid:9) that a substantial number of households with little or no land were fuel deficient.

If fuelwood consumption rises at the modest rate of 2 per cent per annum, and consumption at the turn of the century is of the order of 145 mt there should be scope for new and improved livelihoods for those, currently three to four million people (sec 7.1), engaged in supplying fuelwood to urban areas.

INDUSTRIAL WOOD

Demand for industrial wood exceeds domestic supply. Recorded production of industrial wood from India's forests declined from 13.5 m cu m (= 8.1 mt) in

1979-80 (World Bank 1988) to 12 m cu m in 1985 (FSI 1988:46), whereas the demand in 1985 was 27.58 m cu m (table 2.18).

Table 2.18: Demand for industrial wood

Sector	Demand in million cu m
Pulp and paper	6.57
Packing cases	6.81
Agriculture implements	5.43
Construction industry	2.50
Plywood	1.71
Matchwood	0.44
Railways	0.50
Fibre and particle board	0.23
Furniture	0.36
Sports goods	0.03
Others, incl. mining	3.00
	27.58

The Asian Development Bank (ADB 1987) estimated the demand to rise to 38 m cu m by 2000 A.D. by which time domestic supply would be 33 m cu m, 25 m cu m from government forests and 8 m cu m from new private plantations. Looking at the present declining trend, it is difficult to accept the ADB's prediction of an increase in the production from government forests from 12 to 25 m cu m, unless drastic changes are made in the present policy of plantation and protection. Therefore, the gap between demand and supply of industrial timber is likely to continue.

One of the largest users of purchased wood products are paper, pulp and newsprint units. The Seventh Plan Working Group on Paper Industry (GOI 1985d) estimated that the total quantity of raw material required by A.D. 2000 will be 14 million tonnes as against the availability in 1985 of 4.5 million tonnes. This threefold increase over 15 years, assuming a productivity of 4 tonnes per hectare, will require pulpwood plantations on 2.4 million hectares during 1980-90. The paper industry in a note in 1988 to the government (*Financial Express* 20th August 1988) worked out this figure as close to 3 million hectares. Not all of it should be eucalyptus (although the total new eucalyptus plantation during the period 1980–90 may be close to 2.5 m ha), as part of the requirement has to be met from bamboo and grasses. Of the total eucalyptus planted in India so far, it is estimated (World Bank 1987) that only 25 per cent would go to the paper mills. The rest is not required by them, and has to find other markets.

At least half of the demand for industrial wood has to be met from slow growing long rotation timber (Campbell 1987), whose incremental annual growth is less than that of the short rotation species like eucalyptus. Hence, in terms of area to be planted for reaching the goal of overall self sufficiency in wood, some attention has to be paid to long rotation crops like Sal and Teak.

How does one compare the gaps in demand and supply for fuelwood with that of industrial wood? The Principal CCF Karnataka has estimated (Shyam Sunder and Parameswarappa 1987b:2023) that the deficit faced by the pulp industry in Karnataka in 1985 is 0.2 million tonnes per annum, whereas the firewood deficit is more than 4 million tonnes. The estimate of the firewood deficit may be high because of the tendency of the foresters to overlook non-forest sources, but the USAID World Bank Report (1988:26) also puts commercial and industrial requirements low as a proportion of the total demand for wood, at less than 20 per cent. Requirements for fuelwood exceed those for industrial wood. Fuelwood will remain the largest use of wood, and its provision a major source of livelihoods for the poor.

To conclude this section on demand, future requirements for all tree products, including MFPs, fuelwood and industrial wood, appear likely to continue to rise. The extent to which demand will be met by supply will be partly reflected in prices, to which we now turn.

2.9 Prices

Much of the gains from growing trees on waste and degraded lands take the form of subsistence goods for those who gather them; but part of the potential gain will also flow from the sale of the main types of wood products: poles, timber, pulpwood, and firewood, with the benefits from sales depending on prices and price trends.

POLES

Different products command different prices, and move in different ways. The trend of the late 1980s has been for prices for eucalyptus poles, pulpwood and firewood to converge and become almost identical, with poles tending to decline. A World Bank/USAID team assessed the retail price of eucalyptus poles in Feb-March, 1988 in the north Indian markets at Rs 400 a tonne (USAID 1988), a fall from the earlier price of Rs 500 a tonne. Another study of Andhra Pradesh found the price at the farm gate to be about Rs 250 per tonne (CIDA 1988). The USAID/World Bank evaluation team (USAID 1988) considered that alternate uses for eucalyptus poles would be found, and therefore there was no fear of a further fall in prices. Already eucalyptus from western Uttar Pradesh, Haryana and Punjab was being used to make crates in Himachal Pradesh for carting apples. Its use in brick kilns and sugar cane factories had also increased.

TIMBER

In contrast, timber commands a very high price, with consumers paying Rs 3000-10000 per cu m. Timber prices increased by 14 per cent annually between 1970 and 1980. When deflated by the wholesale price index real timber price rose in the above period by 5.8 per cent annually (Bentley 1984:17). The rise in price of timber during 1975-85 was dramatic, as seen from table 2.19.

Table 2.19: Price index of commodities

	General index of wholesale prices	Index of wholesale agricultural prices	Index of timber prices
1970-71	100	100	100
1975-76	173	157	178
1980-81	257	211	407
1981-82	281	237	556
1982-83	288	248	740
1983-84	316	283	811
1984-85	338	303	946
1985-86	358	310	821
1986-87	377	330	866
July 1987	401	368	945

The fall in timber price in the two years, 1985 to 1987 may have been due to liberal imports of pulpwood, and expectation of a bumper eucalyptus crop from many States. As the price dropped, wood became more competitive for new uses, and the price began to pick up again in 1987, and resume its upward trend, with the tentative index for June 1988 at 1000.

Besides the increase in demand, the main reason for the rise in timber prices has been the sharp fall in supply of timber from government forests in the last fifteen years. This has resulted from deforestation and from the growth in conservation consciousness among State governments. Falls in supply are reported to have been 44 per cent for sawn timber in Uttar Pradesh from 1971-72 to 1980-81 (GOUP 1983a: 64), 66 per cent for wood in Karnataka from 1976-77 to 1984-85 (GOK 1986: 16,22), and 36 per cent for wood in Orissa from 1979-80 to 1984-85 (GOO 1988). In Madhya Pradesh, the largest timber producing State, timber production fell by 44 per cent from 1981 to 1985, as shown in table 2.20.

In such circumstances, a rise in prices is easy to explain.

FIREWOOD

The increase in the retail price of firewood in rural markets of India is shown in table 2.21.

Thus between the period 1973 and 1985 firewood prices at constant prices almost doubled. However, there is some evidence that the trend of steep rise in fuelwood prices has been arrested between 1985 and 1988 (Singh 1988b:46; ODA 1988).

Table 2.20: Production of timber and fuelwood in M.P.

(in thousand cu m)

Year	Timber	Fuelwood	Total	Remarks
1981	1700	4000	5700	The sudden fall in 1984 is
1982	1690	4050	5740	said to be due to the
1983	1500	3500	5000	government's decision
1984	932	1814	2746	to stop felling of trees
1985	944	2029	2973	in 11 districts of the
				State

Source: GOMP 1986: 5.

Table 2.21: Retail price of firewood in rural India

Year	All India average retail price of firewood	All India wholesale price index (1970-71=100)	Firewood prices at constant (1970-71) prices (2) x100/3
	Rs/quintal		Rs/quintal
(1)	(2)	(3)	(4)
1973	9.1	140	6.5
1978	18.2	185	9.8
1985	43.8	350	12.5

Source: UNDP 1986: 113

FODDER

Fodder in the form of leaves and grasses is another forest product the value of which has risen. In Sholapur, a semi-arid district in Maharashtra, prices of sorghum grain rose 40 per cent from 1975 to 1986, but during the same period sorghum fodder rose 670 per cent. These compare with a rise of 208 per cent in the all-India wholesale price index. The jump in fodder prices is partly accounted for by a drought year in 1986, but the increase in fodder prices compared with food remains striking. Moreover, taking averages for two four-year periods, the fodder to grain price ratio almost doubled in just over a decade, from 0.20 in 1971-75 to 0.36 in 1982-86 (Walker 1987). Fodder prices in India have, like timber, also risen faster than inflation or grain prices.

2.10 Conclusion

The future is difficult to foresee. Past price trends may not be sustained. Oversupply of a market can always drive prices down, at least for a time, as happened in northwest India, perhaps only temporarily, with eucalyptus poles. Our best judgement is that continuing economic growth, world shortages of timber and tree products, resilient demand for many of the MFPs, and diversification of tree products, presents a long-term prospect of large increases in demand for most, if not all, of the main tree products. For many people, trees will continue to provide subsistence goods. In addition, and more than in the past, trees can be seen as a major source of future incomes and security for those who grow them, and who gather their products and sell them.

2.11 Location of Poverty and Potentials

Whether poor people can benefit directly from the potentials of lift irrigation and of trees depends partly on location. As we noted in chapter one, for some of the poor there is the possibility of migration. But many of the measures which could enable the poor to gain will be most feasible if they are already living where the resource potentials are. To what extent they do can be examined at two levels: the State level, through State statistics; and the local level, locality by locality.

At the State level, it is noteworthy that most of the 221.5 million of India's rural population estimated in 1984 to be living below the official poverty line are to be found in 12 States—Andhra Pradesh, Assam, Bihar, Gujarat, Karnataka, Madhya Pradesh, Maharashtra, Orissa, Rajasthan, Tamil Nadu, Uttar Pradesh and West Bengal. Together, these States account for 70 per cent of India's landmass, but 87 per cent of its rural population and over 94 per cent of the rural poor. While the general analysis applies also to other States, we will focus on these twelve.

They can be classified according to their endowments per poor household, and whether these are above or below the national average as in table 2.22. The detailed figures State-wise are presented in table 2.23.

Table 2.22: Potentials per poor household compared with the national average

| | | Reclaimable wastelands per household | |
		Below	Above
		I	III
		Bihar	Karnataka
Untapped	Below	Tamil Nadu	Rajasthan
groundwater		West Bengal	
per household		II	IV
		Assam	AP
	Above	UP	Gujarat
			MP
			Maharashtra
			Orissa

Any conclusions drawn from these categories and figures have to be carefully qualified. The estimates do not include lift irrigation from surface water, the scope for which is sometimes considerable in undulating and forest

Table 2.23: Spatial distribution of rural poverty — Unutilised groundwater and reclaimable wastelands

Category	State	Number of rural poor (1983-84)		Ground water potential (ham/ poor family)	Reclaimable wastelands (ha) per rural poor family			
		(m)	(%)	(1986)	Private	Forest	Revenue	All
I	Bihar	32.9	14.9	0.40	0.40	0.26	0.03	0.69
	Tamil Nadu	14.7	6.6	0.64	0.86	0.36	0.08	1.30
	West Bengal	18.4	8.3	0.39	0.20	0.11	0.02	0.34
II	Assam	4.49	2.0	2.0	0.59	0.94	0.23	1.77
	UP	44.00	11.9	0.82	0.35	0.17	0.06	0.58
III	Karnataka	10.30	4.65	0.6	1.49	1.03	0.57	3.09
	Rajasthan	10.50	4.7	0.53	2.88	0.96	1.62	5.45
IV	AP	16.44	7.4	1.0	1.23	1.19	0.29	2.71
	Gujarat	6.77	3.0	1.2	1.57	0.55	0.94	3.05
	MP	21.80	9.85	1.4	1.01	1.73	0.60	3.33
	Maharashtra	17.61	7.95	0.87	1.17	0.84	0.42	2.44
	Orissa	10.80	4.9	1.00	0.59	1.57	0.20	2.36
	Other States & UTs	12.80	5.78	0.74	1.08	3.77	0.46	5.31
	All India	221.5	100	0.79	0.84	0.86	0.31	2.01

Technical notes:
i)   *Sources:*
a.   GOI 1988e
b.   MWR (1986: 34)
c.   Statewise figures for reclaimable wastelands are taken from table 2.13.
ii)   In computing resource potential per rural poor family, family size is uniformly assumed as 5.3.

areas. Nor do they include the growing of trees on the land of resource-poor farmers whose land is not classified as degraded, such as many marginal farmers in fertile areas. More seriously, estimates are in every case for large geographical areas with widely diverse conditions. Bihar is an aggregate of two sharply contrasted zones—North Bihar with its excellent groundwater and fertile soils, and South Bihar with its hills and forests. North Bihar may well belong in category II and South Bihar in category III. The potential of wastelands also varies enormously, depending on soils and rainfall. Wasteland or forest in West Bengal, for example, with a high rainfall, can have many times the potential of wasteland in dry parts of Rajasthan. Also, estimates themselves have been changing and can be expected to continue to do so as the reality changes and as measurements improve.

The value of the table is not so much that it indicates that some States have more or less than others, but that it shows that all States have very substantial endowments per poor household. The uneven distribution of resources means that in many places endowments per household will be higher. An earlier calculation suggested that on an average either one hectare of trees or one hectare metre of water from lift irrigation could enable a household to meet half the poverty line consumption level. This estimate will be high or low depending on local conditions of topography, soils and rainfall, but the scope for generating complete new livelihoods is evident. '

A more general aim can be to strengthen and support the existing livelihood strategies of poor households where they are, adding new sources of subsistence and income. This needs less water from irrigation, or fewer trees, than creating complete livelihoods. It can help households to diversify and to reduce risk. The conclusion seems secure: that as supplements and complements to existing livelihood strategies, lift irrigation and trees present an untapped potential for crores of poor rural people, a potential the value of which has risen and may well continue to rise.

Two major questions have immediately to be confronted.

The first concerns location at the micro level. The distinction (section 2.1) between core and peripheral areas and poverty helps here. There will be many local exceptions, but as noted the core poor are often closer to groundwater, while the peripheral poor are often closer to surface bodies of water and to reclaimable waste. Those poor people who start in a favoured position through proximity are, then, marginal and small farmers in core areas with groundwater, and those in peripheral areas who have land close to surface water, who have land on which they can grow trees, or who are near reclaimable waste, including forest fringes. In searching for strategies, these questions of location provide a starting point in seeing where to concentrate.

The second question concerns who gains and who loses. It is one thing to establish, as this chapter has sought to do, a vast potential for direct benefits to crores of poor people through the exploitation of untapped potentials. It is quite another for this to be made to happen in practice. Unless this question is faced and answered, any programmes based on the analysis of these first two chapters could suffer the fate of so many of their predecessors; the gain would be captured by the less poor and the more powerful, with the poorer and weaker gaining little, or nothing, or even losing. Crucial but neglected questions of practical political economy are therefore next on the agenda.

CHAPTER THREE

Who Gains and Who Loses?

ABSTRACT

In the normal course of events, it is mainly those with more wealth and power who are able to gain access to and appropriate the benefits from lift irrigation and trees.

Inequalities in the ownership of lift irrigation systems (LISs) are sharp, and increase as one moves from water abundant (WA) to water scarce (WS) areas. State tubewells have suffered from inefficiency, poor management, and domination by local bigwigs. Spacing and licensing norms have denied late-coming resource-poor farm families (RPFs) means to acquire their own LISs for access to water.

With trees the pattern has been similar. With social forestry it has been mainly the larger farmers who have used programme incentives to convert their farm lands, often irrigated, to plantations. It is the state, the Forest Department bureaucracy, the contractors, organised thieves and the pulp industries which have derived the major benefit from depleting the forests, while women, tribals, the landless and RPFs have been the losers.

The question is whether these trends can be reversed so that the poor will in future gain more. Learning from the past, practical political economy seeks feasibility through approaches in which either all gain, or the poor gain without the powerful directly losing, or where countervailing power is created to induce the wealthy and influential to accept losses. Lift irrigation and trees will be examined in this perspective, searching for practical ways in which the poorer can gain more than they would have done.

3.1 Appropriation and Access

Who gains and who loses from the potentials of lift irrigation and trees is determined largely by processes of appropriation and access. Both water and trees have historically been common property resources (CPRs). Sequences of exclusion and appropriation have varied. Open access, where all comers can use a resource freely, can be distinguished from community or group access, where it can be used only by the community or group, and private access where the resource has been appropriated by families, households or individuals. Water for lift irrigation and trees have different physical and legal characteristics which affect the ease and nature of appropriation and access.

As a form of CPR, groundwater has peculiar characteristics. It is taken as belonging to whoever owns the land above it and can extract it. Thus a person with only a few cents of land can sink a deep tube and make a living by selling water to nearby farmers, even though the water extracted flows in mainly from underneath their land. One farmers' extraction can also lower the water table for his neighbour, and even make his tube or well run dry, but this is generally accepted as legitimate, even though the water, again, comes from under his neighbour's land. Spacing regulations which require minimum distances between wells or tubes are intended to limit extraction. But groundwater retains some of the character of an open access resource, the appropriation of which depends mainly on a capital asset, a lift irrigation system (LIS) installed on a site. Small and marginal farmers are at a disadvantage from their lack of land to irrigate and their lack of capital for the LIS, but importantly, a well combined with a water market can compensate for their lack of land because of the volume of water to which they can gain access.

Open bodies of water are similar. Lakes, dam reservoirs, rivers, streams, canals, drains and standing water after floods are all sources from which water is appropriated and pumped. Access and appropriation require an LIS. Here again various regulations apply. Limits are sometimes placed on the amount of water that can be pumped up out of a reservoir. Pumping from canals is often prohibited. As with groundwater, those who appropriate open water usually do so at the cost of others whose access is diminished or made more difficult. While the regulations are designed to protect downstream users, piracy is common.

With trees, there are many variations in rights and access. Tree tenure and rights are linked in different and sometimes complicated ways with land tenure and rights (Raintree 1987). At the simple extremes, the State has complete and exclusive rights to trees in Reserve Forests (40 m ha in 1986-87), and private owners of land may have complete and exclusive rights to trees on their land where there is no government regulation limiting them. But in between, there are many overlaps and combinations of State, community and individual rights. In Protected Forests (22 m ha) people have rights of collection of fuelwood and other subsistence items. Many of what are known as "unclassed forests" (13 m ha) are village or community forests with various forms of group access. And on privately owned land, there are quite often State restrictions on felling trees of certain species. As with groundwater and open bodies of water, extra-legal appropriation is widespread. Changes over the last 25 years in the area of legal categories of forest land are shown in table 3.1.

The rights, conventions and practices which determine who has access to and can appropriate and use water and trees, are not static, and are affected by Government regulations and programmes. In order to understand how, in future, the poor can gain more through them, we must first examine the normal processes of appropriation and access which have obtained in the past.

Table 3.1: Changes in area of forest land

Category	Area in	
	1960-61	1986-87
	(in million hectares)	
Reserve	31.6	40.2
Protected	24.1	21.7
Unclassed and others	13.3	13.3
Total	69.0	75.2

(NCHSE 1987; FSI 1988:2)

3.2 Who Gains from Lift Irrigation?

Gain from lift irrigation development in the last three decades has been heavily tilted in favour of the less poor. This conclusion is based on four major points:

1) Ownership of private lift irrigation systems (LISs) has been skewed to the resource-rich and more so in WS than WA areas.

2) State tubewells have not performed well and have tended to serve the less poor.

3) Exploitation by resource-rich farmers can lower water tables and cause external diseconomies to others, and makes access harder for the resource-poor.

4) Laws and regulations have helped the affluent farmers to preempt ground water resources and exclude others.

UNEQUAL OWNERSHIP

Ownership of a lift irrigation system (LIS) is the best means of direct access to groundwater. But the distribution of LIS ownership is unequal. This is not surprising. Modern water lifting technology is capital intensive. The risk of capital loss in establishing LISs is high in many hard rock areas. The indivisibility built into the technology especially below a certain scale of operation makes it unattractive for small holders, especially if holdings are fragmented. Over 90 per cent of the lift irrigation potential utilised in the country at present has been developed at private initiative. Over 3.36 m shallow tubewells and 8.7 m open wells are owned by private farmers. While human and animal-powered water lifting devices are still in use to draw water from shallow open wells and surface bodies, some 5.7 m electric pumpsets and 3.5 m diesel sets, all privately owned, account for the bulk of the existing lift irrigation capacity (MWR 1986: 35-40). The pattern of ownership of private LISs is highly skew. Table 3.2 illustrates the extent of inequality in Gujarat which matches the degree of inequality in land holdings. Over 58 per cent of land-owning families with less than 3 ha owned just over 20 per cent of the land and 25 per cent of the modern LISs, while 24 per cent of the farmers with over 5 ha owned 61 per cent of the land and 53 per cent of the modern LISs.

The extent of inequality in LIS ownership varies across regions. In WA areas of the northern river basins where the cost of installing an LIS is low and risk of well failure minimal, resource-poor farmers can secure direct access to groundwater with relative ease. Studies of LIS ownership in WA areas in the south, such as coastal Andhra Pradesh (Shah and Raju 1986) as well as in the northern plains (Shankar 1987a; Pant 1984) show the ownership of modern LISs to be widely shared.

In WS areas, in contrast, access for the resource-poor is more difficult. In the hard rock water-scarce areas of Southern Peninsula and Deccan Plateau, where water tables are deep and the risk of well failure high, resource-poor families are at a disadvantage in gaining direct access to groundwater. In many parts of Gujarat where costs of installing a modern LIS can be as high as Rs 80,000 or more, LIS ownership is concentrated among the resource rich (Shah and Raju 1986) (see table 3.2). Field studies suggest similar tendencies in water stress areas of southern States like Karnataka (Prahladachar 1987), Tamil Nadu (Guhan and Mencher 1983) and Telangana region in Andhra Pradesh (Shah 1986). There is also evidence that affluent farmers are the first to exploit groundwater (Guhan and Mencher 1983; Shah and Raju 1986) and smallholders begin to follow somewhat hesitantly with a lag which at times may be longer than 15-20 years.

Table 3.2: Inequality in private ownership of Lift Irrigation Systems: Gujarat 1977

Land holding sizes (hectares)	Percentage of land owned	Percentage of all holdings	Percentage of LIS with diesel or electric pumpsets owned
0-1	3.3	24.2	4.1
1-3	17.2	34.1	21.0
3-5	18.4	17.5	21.9
5-10	32.4	17.2	35.3
10+	28.7	7.0	17.7
	100.0	100.0	100.0

Source: Shah 1984:12

The resource-rich have thus led in gaining access to and preempting appropriation of water from lift irrigation. The benefits of huge subsidies on power supply to agriculture have been distributed according to the owner-ship pattern of electric LISs which is biased in their favour (Repetto 1986:13). On the other hand, moves to provide subsidies on capital costs to enable the resource-poor to own modern LIS have been hamstrung by bureaucratic hassle and by conflicting regulations which hit them particularly hard. Official efforts to help the resource-poor gain access to water through LISs have not been very effective.

STATE TUBEWELL PROGRAMMES

State tubewell programmes launched by many States, especially in the North, were primarily aimed at broadening access to groundwater. The generally poor service provided by State tubewells (see chapter 4) has reduced their effectiveness in achieving this goal.

Even with better performance, however, State tubewells could not make a major impact since their share of total lift irrigation is small. Against over 9 m modern LISs owned by private farmers, there are a mere 40,000 State tubewells 85 per cent of which are in the seven States of Uttar Pradesh, Bihar, Orissa, Gujarat, West Bengal, Haryana and Punjab. Although an average State tubewell has a much greater pumping capacity and potential command area than an average private LIS, the actual areas served by State tubewells are less than their potential and have shown a tendency to decline over years (Shankar 1981). Even in States which have taken major initiatives in launching State tubewell programmes, private ownership of LISs predominates. In Uttar Pradesh, which had over half of the nation's State tubewells in 1981, for instance, for every 1,000 ha of farm land, there were only 1.2 State tubewells but 68.5 LISs with private farmers; in West Bengal, the figures were 0.44 and 25.6; and in Bihar, 0.64 and 27.9 (Sharma 1984). Moreover, as we examine in detail in chapter 4, poor management, long shutdown periods, delays in repair works and lack of maintenance have hit the operational efficiency of State tubewell programmes. To the extent then, that State tubewells have potential to serve smaller and poorer farmers, they have achieved relatively little because of the limited areas they supply with irrigation and their inefficient operation.

In their siting and in the access they provide in practice to water, State tubewells tend to favour local bigwigs, who are the wealthier and more influential (see, for example, Pandit 1983; Shankar 1981; Datye and Patil 1987; Singh and Satish 1988). Micro-level evidence of this in South Asia comes from Bangladesh (Hartmann and Boyce 1983:256-7; Howes 1984, 1985; Mandal and Palmer-Jones 1987) and also from India, notably from Shankar's (1981) study of 36 State tubewells in Uttar Pradesh. Although patterns of control, distribution and access have been found to vary, the poorer and weaker generally lose out. Whether through bribery or other forms of influence, State tubewells tend to be sited on or near the land of the wealthier and more powerful, who then get water more easily and with lower transmission losses than those whose land is more distant. For others, proximity does not necessarily guarantee supply. Shankar reported that it was a common observation in the villages where tubewells were located that some of the fields lying close to the tubewells were unirrigated whereas distant fields were irrigated. "The unirrigated fields generally belonged to poorer households who manage to get water only after the fields of bigger cultivators have been irrigated." (ibid: 47). Even force was used: "There were cases when powerful persons intercepted the water going to the field of persons who were comparatively weak. At Parsanipur when a weaker farmer protested he was beaten by the powerful one." (ibid: 48-9). Operators are themselves liable to be either water lords in their own right, or more often pawns in the hands of dominant individuals or groups. Caste, lineage and faction can cross-cut wealth, power, poverty, weakness, and location, as factors governing access to State tubewell water, giving relatively good access to some of the poorer belonging to a caste, lineage or faction which controls a tubewell. But in general, and especially where water is scarce and its supply unreliable, the poor tend to get it last, in least adequate quantities, least predictably, and at highest cost.

EXTERNAL DISECONOMIES

With both access through LISs and access through State tubewells, the less poor have gained but the poorer may appear to have lost not in absolute but only in relative terms. But in situations of unregulated private exploitation of groundwater, the resource-poor are often left worse off in absolute terms as well. Large-scale development of tubewell irrigation in parts of Uttar Pradesh and Gujarat, for instance, has resulted in the lowering of water tables to depths which are still easily accessible to deep and indeed shallow tubewells. But this has reduced substantially the yields of traditional shallow open wells still retained and used by poor people with the help of *rahat, chadas* or Persian wheels, and using human or animal labour (Dhawan 1982:148). Similarly, in parts of Bihar, such as the Chotanagpur region, the development of tubewell irrigation threatens the *kaccha* and *pucca* open wells which use traditional *danri* or *lattha* for human-powered water lift to irrigate small vegetable plots.

In hard rock areas of the south and in States like Gujarat with deeper and smaller aquifers, external effects of private exploitation are even more severe. In the much publicised Mehsana district of Gujarat, and in parts of Coimbatore District in Tamil Nadu, water extraction by existing and new pumps and wells has exceeded recharge to such a degree that the water tables have fallen rapidly, in Mehsana by some 5 to 15 feet per annum. Consequently, wells have had to be deepened frequently, and at heavy cost.

If water rights are viewed on a "first-come first-served" basis, then the late exploiters are imposing diseconomies on the early exploiters. Another view, however, is that late-comers and the resource-poor who have not yet been able to join the race have as valid a right of access to water as those who by the virtue of their resources and initiative secured early access. In this view, the phenomenon can be seen as a massive diseconomy imposed by early exploiters (who benefited from high water tables and low extraction costs) on the late exploiters, especially those who would have gained access to groundwater but for the high and sharply rising cost of doing so. Such diseconomies would have been less serious had their incidence been distributed equally on the poor and the not-so-poor. This is usually not so since it is the resource-poor who join the game late.

The ingress of sea water on some coastal aquifers of Tamil Nadu and Gujarat has demonstrated another way in which unregulated private exploitation results in the loss of livelihoods of poor people. On the Saurashtra coast in Gujarat, for example, due to rapid exploitation of groundwater for sugar cane and banana plantations 12,000 wells became saline over six years between 1971 and 1977; 0.12 m ha of land belonging to 0.13 m families in 800 villages suffered a 60-70 per cent drop in crop yields and indeed in their market value (Menon 1985; Shukla 1985). The resource-poor suffered the most. For, no sooner did the symptom of saline ingress begin to appear, than many resourceful farmers sunk wells further from the coast and began to transport water to their farms in pipelines (Mehta 1986, pers. comm.). Also, while several tens of thousands of affected families abandoned their fields to join the reserve army of labour in towns and cities, many of the better-off families bought up their land and property at reduced value. Frantic efforts by the State government to arrest the process of "salinity ingress" and to restore the productivity of land have slowly begun to yield results in some parts of the coastal strip in Saurashtra. However, many families which have now begun to return to their villages find it difficult to buy back their property and land, the prices of which have risen again.

INEQUITABLE REGULATIONS

Politicians, administrators and technocrats have begun to appreciate the ecological dimensions of unregulated over-exploitation of aquifers. The pace and intensity of response to over-exploitation has increased with the acuteness of the problem. Because of the unwritten norm that those who have enjoyed the benefit of access in the past cannot be denied it in future, the standard official response to over-exploitation is to exclude new claimants of access to aquifers. Regulations to achieve this have typically included: (a) spacing norms to be maintained between existing modern LISs and proposed ones; (b) licensing LISs; (c) tying institutional finance and electricity connections to compliance with spacing and licensing norms; and (d) categorising areas into *white* (safe for further groundwater exploitation), and *grey* (safe for controlled increase in further exploitation), and *dark* (unsuitable for any further exploitation), and then targeting institutional finance and other support (including electricity connections) primarily to white and to a lesser extent "grey" areas to the exclusion of those which are "dark".

In practice, however, most State governments have found it well-nigh impossible to monitor and control private well construction. The only way to exercise a modicum of restraint has been to instruct the nationalised banks and State electricity boards to insist on compliance with the norms before processing applications for new wells. This has often meant that those who can raise their own finance and afford the somewhat higher fuel and other operating costs of diesel engines are virtually untouched by the spacing norms and licensing regulations. It is generally the resource-poor who depend on institutional finance and prefer the cost-effective electric pumpsets whose access to groundwater is thus curtailed. In the village of Iruvelpattu in Tamil Nadu, Guhan and Mencher (1983:1020) described this process of exclusion of the resource-poor from benefits of groundwater thus:

In Tamil Nadu groundwater clearance in terms of spacing of wells has to be obtained to qualify for a land development bank loan for digging a well or acquiring a pumpset. Subsequently, in the early 1970s, electric connection to pumpset was also made subject to groundwater clearance. Most wells in Iruvelpattu were put up by the early 1970s and with the own resource of land owners. Since 1972 a waiting list has accumulated and there are now 15 applicants on it. The richer land owners have thus been able to avail themselves of the benefits of electricity before the regulation and have, in the process, effectively privatised groundwater. It is the late-comers — and particularly the less affluent—who depend on land development loans who are subjected to "groundwater discipline".

Predictably, the regulations have also encouraged illegal "rent-seeking" on a large scale. For example, the rent collected per new connection in Pandalparru village of West Godavari district in Andhra Pradesh was informally reported to be anywhere between Rs 5 and 10 thousand (Shah and Raju 1986) while in Mehsana district of Gujarat, it is believed to be much higher. In Kheda and other districts of Gujarat boring beyond a depth of 150 feet is banned. Most prospective tubewell owners have to make unofficial payments for certificates that show the depth as 145 feet when it is usually over 200 feet deep (Shah 1988).

Often the "exclusion effect"of such regulations is quite drastic. In many parts of Gujarat, enforcement of spacing norms would deny farmers located in an area of 500 acres round an existing tubewell (over 150' deep) an opportunity to establish their own LIS. With respect to State tubewells, spacing norms are even more stringent. Indeed, it is not unusual for an electricity board to withdraw a private connection falling within the command area of a State tubewell. These problems are not peculiar to Gujarat. In a recent field study of government-managed LI schemes in Nadia district of West Bengal, Sen and Das (1987:529) note:

> Because of the increasing length at the field channel, the flow of water at the tailend reduced considerably, making the quantum of water inadequate. On the other hand, the government policy did not encourage them to instal private source of irrigation within the command to supplement water supply. Quite a good number of farmers particularly in DTW (Deep Tubewell) expressed their unhappiness over such restrictiveness.

Spacing norms are aimed at minimising interference between modern LISs lest a new LIS should reduce the water output and the viability of an existing one. Strangely, no State groundwater department has specified similar spacing norms for LIS vis-a-vis an open shallow well. A large farmer can and does, without any let or hindrance, locate a modern LIS close to an open well belonging to his resource poor neighbour, even when this will dry it up.

All in all thus, the normal course of the private exploitation of ground-water has been regressive and inequitable; and the manner of working of various regulatory mechanisms has only made it more so. This does not imply that such regulatory mechanisms are not needed; what it does imply is a need to search for and to devise more effective instruments of policy. These, while providing the necessary control on private exploitation of ground-water, should not oblige the poor alone to bear the burden of such control but instead enable them to enlarge and increase their share in the irrigation surplus.

3.3 Who Gains and Who Loses from Trees?

In the past, normal processes of appropriation and access to government lands and programmes have meant that losers have been women, the poor and forest dwellers; and gainers have been industry, contractors and forest offi-cials, as shown in table 3.3.

Chapters 7 and 8 discuss these factors in detail. Here we shall illustrate with a few examples.

Who Gains and Loses from Government Forests

When an area has been declared a Reserved Forest, all the rights of local people have been extinguished except those explicitly mentioned. As has been widely documented, this process has dispossessed millions of poor people of the rights and access they earlier enjoyed, especially the tribals. Although some rights of access often remain, two processes have constrained and diminished them. The first is the removal of the resource, either through deforestation or through industrial forest plantations. The second is harass-ment by petty officials at the local level, exploiting their *de jure* and *de facto* power over those who use or wish to use the forests.

Loss of access through the removal of trees has occurred either through deforestation or through plantations. Deforestation has taken place through official felling, illegal felling by contractors, and through the activities of local forest dwellers. The major gainers have often been contractors and forest officials.

For their part, plantations have usually been single species, or involving only a few species, equally entailing loss of diversity and access; and often on a large scale, and in practice hardly pursuing an objective of benefiting the local people. In Kerala, for example, since 1970, 1.5 lakh hectares of area has been brought under man-made plantations replacing mixed forests (FAO 1984:37). Although watershed protection was mentioned as one of the objec-tives in the working plans, no prescriptions existed and no steps were taken to enhance protective value of forests. The same FAO study observed that timber production and revenue maximisation got the highest priority, while watershed management was ignored.

The effects on local people of the loss of forests can be illustrated by a

Table 3.3 Main gainers and losers from afforestation programmes

Land	Programme	Gainer	Loser	Reasons
Forest	Production forestry	Industry, local officials	Forest dwellers, artisans	1. Deforestation increased the distance to be travelled for collection of livelihood goods 2. Mixed forests which provided livelihood goods were replaced by plantation crops 3. Industries were supplied cheap raw material at the cost of artisans
Community land	Social forestry	Panchayat elite, urban consumer	Graziers, weaker sections	1. Grazing lands were taken over by Govt. and were planted with non-browsable species 2. Species like casuarina and eucalyptus were classified as fuelwood species, although these provided cash to the rural panchayats, and fuelwood/poles to the urban consumer, thus bypassing rural consumers 3. Distribution arrangements were not properly worked out allowing the powerful to walk away with the "cake"
Private land	Farm forestry	Rich farmers, absentee land-owners, contractors, petty officials	Women, landless labourers, small farmers	1. Tree farming on agricultural lands reduced employment, esp. for women 2. Stringent felling and sale restrictions helped intermediaries and petty officials at the cost of small producers 3. Serious efforts were rarely made to reach the resource-poor farmer

recent study of areas in Orissa and Chattisgarh which were heavily forested a few decades back. The distance required to collect forest products is reported to have multiplied severalfold, as indicated in table 3.4.

With the loss of forests also goes the loss of diversity of products to which poor people have access. For example, medicinal herbs which were available in the past are not available now in forest areas. This leads to more incidence of night blindness, dental caries, anaemia, gum-bleeding and other diseases (Fernandes et al. 1988:244)

Perhaps more seriously, many local cottage industries depend upon forest

Table 3.4: Distances covered to collect from forests in Orissa and Chattisgarh: twenty years ago and present

S.No.	Collection of	Distance covered (km)			
		Orissa		Chattisgarh (M.P.)	
		Past	Present	Past	Present
1.	Flowers	1.7	6.5	1.8	3.8
2.	Leaves	1.6	7.2	1.7	3.9
3.	Fruits	1.7	6.2	2.1	3.5
4.	Seeds	1.7	6.6	1.4	4.4
5.	Fodder	1.3	7.2	N.A.	N.A
6.	Bamboo	2.1	8.9	1.3	5.5
7.	Firewood	1.6	6.2	1.3	3.7
	Average	1.7	7.0	1.6	4.1

Source: Fernandes and Menon 1988:15.

products, as with basket-making, rope-making and *bidi*-making, and many livelihoods are based on the diversity of forest resources. There is often a straight conflict of interest between those who live in and near the forests, and official and commercial interests.

This conflict gives rise to and is reflected in discrimination against those who live near and depend upon forests for their livelihoods. Both cottage industries and large-scale industries such as pulp and paper, rayon, panel products and the match industry, require raw material from the forests. Besides wood, industries use non-wood forest produce too. A substantial part of this is collected by tribals and sold through contractors or forest corporations. The relationship between tribal and forest labour on the one hand and the employment agencies on the other is largely exploitative. Despite the fact that government revenues have increased, wages have often remained stagnant at below subsistence level (Gupta and Guleria 1982b:45; 87, 104).

Several cases have been reported where officials have discriminated against local cottage-scale units, instead of making efforts to help them as they should according to declared official policy. At the same time, highly privileged prices have been standard practice for industries. Till 1981, Karnataka supplied eucalyptus to the paper industries at Rs 24 per tonne (Shyam Sunder and Parameswarappa 1987b:2025), when the cheapest wood in the market sold for Rs 300 a tonne. Another report (CSE 1985:91) has mentioned that in Madhya Pradesh in 1981-82 industrialists paid the Forest Department 54 paise for a four-metre bamboo, while forest dwellers paid a little over Rs 2 a bamboo supplied by the Forest Department. Until recently paper mills in Karnataka were getting bamboo at Rs 15 per tonne while the villagers had to pay Rs 1200. The paper mills had also steadily overexploited the bamboo forests in the State and then inflicted the same damage on other areas, getting their bamboo more and more from other States like Tamil Nadu and Madhya Pradesh, and occasionally from as far away as Meghalaya. Shortage of bamboo affected basket weavers, who were increasingly subject to unemployment.

and whose earnings per day declined from Rs 8 per day in the early seventies to Rs 6 per day in the early eighties.

Although the Government of India has put several restrictions on the use of forest lands through the Forest Conservation Act, it has not used its law-making powers to increase the price of raw material from forests to industries to bring it to par with the market prices nor to reduce the prices to cottage industries and other local users.

In practice, government interventions, even when intended to help the poor, have a tendency to do the opposite. Two villages in district Sarguja in Madhya Pradesh were studied (Dasgupta 1986:44-49) regarding collection and marketing of Sal seeds. It was noted that majority of the collectors were women. Before 1973 the tribals collected Sal seeds for their domestic consumption only. When Sal seeds became an important source of oil, the State government nationalised Sal seeds and obtained monopoly rights for its collection. The poor could then sell seeds only to the agents/contractors appointed by the government, who in turn supplied them to private oil mills after paying royalty to the State government. During 1981 it was noted that of the price of Rs 2.20 per kg, paid by the mill the percentage share of various agencies was as follows:

Table 3.5: Percentage cash shares from Sal seed collection

	Agency	Percentage share
1.	State government as royalty	45
2.	Agents/contractors	36
3.	Tribals	19
	Total	100

Thus the tribals who worked hardest only got less than one-fifth of the total income generated by their labour.

Women also often lose out in benefits from forests and forest activities. They often get lower wages than men for similar work (ILO 1987: 49; CIDA 1988:72), are not paid regularly, and are subjected to harassment if they complain. Women are collectors of nationalised minor forest products (Pant 1980), yet hardly any rules exist for regulating their working hours, or for safety precautions, provision of latrines, job recruitment, leave and other benefits, training policies, productivity-linked bonuses, compulsory insurance against accidents, shelters, civic amenities, creche arragements for the care of children and infants, or medical care. The same is true of forestry works undertaken under NREP or RLEGP budgets which flow from the Department of Rural Development, which supposedly looks after the interests of the poor.

In contrast, contractors and government officials are major winners. As timber prices rise and discipline within the forest service declines scope for illicit felling increases. The value of timber stolen or forcibly removed from one forest division of North Bengal alone by merchants and smugglers is more than Rs 12 million in a year (Ray 1988). Or again, a study (Jha, *Times of India*, Feb. 26 & 27, 1982) showed that in Maharashtra, where a truck of timber (teak) costs Rs 30,000 in the market, the thieves paid tribals Rs 500 to fell trees and chop it up. Then they paid Rs 5,000 to 7,000 in bribe to the forest officials and local politicians. This still left them with a margin of Rs 15,000 to Rs 19,000 per truck, a return on investment of over 100 per cent in a single deal that was consummated within days.

WHO GAINS AND LOSES FROM COMMUNITY FORESTRY

Community forests are of two types: those which have been traditionally managed by a community; and those which have been planted as part of social forestry programmes, many of them as village woodlots.

With traditional community control and management, access to tree products has generally been equitable. To take what may be a typical example, in a hill village, Silpar, District Almora (U.P.) an informal panchayat has been in existence for the last 18 years for the protection of trees on common land (Tripathi 1987:132-34). There is no watchman; every family is equally responsible for the protection of forest. When any unauthorised felling is reported the panchayat charges a fine and half of the recovered amount is given to the person who took the initiative in reporting the offence. After the rainy season, grass is allowed to be cut on the basis of a permit for which the panchayat charges Rs 2 per family. Due to a clear understanding among villagers and their active involvement, forests on common land are being managed efficiently, and each family benefits from such management.

Exceptions to such equitable access occur especially with encroachments. An example here is a *gramdan* village, Govindpura, in district Banswara (Rajasthan), with 102 tribal families. In *gramdan* villages 75 per cent of total private land is pledged to the village body which manages the land on behalf of the community. This village has about 80 ha of common land but almost all of it is encroached by individuals (Bhattacharjee 1988a). The rich and the influential farmers have encroached by far the most, with 8-20 ha each, while poor have had to be content with less than one ha. Rich forests on this common land have disappeared in the last 20 years.

The Gram Sabha took up afforestation with government and Panchayat Samiti funds on 20 ha of this land. It was clear to everyone in the village that only those rich families who had encroached would have the usufruct from such trees. Thus public funds were used by the Gram Sabha to help the influential, a pattern quite common in other rural development projects too.

With government-managed community plantations, the pattern has commonly been less equitable than with traditionally managed forests.

In community plantations, who gains and who loses has been affected by the choice of species. Fodder is crucial to the economy of Indian villages. Realising this, land laws of most of the States forbid the use of grazing lands for purposes other than producing grasses and fodder. Yet Forest Department (F.D.) has planted non-browsable species like eucalyptus on such lands in Gujarat (PEO 1987), Karnataka (Brokensha 1988), and other States (IIM 1985), thus depriving the poor villagers and sheep owners of an important resource.

The poor tend to lose not only fodder but also other benefits from the trees themselves. A World Bank/USAID team after touring Uttar Pradesh, Gujarat, Himachal Pradesh and Rajasthan in February/March 1988 found that commercial species planted by the F.D. on grazing lands tempt the panchayats to sell in the markets, rather than distribute in the village. On these same lines, the powerful non-officials controlling Mandal Panchayats in Karnataka insist on auctioning eucalyptus, rather than distributing it to villagers. In village Medleri, district Dharwar (Karnataka) a local voluntary organisation had to obtain a stay order from the High Court against the auction of eucalyptus to urban contractors *(Indian Express* 23rd April, 1988 and *Deccan Herald* 23rd July, 1988), pleading for equal distribution to all families within the village.

The Tamil Nadu Social Forestry Project also did rather little to help the poor. It began in 1981-82 with the primary objective of meeting the fuelwood and fodder needs of the poor. Most of the community forestry plantations were on village tank foreshores. Its evaluation (SIDA 1988) indicated that output from tank foreshore plantation is not being used to meet local demands for fuelwood, but was being sold to urban areas. The Additional Chief Conservator of Forests, Tamil Nadu admitted (Wilson 1986:309) that only 5.7 per cent of the total quantity of wood produced in community forestry programmes was actually utilised by the rural people; the rest was all sold to the urban areas. The panchayats utilised the proceeds for purposes such as repair of roads, schools and drains, but there were also instances of questionable utilisation, like payment of telephone bills and travel of the *Sarpanch* (Shepherd 1987). Providing tree cover to common lands also meant depriving access of the poor to grazing lands. The government did not issue clear instructions as how to tackle such conflicts. It advised consultation of all departments and panchayats which virtually meant the F.D. could continue planting non-browsable crops on lands meant for grazing. Women's involvement in decision making was negligible. The study concluded that villagers were indifferent because they were not consulted, because the trees were planted not by villagers but by outside labour hired by the F.D., because it was not clear who owned the trees, and because 50 per cent of the produce was to go to the F.D.

The pattern presented by these two examples is also reflected elsewhere (CENDIT 1985a; SIDA 1987). It is reasonable to conclude that with officially sponsored community woodlots the benefits to the poorer, beyond wage labour, have been disappointing.

WHO GAINS AND LOSES FROM FARM FORESTRY

A study of Uttar Pradesh (Gupta 1986) shows that farm forestry has been more popular with relatively large land owners, absentee land owners including urban dwellers, and businessmen. Not only is their orientation towards cash incomes higher and their capacity to respond to new enterprises better, but also tree crops offer the advantages of ease in labour management. Market-oriented farm forestry enables the rich to save taxes on the unaccounted income from other economic activities, as incomes from forestry and agriculture are exempt from many taxes.

In the Tamil Nadu Social Forestry Project, during 1982-87, 90 million seedlings were distributed, but only a small proportion reached poor households. Even where the poor planted trees, survival rate and yields were low (Varadan 1987). One study (Andersen 1988:26) indicated that only just over 10 per cent of the seedlings reached the poor, consisting of the landless and the marginal farmers.

Half of the block plantation (planting in the fields, as opposed to in strips) by farmers has been on previously cropped lands (IIPO 1988:61). Similar conclusion was reached by an ILO study which estimated that 50 per cent of the land covered under the farm forestry component was good agricultural land (1988:17). How does it affect employment?

Tree planting on land previously used for agricultural crops tends to displace labour and to substitute male for female employment (ILO 1988:21). A study of eucalyptus plantation under the farm forestry programme (Malmer 1987) on lands which were previously being used for groundnut cultivation, has found that instead of women's employment which groundnut cultivation generated, eucalyptus required digging pits and felling trees, both of which are done by men. Averaged over a rotation cycle of ten years, total employment per hectare per year dropped from 112 to 45. Female employment dropped from 100 days to nil, while male employment rose, but only from 12 to 45. Thus not only was total employment reduced when plantation trees replaced agricultural crops, but women were also thrown out of employment.

The adverse impact of tree plantation on crop lands has also been commented upon in a FAO study (1988:48) on farm forestry in Gujarat.

As we shall describe in greater detail in chapter 8 (sec.8.5) restrictions in force (1988) in several States prohibit the harvesting of all or certain trees on private land, and transit regulations require permits to move timber or tree products. The gainers from these restrictions are officials who have to be paid off, and contractors who are able to negotiate with them. The contractors benefit from their strong bargaining position with farmers who are unlikely to have the necessary contacts and skills to deal with the officials. The farmers lose, receiving only very low prices for their trees. Small farmers, and farmers with small lots of trees to sell, are the weakest, and are liable to get the worst prices, if indeed they are able to sell their trees at all.

The evidence presented above for forest, community and private land emphasises the negative. There have been exceptions where the poor have benefited from tree programmes. The Group Farm Forestry programme in West Bengal (Shah 1987a) is one example, with farm forestry. The Forest Farming for the Rural Poor programme of Orissa, despite problems (sec.8.4) is another. The Forest Department in Karnataka has done excellent plantation of fodder trees in some villages of Uttara Kannada (Gadgil 1988). But such programmes have tended to be small-scale and based on exceptional and sustained good leadership in Forest Departments. But it has been much more common, as we have indicated, for the rich and powerful to gain from trees, and for the poor to gain little or to lose.

3.4 Practical Political Economy

With ground and surface water for lift irrigation, and with trees, then, the normal processes of appropriation, regulation and access have tended to benefit the more powerful and wealthy more than the poor. A common response to such processes is to call for the exercise of "political will", followed by recommendations which mean that these same powerful and wealthy people must lose. However desirable that may be for equity, it is rarely practicable without countervailing political power exercised by the poor and by others on their behalf. Calls for "political will" can be an escape from thinking through feasibility in realistic detail.

The problems must not be minimised. There is competition for untapped resources and latent potentials. Rural elites and bureaucracies would like to be the main beneficiaries. Further, rural elites may see themselves as losers when the poorer gain more adequate, secure and independent livelihoods. Self-respect gained by the poor is deference lost by the not-poor. A poor and weak labour force is also more docile, easier to manage, and cheaper than one which has some independent means of livelihood.

In terms of gainers and losers, strategies can be classified as the following four types:

Type	Rural elite	Poorer rural people	Political feasibility
A	Gain	Lose	High
B	Gain	Gain	↑
C	No change	Gain	
D	Lose	Gain	Low

Type A programmes in which the poorer lose are unacceptable. Type D programmes in which the rural elite lose are attractive, though not to the rural elite, and are difficult to implement without strong countervailing power to their local influence. In most of India, such conditions do not exist. Partial exceptions are Kerala and West Bengal where left wing governments have implemented land reforms. We are not saying that nothing should be attempted from which elites lose, but only that such approaches may not be feasible, at least to start with.

It is, thus, with types B and C programmes that the major practical opportunities lie. In type B "all gain" approaches, rural elites gain along with the poor. In the Chinese phrase, all boats float higher. With C approaches, rural elites lose through not being the direct gainers from exploiting the resource potential, but they do not have to give up what they already hold. Where resources are vast, there is usually much scope for B and C approaches. Fortunately, as we have seen, that is the condition in much of rural India with water for lift irrigation and with trees.

In terms of practical political economy, B type approaches where all gain can be the only feasible approach where the poor are weak and unorganised, at least at first. Where they are stronger and organised, C and even D approaches become more feasible. Empowerment of the poor to claim their rights is a key objective in any strategy, and the establishment of preconditions for empowerment. For this, the democratic constitution, the exercise of free elections, and the growing awareness and sophistication of the electorate augur well, and may generate political support for programmes which, in reality as well as theory, enable the poorer to better their condition. The most serious problems arise when the interests of the poor conflict with those of political leaders, officials, contractors and/or industrial interests. In such cases, countervailing power and coalitions are needed to persuade losers to accept their losses, a theme to which we return in chapter 10 (sec. 10.4). But those are not the only opportunities, and there are many fine shades and degrees of conflict and of gains and losses.

In the chapters which follow now, our purpose is to re-examine water from lift irrigation, and trees, from the standpoint of a practical political economy which bears this in mind; and to search for realistic policies and programmes which by involving less direct conflict of interests, will have a better chance of effective implementation and truly serving the poor.

PART TWO

Lift Irrigation and the Poor

CHAPTER FOUR

Access to Water through Groups

ABSTRACT

Many factors curtail poor people's access to lift irrigation (LI) potential. Capital investments to establish lift irrigation systems (LISs) are high and chunky and increase sharply moving from water-abundant (WA) areas to water-scarce (WS) areas. Risks of capital loss from well failure usually deter individual poor families in WS areas. The large overheads give economies of scale in LIS operation which resource-poor farmers with small and fragmented holdings find it hard to exploit.

These constraints suggest group organisation to improve poor people's access to LI water. Three forms of group are found: public tubewells established and operated by many State governments; NGO-induced LI groups, especially in WS regions, significant for their experiments in equitable distribution of water where it is scarce and liable to be pre-empted by the rural elite; and spontaneous LI groups which are small, informal and underperceived, but the most extensive type.

Public tubewells and induced LI groups account for only 2 to 4 per cent of the LI area already developed. Collective action for shared LI is hard to start and sustain. Public tubewells have a record of poor performance. Need and technical and economic feasibility are not enough for survival without good management. Factors in success are a dependable and adequate water supply, size of group, and leadership.

4.1 Types of Conditions and Groups

For the development of ground water and surface water, and especially to improve the access of resource-poor farmers (RPFs), groups have frequently been formed by government, NGOs, and farmers themselves. These can be classified in many different ways, for instance by :

source form which water is lifted	groundwater from confined, semi-confined or unconfined aquifer; reservoir, lake or pond; river; canal; drain; etc.
height of lift	low-lift, shallow, deep, etc
size of the area irrigated	from less than a hectare to hundreds of hectares
numbers of farmers involved	from three to hundreds

energy source	mainly electric and diesel, but also animal, wind, producer gas, etc.
horsepower of electric or diesel pump	mainly 3 HP and above

All of these in various ways affect who can and does have access to lift irrigation water. In addition, two other factors have a strong bearing on the formation and survival of groups. These are first, common patterns of physical and social conditions including water abundance or scarcity, topography, and distribution of land ownership; and second, the institutional origin and maintenance of the group.

First, patterns of physical and social conditions is a subject deserving its own theoretical and practical development. It includes questions of abundance, replenishment, reliability, and flow size of water in an aquifer or other source, of topography and soils, and of ownership or access to land which can be commanded by the water. For policy purposes, though, broad classifications are needed. In this chapter we will use the twofold classification of untapped potential outlined in chapter 2 which divided areas into water abundant (WA) and water scarce (WS).

Water-abundant (WA) areas include most flat alluvial plains and deltas, and water-scarce (WS) areas include most hilly and undulating regions. As we identified in chapter 2, WA areas tend to be accessible, with better infrastructure, larger villages, more unequal landholdings, and higher proportions of landless households (Dasgupta's "A villages"), while WS areas tend, in contrast, to be less accessible, with poorer infrastructure and communication, smaller villages, more equal landholdings and lower proportions of landless households (Dasgupta's "B villages") (Dasgupta 1984).

Second, institutional origins and maintenance of groups vary. They fall into three classes:

Public groups: State, panchayat and community LISs which have been set up as part of State or local government programmes, with government financing, implementation and management.

Induced groups: cooperative, communal and group LIS projects which have been initiated by NGOs, usually with the intention of self-management by the groups themselves.

Spontaneous groups: private, family, neighbour and company groups which have formed on their own to install and operate joint lift irrigation facilities.

In discussions of lift irrigation, the importance attributed to irrigation by groups has been disproportionate to the area they irrigate. The scale of public and induced group lift irrigation is small compared with private lift irrigation. In fact, public and induced groups account for only a very small proportion of the area irrigated by lift. Of the 34.5 million hectares of gross irrigated area reported for LI for 1984 (NIRD 1985), our estimate is that induced LI groups accounted for only some 30,000-60,000 hectares, or 0.1 to

0.2 per cent, and public LISs accounted for some 600,000 to 1,200,000 hectares, or 2 to 4 per cent.

There have been obvious reasons why public and induced groups have attracted attention. Public tubewells and other lift irrigation groups have not only represented substantial investment, but have performed badly, attracting adverse evaluations by government, banks and social scientists. For their part, induced groups, though responsible for much less area irrigated than public groups, have been promoted by NGOs often to serve smaller and more marginal farmers, and sometimes with novel approaches to access and distribution which have intrigued and interested social scientists and policy makers concerned with equity. Spontaneous groups, in contrast, have received little attention although they must account for much more lift irrigated area than public and induced groups taken together.

4.2 Why Groups?

The main rationale for lift irrigation groups is to enable resource-poor farmers to gain or improve their access to water. This rationale is based on the desirability of offsetting the normal patterns of appropriation by the better off and more powerful ones outlined in chapter 3. But there are also other reasons for group approaches.

Non-farming outsiders—in government organisations and NGOs in particular—often prefer groups to individual lift irrigation development. The reasons include ideology, convenience and patronage. Ideologically, both government officials and NGO workers tend to prefer "communal" to "individual" control over natural resources. Official preferences sometimes reflect a hangover from the days of Community Development, while NGO workers sometimes idealise traditional and cooperative sharing, and the somewhat romantic notion of building group strength and solidarity through the sharing of a common resource. For convenience, too, groups are preferred for their administrative economies of scale. Fewer paper transactions are required per unit of funds disbursed, and larger total sums of money may be involved than where development is on an individual family basis. Opportunities for patronage are also presented, for example in awarding contracts, and in the appointment of staff such as pump operators.

Four other reasons affect the preferences for group organisation for lift irrigation on the part of both outsiders and of resource-poor farmers themselves. These are: (1) Viability and scale; (2) High capital costs; (3) Risks of capital loss; and (4) Hassle and access to credit, machinery and technical advice.

1) VIABILITY AND SCALE

Viability of lift irrigation increases with scale in three sets of conditions. These may occur separately or together.

a) The first concerns economies of scale. Other things being equal, both capital and running costs per unit of water pumped decline with scale (Jairath 1984; Patel and Patel 1971). Overheads are a very important component of total costs of running pumping plants. Where power is charged on a per hp basis almost all costs are in the nature of overheads. The recurrent overheads for a pump operator and water distributor as also of depreciation, interest, etc may be the same for a group of 15 as for a group of 100.

b) The second concerns physical and social conditions which require or favour larger-scale lift irrigation systems (LISs). The most common are where the height of the lift required is considerable in order to bring water to the fields of cultivators. Physically, this can occur where groundwater is deep, or where water is to be lifted from a river, reservoir, pond, drain or other surface source up a slope in order to reach the command area, as in undulating country. The higher the lift, the more powerful the pump has to be to raise the same flow of water. The more powerful the pump is, the higher is the capital cost, the more difficult it is for a RPF to purchase and install it and the more important become the economies of scale. For their part, social conditions favouring larger scale LISs are where there are several or many small holdings close together which otherwise lack access to water. Both these physical and social conditions tend to occur in B type villages, and in peripheral locations.

c) Viability increases with scale where group action is required for operation, maintenance or control. A percolation tank from which water is lifted may need periodical desilting. A dam wall or spillway may need maintenance. An open well may need deepening. A watershed may need protection. Or group solidarity may be needed in order to resist subversion or sabotage by the richer and more powerful. Group action for any of these can occur without shared LISs, but is likely to be stronger where LIS sharing takes place.

2) HIGH CAPITAL COSTS

The cost of securing access to modern water lifting technologies—and, through them, to ground and surface water—varies widely across environments and is often beyond the resources of an individual poor family. In the Gangetic plains, where the water table is relatively high and the top soil is underlain by layers of sand and silt, a shallow tubewell may cost only Rs 10-15,000 (Pant 1984; Shankar 1986) and a simpler bamboo tubewell, only half as much in real terms (Appu 1974; Pant 1984). Here, access to the aquifer and to the modern lift technology is likely to be more equitable than, for example, in hard rock areas of southern India with deep water tables and with layers of hard rock requiring complicated and costly drilling operations. In such areas, a tubewell with an economic discharge may cost anywhere between Rs 30 and 250,000 (Dhawan 1986; Copestake 1986: 11-14; Nagabrahmam and Raju 1986:17). Substantial variations in the cost of open or tubewells may also exist within the same environment. For instance, in the mid eighties to install a shallow tubewell complete with a pumpset and engine/motor cost less than Rs 15,000 in parts of Panchmahals district in Gujarat and these LISs were widely used by small farmers (Shah 1985); but less than 20 miles away, in Kheda district, a tubewell could produce economic discharge rates only from a depth of 150 feet and cost upwards of Rs 80,000 (Shah and Raju 1988:9). It is rarely feasible for even a large farmer, let alone a resource-poor family, to raise internal resources to finance such large investments; and institutional finance is notoriously scale-biased with the credit-worthiness of a borrower directly related to owned land. It is therefore hardly surprising that ownership of modern waterlifting devices is highly skewed in favour of larger farmers and the skewness tends to increase across regions as the cost of their installation increases (Shah and Raju 1988).

The difficulty faced by poor people in raising capital is illustrated by the example of the Pani Panchayats (lift irrigation water cooperatives) of Purandhar Taluka, Pune district, in Maharashtra, where small landowners struggled to raise their required down payment of 20 per cent of the capital cost for installing group lift irrigation (the balance being 50 per cent bank loan and 30 per cent grant). Many settled for a smaller share of water than their entitlement because they could not raise enough; but the extremes to which they were prepared to go is shown by their willingness to sell cattle, sheep, goats and utensils, and a few even their *mangal sutra*[1] in order to secure a share of the group's water (GGP 1983:9).

3) RISKS OF CAPITAL LOSS

Just as there is risk involved in owning and operating LIS which can be reduced by exploiting the potential to share/sell water and thereby, to recover part of the cost of running a well, there are also risks of well failures particularly in hard rock regions with discontinuous aquifers. The risk may be in terms of not striking water at all after having incurred the expenditure on drilling or blasting, as the case may be (Shah 1985:5; Dhawan 1984:5; Nagabrahmam and Raju 1986:25) or of investing in wells which turn out to have much lower yields than expected (Dhawan nd:5). There is also the danger of once productive wells failing either for natural reasons or due to over exploitation by deeper tubewells (Dhawan 1982:146). There are also situations, as in Mehsana district of Gujarat, where bores must be deepened every year to chase a declining groundwater table in order to salvage the original investment (Shah 1986:8). Investment in wells or tubes in such situations presupposes a substantial capacity to absorb financial risks which individual resource-poor families almost never possess although groups of poor families are known to have taken such risks.

4) HASSLE AND ACCESS

The difficulties faced by small and marginal farmers in gaining access to

[1]Necklace offered to a newly wed bride by the groom's parents. The ornament has a high sentimental value, is passed on from generation to generation and is rarely sold.

credit, purchases of machinery, contractors for boring and installation, electricity connections, and even diesel purchases, are well known, and in Bihar, at least, are probably a major factor inhibiting the exploitation of ground-water. One argument for groups, appealing in principle to both small and marginal farmers, and to NGOs and government organisations wishing to help them, is that they can take such negotiations out of the hands of the farmers themselves, enabling them to gain access to water without such hassles and the additional costs and risks which go with them.

These factors, together with the priority given to irrigation development by government, NGOs and farmers alike, have generated and encouraged a succession of programmes and initiatives for public lift irrigation, for induced lift irrigation, and for spontaneous groups in many parts of India. A review of the experience with groups of these three types will help us to assess their strengths and weaknesses and evaluate options for future policy.

4.3 Public Lift Irrigation Systems

Public LISs take various forms, including pumping from open bodies of water, but the most common are public tubewells. The public tubewell programmes launched in various States, and on the largest scale in some of the north Indian States in the sixties and later, were intended to achieve benefits of scale (Abbie et al. 1982:35-36) and to augment and broaden access to groundwater for resource-poor families who were unable to invest in their own tubewells. In addition to the other arguments, the case for public tubewells was also based on the depth and quality of aquifers. Where aquifers near the surface were unsatisfactory, or liable to drop seasonally or permanently below the level from which centrifugal pumps could lift, larger pumps could tap deeper aquifers to provide a better water supply in volume and reliability than smaller individually owned pumps. A public tubewell could then, in theory, supply water to resource-poor farmers who would either have no water, or water that was unreliable.

The force of these arguments varies by individual tubewell, by hydrogeological zone, and by social conditions, but whatever their force, the recorded overall performance of public tubewell programmes has been so bad that the evidence might, to anyone coming to it fresh, be hard to believe. It is, however, consistent and we consider substantially true.

Since some 70 per cent of public LISs have been in Uttar Pradesh, Bihar and West Bengal, and over 85 per cent of them in the Gangetic plain most of the evidence will be taken from that area, though other evidence will also be drawn on.

Performance of public LISs can be conveniently gauged against four criteria: survival, that is, numbers of pumps continuing to function; area irrigated compared with area planned; operating hours; and access of resource-poor farmers to water.

1) SURVIVAL

Many public LISs have ceased to operate. None of the 15 public river LISs in Bharuch district, Gujarat, was said to be operating in early 1987. During 1981-82 in Uttar Pradesh, 11.5 per cent of public tubewells were reported not to be working, while for Bihar the figure was 33 per cent (Sharma 1988:18).

2) AREA IRRIGATED COMPARED WITH AREA PLANNED

A formidable literature on the working of public tubewells indicates that the average area actually irrigated by them falls far short of that projected at the time of planning. Examples are given in Table 4.1.

Table 4.1: Public tubewell performance

Region	Period	Area planned to be irrigated (ha)	Area reported to be irrigated (ha)	Percentage utilisation reported (rounded)	Source
UP				15-26	Singhal nd:13
UP (of public tubewells which were working)	1980-81	100 per well	42	42	Sharma 1984:18
Bihar (of public tube-wells which were working)	1980-81	100 per well	21	21	Sharma 1984:18
UP	1979-80	120[1]	57.1	48	Shankar 1981:12[2]

[1]"rated capacity"
[2]citing the Draft Sixth Five Year Plan (1980-85)

3) HOURS OPERATED AND FINANCIAL VIABILITY

In Uttar Pradesh the hours reported operated per annum by public tubewells showed a steady decline over 13 years from 1966-67 to 1978-79, from an average annual utilisation of 3,335 hours in 1966-67 to 1,466 hours in 1979-80 (Shankar 1981:14). Several factors explain this trend. Deteriorating power supply has been cited as an important cause by researchers. But equally important has been the declining quality of irrigation service offered by public tube-wells. This and other problems, have reduced their competitive edge compared with increasing numbers of private LISs which have cut into their command areas (Pant 1984).

State tubewells in several States but especially in Uttar Pradesh, are a major drain on the public exchequer. Singhal (1988:5) estimates the annual loss to the government from State tubewell irrigation at Rs 1,598/ha. Similarly, quoting from the Memorandum of Budget Estimates 1987-88 (p. 45 of Appendix), Shankar (1988:1) shows that the Uttar Pradesh government lost Rs 117 crores on State tubewells which is 16 per cent of a total capital investment of Rs 740 crores. This compares poorly with even canal irrigation where the annual loss is Rs 157 crores or 6 per cent of the total capital investment of Rs 2,607 crores.

4) ACCESS OF RESOURCE-POOR FARMERS TO WATER

In addition to these indicators of poor performance, there is widespread evidence in South Asia as a whole, including especially Bangladesh, (Hartmann and Boyce 1983:256-257; Howes 1984) that water pumped from public tubewells tends to be captured by the wealthier and more powerful to the detriment or exclusion of the poorer and weaker. Wells tend to be sited on the land of the wealthier and more powerful in the first place, often through bribery and other forms of influence, and requirements that the poor be involved are often evaded. If water is scarce, it is the poor who get it last, if at all, or who have to pay most for it. For the poor and powerless, the water supply is also much less reliable than for the rich and powerful.

The reasons for poor performance are many, frequently documented, frequently lamented, and best presented as a simple list:

— mechanical breakdown resulting from poor maintenance, lack of spare parts, and indifference or difficulty in obtaining and fitting spare parts
— lack of power, through electric power cuts or through shortages or difficulties in obtaining diesel
— land tenure with fragmented holdings and/or with land across which owners are unwilling to permit channels to pass
— construction of private tubewells in the command providing an alternative and more reliable source of supply
— influence and monopolisation by more influential farmers or factions
— absenteeism, indifference, incompetence and favouritism on the part of tubewell operators

The operator is sometimes given the major blame. Thus Pandit (1983:119) has shown that usually the operator shows "neither response nor responsibility to his duties nor he runs the tubewell according to farmers' call and requirements". The tubewell operators are in a powerful position to bestow favours. "As nobody wants to displease the operators, no one complains against them to the higher authorities and even if one does, it is seldom attended to. Cultivators want to be on good terms with them for getting water and the latter move about like *nawabs* whose favour is sought by everyone" (Shankar 1981:35). With alliances between tubewell operators and local bigwigs, small and marginal farmers are at a severe disadvantage in gaining access to water.

In attempts to prevent or overcome such problems, various measures have been proposed or undertaken. In West Bengal, a system of beneficiary committees has been introduced to manage public tubewells. Spout Committees, one for each spout command, are formed in Deep Tubewell as well as River Lift Systems for better management of water distribution. They are intended to help local extension staff in working out the cropping pattern for spout commands, to decide on the sequence of irrigation to each plot and to facilitate phased sowing of crops on different plots. All Spout Committees together elect a central committee, which co-opts the local MLA, VLW or Extension Officer. It is uncertain if these committees are able to play a major role; but the lineman who manages the flow of water is recruited by the Central Committee and paid by farmers at a rate of Rs 24 for boro and Rs 15 for other crops per acre (Sen and Das 1987:528).

West Bengal has also effected other improvements in public LISs. Underground pipelines are provided at least for a part of the command; a seven-day rotation for each spout command has been implemented so that the farmer can divide his plot into equal parts according to the requirements of irrigation intervals of the crop. Thus the farmer could either take his entire water share every week to irrigate a third of his plot or, by arrangement with other farmers, use three-weekly rotations and get three times his weekly quota. Rosters are apparently maintained for spouts and plots in each spout.

While West Bengal public LISs appear to be operating somewhat better than in other States, problems of equity and managerial effectiveness remain. Unauthorised cultivation in the command is a major cause of losses of revenue and insufficient supplies for tail-enders; this is often facilitated by the "unholy agreement (in the form of bribes) between field level irrigation officials and the farmers" and is hard to curb as "most of these unauthorised irrigators were taking refuge to political parties in power. The extent of area under unauthorised irrigation in a sample of public LISs in Nadia was 74% for deep tubewells, 19.5% for (shallow) cluster tubewells and 66% for river lift systems" (ibid: 530-533).

Official policies and programmes lay great stress on public LISs as an equitable alternative to unregulated private exploitation of LI potential. As a result, new and bigger efforts continue to be made to improve their performance. A large scale and well-known attempt of this variety has been the "World Bank Tubewell" programme in Uttar Pradesh whose government has been the most serious about its public tubewell programme.

The programme attempts a technological fix. A modern pumping plant—complete with automation in the controls of prime mover, a capacitor, electronic hour meter, etc.—is fed by a dedicated powerline with at least 16 hours of power per day. Water is pumped to an elevated regulating tank with about 10 minutes' storage and then conveyed through two loops of buried (PVC) pipe distribution, each loop serving 37-50 ha with a discharge of 7.5 m³ per hour (about 0.74 cusec). It has been stated that "this system, besides eliminating conveyance and operational losses, increases reliability of the irrigation service at any outlet. It also does away with problems connected with right of the way, thus saving land which otherwise would be needed for surface canals" (Datye and Patil 1987:219). While a mid-term review of the World Bank (cited in ibid: 219) expressed satisfaction with technical performance, it noted that the expected switch over from "protective" to "productive" irrigation was nowhere in sight.

More recent reviews, by independent scholars, though few, are more detailed and insightful. Singh and Satish (1988) on the basis of a study in Gorakhpur and Varanasi developed a favourable impression of benefits accruing to farmers, effectiveness of the control system, etc. but concluded that "all is not well with the management of (World Bank) public tubewells. Performance is already on a decline and the coumulative effect may become noticeable in a decade. Notice the defects in "Kundis"—leakages and breakdowns, the steady increase in the hours required per watering per acre, farmers' dissatisfaction with the system of water allocation, the failure of the farmers' committees to manage the farm distribution system and animus between water users wherein the individual's might gives the right to water" (ibid: 35).

A brief visit by Chambers and Shah to Deoria district in eastern Uttar Pradesh in February 1987 found other weak points with World Bank tubewells. Of the four they visited, three were not working due to faulty construction of pipes by contractors. This, albeit, can not be generalised, and could be rectified, though at a cost. More serious was the view of a local farmer, not to be lightly dismissed, that the World Bank tubewells would first cause the group and individual pumps in their commands to fail by offering cheap subsidised water and then would themselves fail. Many of these tubewells at least in Deoria district were concentrated in blocks which already had irrigation groups and private tubewell owners; many of these were directly hit. The competition between the World Bank tubewells, with their subsidies and privileged power supplies, and local groups and private water sellers was patently unfair; as a result, several groups became defunct and private pumpers sold off their pumps. They were feeling bitter, and perhaps rightly so. Other small farmers, lured by cheap prices of World Bank tubewell water, had stopped buying from their group tubewell or neighbouring tubewell. They too were bitter since the World Bank tubewell, once stopped, took several months to get repaired. A more formal study by Nagabrahmam and Ballabh (1987) confirmed many of these points.

The real costs and benefits of the World Bank tubewells are complex, but the costs include the undercutting of existing private suppliers of water through water markets and of small farmer LI groups. Widespread replication of these tubewells is planned; but we are sceptical of substantial net benefits of each replication unless it is accompanied by comprehensive planning (especially, of the location of clusters of such tubewells) and monitoring of their overall social effects.

In general, the poor performance of public tubewells presents such strongly interlocking weaknesses that we doubt if they will emerge as an effective large-scale means of supplying water to resource-poor farmers. In WA conditions, like those of the Gangetic basin, other means must be sought.

4.4 Induced and Spontaneous Groups

Induced and spontaneous groups take many forms. As types they shade into each other according to the degree of external influence and support as against local initiative and self-reliance.

Induced groups include those of the Sadguru Seva Sangh in the Panch-mahals district, Gujarat; the Vaishali Area Small Farmers' Association (VASFA) and the Indo-Norwegian Agricultural Development Project (INADP) in respectively Vaishali district, Bihar, and Deoria district, Uttar Pradesh; the Association of Sarva Seva Farms (ASSEFA) in Madurai district, Tamil Nadu; the group wells for weaker sections of the Mulkanoor Coopera-tive Rural Bank (MCRB), in Karimnagar district, Andhra Pradesh; and of the Gram Gaurav Pratisthan (GGP) in Pune district, Maharashtra. A special category of induced group are the landless irrigation groups of Bangladesh (sec. 4.5).

Spontaneous groups include the "water companies" of the villages in Kheda and other districts of Gujarat (Shah and Raju 1988) which exist almost entirely to sell water, and which issue printed receipts, keep accounts, and manage their operations quite professionally; and the cooperation between relatives and neighbours with little land as reported for Allahabad district (Shankar 1987).

To describe each set of groups in turn would be laborious. The interested or sceptical reader is referred to the sources which are mostly available publicly. To identify those elements which are common to successful groups, we are inevitably forced to simplify realities which are complex, diverse and dynamic.

In this chapter, we will apply to these approaches two overarching criteria:

a) Survival, stability and effectiveness: whether the group survives and achieves effective irrigation.

b) To what extent the group serves poorer people, and with what degree of equity.

Policy questions of replicability, scale and speed will then be taken up in Chapters 6 (sec. 6.7) and 10 (sec. 10.3).

Reviewing the evidence, six factors stand out as influencing the chances of survival, stability and effectiveness, of induced or spontaneous group LI systems. These are:

homogeneity of the group
group size
supporting services

water availability
alternative water supplies
economic and financial viability

1) GROUP HOMOGENEITY

Some groups fail because of factionalism. Group homogeneity is frequently
mentioned as a factor in success. Group homogeneity is linked with group
size, since small groups tend to be more homogeneous, as occurs with some
spontaneous family groups where, for example, a number of brothers share a
LIS.

2) GROUP SIZE

Group stability and effectiveness appear to be distributed in a U-shaped
curve. Large lift irrigation projects, with hundreds of members, typically
have a supporting bureaucracy and services, and are usually stable in size or
expand. The groups of the Sadguru Seva Sangh in Gujarat average 117
members, and have proved very stable.

At the other extreme, very small groups also appear generally stable.
There is a tendency amongst intermediate sized groups, let us say in the range
of 8 to 50 members, to shrink, losing members over time. Of the 42 INADP
groups in Deoria district, Uttar Pradesh, one was exceptionally reported to
have expanded in members, but several had shrunk, and 3 had sold out or
been taken over by one person (pers. com. Singh 1987). The best documented
case is that of landless group tubewells initiated in 1983-85 in Tangail district
in Bangladesh by the Grameen Bank. Of 11 tubewells studied, 9 were reported
in early 1987 to have reduced their members, in four cases selling to a reduced
number of members and/or non-members. The scale of reduction was from
an average starting number of 24 members (range 10 to 50) to an average later
of 8. But even 8 can be too many for ease of sharing. Among the Bangladesh
groups too—those with 10 and eight members respectively after the first
reduction in numbers, subsequently sold out (Mandal and Palmer-Jones 1987
draft: 11). Among spontaneous groups in Andhra Pradesh which began with
three and ten members, members withdrew from the larger groups. And the
failure of an ASSEFA group was attributed to its having "as many as seven
members" (Nagabrahmam and Raju 1986: 6 and 20).

Indeed, spontaneous groups are almost invariably small in numbers. Of
11 group wells in Anklav village in Gujarat, the median size of the groups
was four, with a range of two to seven (Nagabrahmam and Raju 1986:16). In
Pandalaparru village in Andhra Pradesh, six group wells had three to four
members each (ibid: 6).

In his survey in Allahabad district (table 4.2) Shankar (1987) found shared
ownership was prevalent for households with small operational holdings.
Sharing declined as size increased, with an average of three households per

Table 4.2: Numbers of households and tubewells by size of operational holding

Size of operational holding (ha)	Number of households	Number of tubewells
less than 1	36	12
1 to 2	65	29
2 to 3	48	31
3 to 4	26	17
4 to 10	50	51
All	225	140

The sample of 140 tubewells in Bahadurpur block, Phulpur Tehsil, Allahabad district, surveyed in 1985-86. (Shankar 1987:3A).

tubewell among those operating less than a hectare, and apparently no sharing among those operating more than 4 hectares.

Here as elsewhere several landholdings and indivisible engine sizes with 5 or 3 HP as the normal minimum available, have combined to encourage spontaneous group formation.

A plausible explanation of the U-shaped curve may be that very large groups

— are less likely to be formed unless there is an adequate water supply
— are likely to be linked with a competent supporting organisation
— are likely to throw up their own leadership which, with a vested interest or not, will ensure continued operation
— will have one or more employees with responsibilities for day to day operation

Middle-sized groups, may lack these advantages. At the other extreme, very small groups, say of six members or less, may be able to manage on a face-to-face informal basis without a need to organise.

3) SUPPORTING SERVICES

Supporting services include a reliable and adequate power supply, and mechanical repairs and spare parts. Where medium and large groups have survived, as with the INADP groups in Deoria, the GGP Pani Panchayats in Pune, and above all the Sadguru Seva Sangh groups in Panchmahals, there has been good technical backup. In this, the Sadguru Seva Sangh appears exceptional, able to claim that the farmers had never suffered crop losses on account of machinery breakdowns, breakages of pipes or the like (Jagawat 1986:6).

4) WATER AVAILABILITY

Without water, no group can work. Many of the GGP groups suffered severely in a succession of droughts. Intensified competition for water can also destroy a group. But water shortages which are not too extreme can strengthen a group, for example, where equitable measures are agreed to for sharing.

5) ALTERNATIVE WATER SUPPLIES

Farmers prefer water supplies under their own control. For this reason, many farmers who can do so opt out of groups and group sharing, or maintain their position in a group while simultaneously using another supply. In water-abundant areas, field realities are often complicated. Of the 42 Deoria groups, six were said in early 1987 to have more or less ceased to exist because of the installation of World Bank tubewells covering their commands, with the promise, not necessarily fulfilled, of cheaper and more reliable water. One of the Deoria groups, Mukundpur, had ten members, all with land outside as well as inside the command of the group tubewell, and within the command, there were three other tubes as alternative sources of water. As we shall see in Chapter 5, in water-abundant areas, water markets often overlap, presenting farmers with choices which are likely to weaken groups and group cohesion.

6) ECONOMIC AND FINANCIAL VIABILITY

Finally, the survival or otherwise of a group depends on its economic and financial viability. There is much variation. In 1985/86 almost all the Deoria group tubewells were disconnected from their electricity supply for failure to pay their dues, though most paid up subsequently and were reconnected. The Sandguru Seva Sangh, in contrast, reported a satisfactory repayment record.

These six factors interlock. They are presented diagrammatically in table 4.3.

We emphasise that these are tendencies, not absolute rules explaining effectiveness—or lack of it—in groups. For example, a group of say 25 members may be stable because of other factors such as exceptional leadership and special advantages.

The mutual reinforcement of these factors can be illustrated by cases. In his study in Salem district, Palanisami (1981:1) found that many big diesel engine schemes were idle because of differences of opinion among the farmers running the schemes, whereas small schemes were performing better. One of the ASSEFA groups failed because although it had only seven members, water was limited through slow recharging and each member had to wait a fairly long time for a turn.

Finally, homogeneity, size, services, water availability, alternative water supplies and economic and fiscal performance are not the only factors affecting survival, stability and effectiveness. Other factors can also be decisive including group leadership, social effects of irrigation (for example where it is highly valued because it removes the need for seasonal outmigration), theft of a pump, transformer or electric cable, diminishing water supply as a water table drops, water logging which reduces demand for water, and damage by flooding. Given qualifications such as these, and such disparate and scattered

Table 4.3: Factors in the survival, stability and effectiveness of induced and spontaneous LI groups

Tendency to	Homogeneity	Number of members	Services	Water avail-able	If alter-native water	Economic and fiscal performance
fail	factions	inter-mediate say 8-50	not available	not available	cheaper more reliable, available to most members	very poor
shrink	factions	inter-mediate say 8-50	inadequ-ate or unrelia-ble	limited unreliable inequitable	cheaper, more reliable, available to some members	poor
be stable or expand	homogene-ous	over say, 100 (expand) under, say, 8 (be stable)	adequate and reliable	adequate or limited but reli-able and equitable	not avail-able or more costly, and/or less reliable	good

evidence as we have our generalisations should be treated as working hypo-theses rather than revealed truth.

4.5 Equity

The issue with equity is whether groups can enable the poorer to gain more from lift irrigation. With public LISs or groups which are dominated by larger farmers, RPFs may gain little or nothing. They can even lose if they start cultivation and then get low yields or lose a crop because they cannot get the last irrigations needed. But there are two conditions in which equity is served. The first is where a group consists of RPFs or landless labourers. The second is where access to water is governed by equitable principles.

1) GROUPS OF THE POORER

LI groups can be designed for the poorer. This intention can be realised either through selection policy, or where group LISs are installed in backward areas, or for both reasons. While some were less poor than others, the Tribals of Panchmahals district who have benefited from the LISs of the Sadguru Seva Sangh were disadvantaged as a whole, and all within the command areas tended to gain by lift irrigation, even though there was no selection process biased towards the poorer. The groups of the Gram Gaurav Pratisthan in

Pune district were automatically the poorer farmers as the better-off had already obtained lift irrigation and were growing sugar cane. Moreover, the groups were unattractive to larger farmers because of their prohibition of sugar cane growing and their limited water supplies. The groups of VASFA in Vaishali district and of INADP in Deoria district were designed for small and marginal farmers, (reportedly 97 per cent of members) and backward groups (reportedly 23 and 78 per cent of members respectively) (Pant 1985:60,63). The ASSEFA small groups in Madurai district were mostly Harijans and backward classes owning an average of only 1.5 acres under previously rainfed conditions (Nagabrahmam and Raju 1986:17).

Where, as in these cases, group members all have some land, two practical points can be noted. First, the location is critical. Much depends on topography and the distribution of landholdings. It can be difficult to serve only SFs and MFs where their holdings are interspersed with those of larger farmers as is often the case in water-abundant areas, though easier in peripheral areas where landholdings tend to be more equal and water scarcer. Second, the smaller the group, the less danger there is of larger farmers joining or wanting to take it over.

A striking case of selecting for the disadvantaged is provided by lift irrigation groups for the landless in Bangladesh (Wood 1982, 1983). A "landless group" is defined as

> A group with no control over the means of production or distribution; landless or marginal farmers with no assets; fishermen with no implements; rural artisans who lack working capital or raw materials; families who sell their manual labour; women of the above groups.

Three NGOs—PROSHIKA, BRAC (the Bangladesh Rural Advancement Committee) and the Grameen Bank—have initiated such groups. PROSHIKA initially spearheaded the approach. BRAC had facilitated the formation of groups. The selection of members required special care, and some groups had to be abandoned, or started again when they were joined by people who were ineligible or intent on subverting the group. Each group drew a loan for an engine and pump, either a lowlift pump for open bodies of water, or a fixed shallow tubewell. Groups then sold water to willing buyers, sometimes selling their own labour together with the water. The numbers of groups have steadily expanded and the approach established as feasible with committed voluntary agency staff. To our knowledge, however, it had not, as late as 1987, been tried in India.

2) WATER ALLOCATION PRINCIPLES

The second main way in which the poorer can gain more is through rights to water. The normal convention, as in canal irrigation, is water entitlements proportional to land holding size: the larger the holding, the bigger the share in water; and the smaller the holding, the smaller the share, in simple arithmetic proportion. But in India there are three remarkable examples of induced groups where allocation is more equitable.

The first example is the Gram Gaurav Pratisthan in Purandhar Tehsil, Pune district (Chambers 1981; Parulkar 1982; GGP 1983; Deshpande n.d; Kohle et al. 1986; Morehouse 1987). This voluntary organisation led by Vilas and Kalpana Salunke had by 1984 initiated some 34 lift irrigation groups which were operating. Others were in process of formation. Much of Purandhar Tehsil has low rainfall and much of the available water in *nallas* had been appropriated by larger farmers. The system evolved for the GGP groups, known as *pani panchayats*, was as follows. A potential command area from a percolation well, percolation tank, or reservoir was identified. Potential beneficiaries with land in the command raised 20 per cent of the capital cost, the remaining 80 per cent being either grant or loan (arrangements having varied over time). The unique provision was water entitlements limited to half acre irrigated per paid up family member, with a theoretical limit of two-and-a-half acres for any one family. (There are, however, some cases where a larger family had entitlements of more than two-and-a-half acres). This provision scored well for equity in allowing larger families more irrigated area up to a limit, but a very poor family could have difficulty raising its 20 per cent of capital cost to buy into the group, or might be rationally reluctant to take the limited risk. (Late entrants had to pay the full 100 per cent if they were accepted.) While the half acre principle is widely known, actual practices vary while broadly converging on the theme of equity (Kohle et al. 1986:48,06).

The second example is not lift irrigation, but small-scale surface irrigation from small tanks, This is the system evolved at Sukhomajri and Nada villages in Chandigarh district (Seckler and Joshi 1981; Chowdhry et al. 1984; Mishra and Sarin 1987; see also sec. 7.3). At these two villages small dams were built as part of anti-erosion experiments and measures. When irrigation from the dams became possible, the villagers considered the water to belong to all, and allocated it equally to each "*Chula*" (hearth or household) regardless of landholding size or landlessness. In consequence, landless households held rights to water which they then traded to others, or used for sharecropping in land from those who were short of water. Although this is small-scale surface irrigation, the principle of equal rights to a new water resource is important, and is being adopted in our third example.

The third example is at too early a stage to be considered established, but is interesting and important as an innovative hybrid of the GGP and Sukhomajri/Nada principles. This is the system of rights being developed with some groups of the Aga Khan Rural Support Programme in Gujarat. The thinking is that where a group LIS is installed, all villagers, on the Sukhomajri/Nada principle, will have water rights. This has been implemented in Parodi village in the Bharuch district where each member household is entitled to 2.5 acres of water irrespective of its landholding within the command area which may be 250-300 acres. About 150 families have formed a cooperative an represent all landholding classes including the landless. The expectation is that large farmers with more than 2.5 acres in their command will be induced to lease out their excess land to the landless or marginal farmers who have more water entitlement than their own land. Water shares are to be non-negotiable so that such lease contracts are encouraged. Interestingly, while cost of irrigation is levied at the same rate of Rs 60 per watering per acre, it is proposed that loan repayment be shared in proportion to the total land in the command and not to water entitlement. This provision is likely to cause resistance from large farmers, and it is too early to say how the proposed arrangements will work out.

In other groups elsewhere in India, too, water allocation to all landholders has been adopted in time of crisis. In rabi 1985 one of the Sadguru Seva Sangh groups in Panchmahals district, finding water much too scarce to irrigate its usual 700 acres, decided that only gram should be grown and that each of its 150 members would receive water for only one acre each, the same area and amount of water for everyone. Four other groups acted similarly in that same season (Jagawat 1986:9-10).

DEGREES OF EQUITY

In normal past thinking, water rights have been linked to land rights. The examples of GGP, Sukhomajri/Nada, AKRSP and the landless groups of

Table 4.4: Equity effects of water allocation principles

Equity	Allocation of water in relation to land-holding size	Equity	Examples
1	*Disproportional:* the larger the land-holding, the more water per unit land.	— — —	large farmers dominating public tubewells
2	*Proportional:* water in proportion to land-holding size	— —	public tubewells in theory. Many LI groups in theory
3	*Equal:* Equal for each landed household member, or, equal for all members, including the landless	0	GGP Sukhokajri/Nada, and AKRSP
4	*Progressive:* the smaller the landholding, the more water per unit land	+	SSS equal water allocations in crisis
5	*Exclusive Rights:* to landless households only.	++	Bangladesh landless groups

Notes: Ranking is difficult between 3 and 4 because of the effects of including or excluding the landless who may be many or, as with GGP, few
—,0 and + signs are used to indicate degrees of negative or positive discrimination affecting the poorer.

Bangladesh show that this need not be so. Moreover, a redistribution of rights to water can produce effects similar to a land reform. Put differently, much common property water for lift irrigation is an unappropriated resource where equal rights or rights which discriminate in favour of the poor, can be justified and established. Policies, decisions, and their implementation can then be assessed in terms of their degree of equality or positive discrimination for the poorer, as in table 4.4.

4.6 Conclusion

The evidence reviewed is not conclusive. Experience with LI groups will grow and better generalisations will be made as more evidence becomes available. But some working hypotheses are supported and some policy questions sharpened.

The evidence suggests that most public LISs have been ineffective, inequitable and uneconomic and may well remain so. Induced LI groups have a mixed record, but if well implemented in water-scarce areas, can bring substantial gains to the poorer. Exceptional NGOs achieve localised water reforms in which the poorer gain much more. But there remain problems of scale. Privately owned LISs whether by spontaneous groups or individuals, account for over 95 per cent of the area irrigated by lift. A small improvement in their role will bring bigger total benefits than scattered NGO-induced groups however equitable and excellent they may be, and however worthy of support. Groups, whether public or induced, do not present a massive, large-scale option. The question is then whether there are other ways the poor can gain. This points us towards private LISs and the buying and selling of water.

CHAPTER FIVE

Access to Water through Markets

ABSTRACT

The private initiative which has developed 96 to 98 per cent of the LI area has given inequitable direct access to irrigation water, but landless people and resource-poor farmers have variously benefited through increased labour demand and wages, opportunities to buy water, and appreciation of land values. It is also common for small and marginal farmers to rely on selling water to make their LISs viable. Private water markets supply many millions of RPFs and a huge area, with 40 to 50 per cent of privately lifted water sold in Uttar Pradesh and Andhra Pradesh, and 70 per cent in parts of Gujarat.

With diesel LISs, water prices vary between regions by a multiple of three. This is explained not by aquifer conditions but by degrees of water sellers' monopoly power and by incremental costs. With electric LISs, water prices are much lower in States with per horsepower based flat electricity tariffs, since these reduce incremental pumping costs close to zero. Where power is charged pro-rata, as in Gujarat until 1987, private water prices have been several times higher. The lower the incremental pumping costs and the lower the monopoly power of the seller, the more equitable is the water market and the greater are the benefits to RPF purchasers of water through good irrigation service at reasonable cost.

Unlike groups, markets can be strongly and quickly influenced by a few public policy instruments with enormously wider impacts. Gujarat's 1987 switch from pro-rata to flat electricity tariffs lowered water prices throughout the State by 25-60 per cent, benefiting some 1.5 to 2 million water buyers, mainly RPFs and their families, with gains to them of some Rs 100 crores per annum.

5.1 Private LIS: Vast Scope for Scale and Speed

When compared with the miniscule share of State tubewell programmes and NGO-induced LI groups in the Indian lift irrigation economy, the over 10 million private owners of LISs in rural India form a whole class by themselves. In 1988, private LIS owners accounted for over 95 per cent of the groundwater development that had already taken place. Their number has swollen rapidly—in recent years at a rate of some 100,000 every year. Privately owned LISs were about half of the total in 1950; in 1987 they were 98 per cent (Kolavalli and Chicoine 1987). The rate of increase in their number itself is expected to increase in the years to come. There is every reason to believe that they will at least maintain their share in the coming two decades as much of the remainder of India's unexploited groundwater potential is developed and appropriated.

It is perhaps important to reform the public tubewell programme and to encourage and support NGO experiments with LI groups; however, it is even more important for policy makers to recognise that neither offers the promise of the scale and the speed necessary to achieve major impacts on rural poverty; and that even with the most optimistic view of their future, State tubewells and NGO-induced LI groups will, for ever, play only a limited role while private pumpers will dominate in the overall LI scenario. Practical political economy in this context requires that ways are found and policies devised to influence the actions and decisions of private LIS owners and thereby to ensure equitable access to groundwater.

5.2 Spillovers of Private Enterprise

Since establishing an LIS may require considerable capital investment, most existing private LIS owners are the non-poor. This scale bias observed in the ownership of LISs has often prompted those concerned about the poor to ask: "who gains from this last frontier? The haves or the have nots?" (IDS 1980). In most situations, however, unequal private exploitation of groundwater is better for the poor people than no exploitation. As a matter of fact, the poor have often gained substantially from private LI development and it is important to look for ways in which the poor can gain much more than they have so far.

Private investment in lift irrigation generates four distinct streams of benefits; not all of these accrue only to those who make the investments. The *first*, which does, is the increased and stable income from higher crop yields, proofing from droughts and erratic rainfall, higher cropping intensity, freedom to increase fertiliser application, access to HYV technology, etc. The *second* is increased and more continuous demand for farm labour which generally results in improved wage rates and greater year-round employment opportunities. This benefit accrues to families which depend partially or fully on agricultural labour for their livelihood and has highly positive impacts on their livelihoods, security, independence and self-confidence (Chambers 1986). The *third*, arises from the fact that private owners of LISs everywhere have strong incentives to share their surplus water-lifting capacity with their neighbours by selling them water. The incentive is to spread the substantial fixed costs of LIS operation over a larger command area to benefit from lower unit costs. Even when somewhat unfair, such water transactions leave those without their own LISs better off with a wider opportunity set. And *lastly*, the exploitation of LI potential in an area rapidly raises the value of land belonging to not only those who own LISs but also those who do not (Shah and Raju 1988; Jagawat 1986).

Where water selling by private LIS owners is substantial and pervasive, the overall benefits of private LI investment to the community far exceed the benefits to the LIS owners. Total land irrigated is greater than the parcels on which LISs are installed. This is especially true when landholdings are fragmented since LIS owners too may purchase water to irrigate their distant parcels unirrigable by their own LISs. The positive effects on labour demand and wage rates are thus augmented. The difference between LIS owners and the resource-poor non-owners in access to attractive enterprise-technology options also diminishes with the latter having the option to purchase water. A piece of land which falls within the command of a private LIS generally tends to be worth more than it was before the private LIS was established.

These "spill over" benefits to non-LIS owners will increase as the number of "water sellers" increases; as more and more resource-poor non-owners gain access to groundwater irrigation through purchased water; and as the sellers compete amongst themselves to sell more water and, in the process, improve the quality of "irrigation service" and push the water price down—both of which may mean that being a "water buyer" is not particularly bad. The "spill over" benefits to the community also increase as the terms of water transactions become more uniform and transactions become more impersonal. When a water buyer can potentially deal with several water sellers, he will be less likely to be subjected to unfair practices. When a parcel of land can receive irrigation from a number of willing water sellers at a cost not substantially higher than what would be incurred with own LIS, the appreciation in its value will be quite as high as that of a parcel with a LIS. With such a highly developed, competitive market for water, thus the differences arising out of differential access to groundwater between those who own LISs and those who do not will be reduced to a minimum.

On the other hand, in a monopolistic market for water, in which sellers can behave in an arbitrary manner and charge water prices substantially higher than their costs, the benefits to non-LIS owners will decrease and the profits of LIS owners will increase. However, even a monopolistic water market will often be better for the resource-poor than no market at all. This latter state would result from a literal interpretation of the stipulations made by most State electricity boards in India to the effect that electric LIS owners cannot use electricity to sell water to others (REC 1980; Swaminathan 1987). If these stipulations were vigorously enforced, which luckily they are not, then they would result in the abolition of water markets and make resource-poor buyers as well as LIS owners worse off.

5.3 Water Markets: Recent Evidence

In spite of their vast potential to enhance equity and productivity, groundwater markets have, until recently, remained unresearched and largely unobserved. Recent field studies have revealed that in many parts of India, notably in Gujarat, well-developed village level groundwater markets may have existed and functioned for as long as 80 years. In several villages of the Kheda district in Gujarat, for example, private LISs, some operating even today, began selling water pumped with a diesel pumpset and conveyed through underground cement pipelines as far back as around 1920 (Shah 1987b).

The earliest formal mentions of groundwater selling by private LIS owners can be traced to the mid-sixties; the references since then indicate that groundwater markets have been far more pervasive and important than had been widely thought. Field studies indicate the sale of water to be a large proportion of total pumpage and a significant source of income for the seller. Patel and Patel (1971) found, in the late sixties, a sample of private LIS owners in Uttar Pradesh selling 35-40 per cent of their water output to other farmers. More recently, Shankar (1987:9-12) found average hours of water sold by LIS owners to be 41 per cent of total hours of pumpage in Allahabad district; he found very little variation in water-selling behaviour across various landholding categories and also that buyers land was 39 per cent of the total land irrigated per LIS. Kolavalli et al. (1988) note water sales to be 20 per cent of total pumpage in *kharif* and 50 per cent in *rabi* for eastern Uttar Pradesh with the annual average of around 40 per cent. Sangal (1982) came up with similar findings for another region; a recent NABARD study in the Muzaffar Nagar district suggested somewhat lower—but quite significant nevertheless—percentages for water sales by both diesel as well as electric tubewell owners (NABARD 1987). Many of these studies (NABARD (1987) and Kolavalli et al. (1988) in explicit terms) note the greater proportion of water sales by SF and MF pumpers as a means to make their irrigation investment viable. But for this sale of water, capacity utilisation of private LISs would be very low and average cost of own irrigation per hour or per acre very high for the owner. In West Godavari district of Andhra Pradesh, electric and diesel LIS owners were found to sell 32 and 44 per cent of pumping hours respectively in 1986 and most of those interviewed would have liked to sell up to twice as much if there had been buyers (Shah and Raju 1988). In Kheda district of Gujarat, where high fixed costs on account of high capital outlays on LISs make water selling even more of an economic necessity, the proportion of total water output of a well sold is of a much higher order. In Anklav village, a sample of 26 electric LIS owners interviewed sold 78 per cent of their annual pumping hours and it was indeed doubtful if any of the private LISs would survive without opportunities to sell water (Shah and Raju 1988). Kolavalli (1987), working in the same area, found on an average two-thirds of the water output being sold by private LIS owners.

5.4 The Compelling Logic of Water Selling

The bulk of the cost of running an LIS is fixed in nature; as a result, the unit cost of pumping per hour declines sharply as hours of pumping per year increase. Figure 5.1 based on a study by Shah and Raju (1988) shows the average pumping costs for a sample of LIS owners in Pandalparru village in the West Godavari district (Andhra Pradesh) and Anklav village of Kheda district (Gujarat). In both, average pumping costs declined by nearly 50 per cent as hours of operation per year increased from less than 1,000 to over 2,000. Having made the investment in an LIS, it thus makes sound business sense for the owner to operate for long hours by selling surplus pumping capacity and to cut prices as long as the price at which water is sold pays for the variable costs of pumping.

There are several ways in which LIS owners interested in high capacity utilisation try to sell more water as shown in the two villages referred to above. In Pandalparru, LIS owners who operated for over 2,000 hours managed to sell more by cutting their price by 40 per cent. Another way most LIS owners as, for example, in Anklav try to sell more water is by offering a superior irrigation service to the buyers of water at the time needed, and in the quantity needed. Several other benefits are commonly offered to buyers. Interest-free credit on water payments until the end of the season—and, often later—is usual in Gujarat. In Gujarat, it is also common for LIS owners to lay underground pipeline networks with outlets at several fields so that the buyers' irrigation costs are reduced (Shah 1987b). Where several of them operate in a community, private LIS owners are often quite keen to establish a long-term relationship with a stable group of buyers since, by doing so, they can reduce the uncertainty in their business.

Perhaps the best aspect of dealing with private water markets from the viewpoint of a resource-poor water buyer is their informality, flexibility and promptness with which irrigation service can be secured. In contrast, public irrigation systems—canals as well as lift—feature none of these.

5.5 Quality of "Irrigation Service"

There are, of course, references to situations in which owners of LISs have used their monopoly of access to groundwater to force buyers into exploitative transactions. Casual observers have often described LIS owners as "water lords" in the same sense as the term "land lord" is used with feudal undertones (e.g. Jairath 1984: 1710). It is unlikely, however, that such monopolistic or feudal elements are very pervasive. For the economic necessity of spreading fixed costs makes feudal or monopolistic behaviour unsustainable over long periods. This necessity induces LIS owners to supply an irrigation service of high quality. The inducements become stronger as new LIS owners cut into the territories of existing ones; as medium and small holders too begin to invest in LISs since their need to sell is greater than that of LIS owners with large holdings; and as fixed costs of LIS operations increase as a proportion of total costs.

A significant body of direct and indirect evidence that has built up over time indicates that private water sellers supply irrigation service of a high quality. High quality of irrigation service implies "adequacy"—water is supplied in quantities needed by the buyer; and "dependability"—water is supplied at the time the buyer wants. Lowdermilk et al. (1978) cited in Tiffen and Toulmin 1987:6 reporting on 378 Pakistani farmers found that those using water purchased from private tubewell owners enjoyed a better control over the water application than those using public tubewell supplies and as a result, obtained higher yields of rice as well as wheat. Significantly, those using purchased private tubewell water in their sample were four times as many as those using public tubewell supplies and three times as many as those with their own LISs. Similar observations have been made by researchers who worked in the northern States in India; Mellor and Moorti (1971), Pant (1984), and Shankar (1981), for instance, show how farmers prefer the considerably more expensive private tubewell water to the subsidised but undependable and inadequate State tubewell supplies. Indeed an analysis of State tubewell performance in Uttar Pradesh by Shankar (1981) directly relates the secular decline in the average hours of operation of State tubewells to the rapidly expanding opportunities to buy water from private tubewell owners. Likewise, in explaining the deteriorating performance of State tube-wells in Haryana, the managing director of the State tubewell corporation directly blamed the operation and growth of private tubewells often established within the command areas of State tubewells.

In Gujarat too, substantial evidence confirms strong farmer preference for the purchased private tubewell water over public tubewell as well as canal water supplies. Jayaraman et al. (1982) found private LIS in the Mahi Right Bank command doing roaring business although they charged 8 to 10 times more than canal irrigation. Kolavalli (1986), who aptly describes private water sellers as suppliers of "on demand" irrigation service, and Brahmbhatt (1986), both working in the Mahi Right Bank Canal (MRBC) command, confirm the higher productivity of private LIS supplies and the resulting preference for them.

Learning from the northern States, the Gujarat State public tubewell administration, in a bid to keep private LIS owners at arm's length, stipulated that they were not to operate within the commands of State tubewells. Recent studies, however, show that this has not helped the State tubewells much; for, private LISs operating from outside the State tubewells' commands have made deep inroads into the latters' territories through elaborate underground pipeline networks (Shah 1987b).

As water markets become more competitive, scope for arbitrary behaviour by sellers decreases. In a backward village of the Balasinor taluka in Gujarat, the *Talati* (village official) narrated an incident of buyers boycotting a seller who withheld supplying last two irrigations to a buyer in 1983 *Kharif* season when the monsoon failed. By the next monsoon, the seller realised that he was not quite as powerful and independent of the buyers as he had thought and that he needed the buyers as much as they needed him. In competitive water markets, likewise, collusive efforts among sellers too generally fail. In Karamsad as well as Navli villages of Gujarat, sellers tried to unionize as early as in the late sixties; in Karamsad village, a pump-owners' association was actually registered and exists even today. Two main items on the agenda of these associations were to boycott a defaulting buyer and to prevent sellers from undercutting each other. In both the villages, after paying considerable lip service to these collective goals, LIS owners went about doing precisely what they thought was in their best individual interests. Undercutting continued apace and minor defaults by buyers continued to be tolerated (Shah 1987b).

5.6 Diversity in the Terms of Water Sale

Measuring the performance of water markets on "dependability" and "adequacy" criteria is difficult and complex. It is easier to find the prices at which water sales are taking place. While sharecropping for water is a widely used practice, cash sale of water on a per hour basis or on a per acre of a crop basis is more commonly found in most parts of India. Field studies reveal substantial variations in water prices in different States and between electric and diesel LISs but a surprising degree of uniformity within a given region in the prices charged by electric and diesel LISs. Understanding the factors that explain inter-regional differences in the terms of private water sales is important since the level of price determines the cost of purchased irrigation to the buyer and the profits made by sellers; further, the relationship between the price charged and costs incurred by LIS owners may also offer insights into the "adequacy" and "dependability" of private water markets.

Table 5.1 presents an array of water prices charged by private LIS owners in various regions of India. In column 2, we note that the prices charged by

Table 5.1: Prices of water sold by electric and diesel LISs in various parts of India

	Location	Electric LISs			Diesel LISs		
		Price (Rs/hr)	HP (Av)	Price (Rs/hp/hr)	Price (Rs/hr)	HP (Av)	Price (Rs/hp/hr)
	1	2	3	4	5	6	7
1.	West Godavari, Andhra Pradesh:1986 (Shah & Raju 1988)	3.0-3.10	8.6	0.35	7.5-7.7	6	1.25-1.28
2.	Western UP; 1984 (Shah 1985), Punjab 1982 (Jairath 1984)	4-5	7.5	0.53-0.67	8.0-10	6	1.33-1.67
3.	Eastern & Central UP: 1986 (Jain & Balabh pers com; NABARD 1987)	4-5	5	0.8-1.0	10-12	5	2.0-2.4
4.	Northern Kheda dist; Gujarat: 1986 (Shah & Raju 1988)	15	14	1.07	15	9-3	1.61
5.	Panchmahals dist, Gujarat 1984 (Shah 1985)	—	—	—	16-18	5	3.2-3.6
6.	Midnapur dist, West Bengal 1987 (Shah 1987a)	—	—	—	14	5	2.8
7.	Charutar tract Gujarat 1986 (Shah & Raju 1988)	25-28	21.2	1.18-1.32	—	—	—
8.	Mehsana & Sabarkantha dists Gujarat 1985 (Shah pers comm)	42-45	30	1.4-1.5	—	—	—
9.	Madurai dist Tamil Nadu : 1986 (Copestake 1986); Karimnagar dist AP 1986 (Shah 1986b)	4.5-5	5	0.9-1.0	16-21	5	3.2-4.2

electric LISs vary across regions by a multiple of 12 to 15. In West Godavari district, electric LIS owners charge around Rs 3 per hour while in Mehsana district of Gujarat, they charge as much as Rs 45 per hour. In the case of the diesel LISs too, prices vary across regions but only by a multiple of about three. What explains such large variations in water prices across regions? Several alternative explanations can be considered.

To start with, we could argue that price variations are explained by differences in LIS capacities. Columns (3) and (6) of table 5.1, however, show that even prices per hp/hour vary by a factor of 2 to 3. Differing aquifer conditions—such as depth to the water table, and regularity and quantum of recharge, — could be another explanation. However, we note that between the sites from the Panchmahal (Gujarat), Midnapur (West Bengal) and West Godavari (Andhra Pradesh), aquifer conditions are not all that different; depth to the water table is 30'-40' and recharge to the aquifer plentiful in all the three locations. And yet, prices per hp/hour charged by diesel LIS owners differ by a factor of 2 to 3. It might be argued that although the price per hour may vary widely, cost per acre of irrigation may not vary all that much. But this too does not have much empirical support. Shah and Raju (1988) note that an average buyer in Anklav village in Gujarat paid over twice as much per acre irrigating water saving grain crops in comparison with what buyers in West Godavari paid for irrigating sugar cane and banana. Earlier, Shah (1985) noted that buyers in Panchmahals district in Gujarat paid Rs 685 per acre of wheat irrigation while those in Meerut district of Uttar Pradesh, with similar aquifer conditions, paid just Rs 133.

It appears that the only complete explanation of water price differences is to be sought in the economic behaviour of water sellers. This is deeply influenced by their relative bargaining power (or "monopoly" power) and the incremental cost of pumping. Factors such as aquifer conditions and water lifting technology seem to enter the price determination process only indirectly through their effect on the sellers' bargaining power and incremental pumping costs. For a given level of incremental cost, water prices tend to increase across regions as the sellers' bargaining or monopoly power increases; likewise, given the structure of the water market reflecting a particular degree of monopoly power enjoyed by an average seller, water prices tend to increase directly and proportionately with increases in incremental cost as long as the prevailing price covers the full unit pumping costs. In order to understand the working of water markets, then we need to identify the factors that affect the "bargaining power" of water sellers and the incremental pumping costs.

5.7 The Balance of Bargaining Power

Measuring "bargaining power" is difficult. However, it is useful to view it as the ability of the seller to raise the sale price of water without losing a substantial chunk of his demand (Shah 1985). The bargaining power of a seller vis-a-vis a group of buyers will decline as the pressure on him to sell water increases. An LIS owner with a large holding would enjoy greater bargaining power than one with a small holding. If a single LIS owner establishes a pipeline network, his bargaining power increases while that of his competitors declines. If many sellers install pipeline networks, all of them will suffer reduced bargaining power. Sellers in a village with good, regular rainfall or good reliable canal irrigation will enjoy lower bargaining power than the class of sellers operating in a region with insufficient, erratic rainfall and absence of alternative irrigation sources. Likewise, a seller who faces high fixed costs will enjoy lower bargaining power than one with a cost structure dominated by variable costs. Table 5.2 lists a set of factors affecting the bargaining power of sellers.

Table 5.2: Determinants of water sellers' bargaining power

High bargaining power	Low bargaining power
Low and erratic rainfall	High and stable rainfall
Water scarce and deep	Water abundant and close to surface
High capital cost of LIS installation	Low capital cost of LIS installation
Low LIS density	High LIS density
Stringent and well enforced spacing/licensing norms	No spacing/licensing norms
Use of unlined field channels by sellers	Use of lined water conveyance systems by most or all sellers
Crops requiring large quantity of water	Crops requiring small quantities of water
No canal water; none or inefficiently managed state tubewells; no electricity	Efficient State tubewells, access to canal water; access to electric power

In table 5.2 we have presented analysis based on information from nine locations in India on some of the factors which, in our view, directly or indirectly affect the bargaining power of a representative water seller. The field studies from which this information is drawn also provide indirect evidence regarding the differing degrees of bargaining power enjoyed by sellers in these locations. In the West Godavari village studied by Shah and Raju (1988), for instance, where the sellers' bargaining power is the lowest, almost all available evidence indicates highly competitive behaviour amongst sellers. The main *kharif* rainfall is plentiful and reliable; the water table is high and the annual recharge to the aquifer substantial; as a result, the cost of securing direct access to the aquifer is very low. The density of private LISs is high and can increase rapidly since there are no effective spacing norms nor any licensing regulations to bother potential entrants into the groundwater markets. Nearly 40 per cent of the village's farmland is partially irrigated by an unlined canal fed by water lifted from river. In several villages of this area, diesel engines have begun to be decommissioned since buying water from electric LIS owners is cheaper than using own diesel LIS. Diesel LISs that still exist operate only in far off and remote areas where electric LISs have not been able to reach.

As a consequence of all these factors, the water market is highly competitive and the price at which water is sold is only marginally higher than the average cost of pumping (Shah and Raju 1988).

At the other extreme, the bargaining power enjoyed by LIS owners is high in Karimnagar district of Andhra Pradesh and Madurai district of Tamil Nadu. This is reflected in the fact that the price charged by sellers is two to three times the incremental pumping cost per hour. Both these districts are remarkably similar in their low and unreliable rainfall, in their limited groundwater potential and the high cost of access, low density of LISs and the difficulties in rapidly increasing it due to stringent spacing norms.

Between these two extremes lie several shades as table 5.1 describes. In several locations, factors with conflicting effects co-exist. In the Panchmahals district in Gujarat, for instance aquifer conditions are favourable; but rural electrification is poor and well densities are low. As a result bargaining power is high; in Midnapur district in West Bengal, which is otherwise similar to Panchmahals, rainfall is higher and more stable so that buyers are not at the mercy of sellers as much as they are in Panchmahals.

From the viewpoint of equity, an ideal water market is one in which water prices are close to incremental pumping costs but allowing sellers "fair" returns; in which active competition prevents the hegemony of sellers; and in which the balance of bargaining power struck between buyers and sellers reflects the mutuality of their needs and interests. One way to make exploitative water markets more equitable is by reducing the bargaining power of sellers where it is very high. Our analysis points at several ways this could be done. Where aquifers are plentiful, increasing LIS density and achieving "saturation" could be effective in reducing sellers' bargaining power. Developing alternative irrigation sources, stimulating investments in pipeline networks, etc. can also be equally effective. All these measures, however, are likely to be slow in their impact. A quicker and surer method of creating equitable markets is through affecting incremental pumping costs.

5.8 Incremental Costs and Water Prices: Diesel LISs

Incremental costs are direct costs incurred by the LIS owner for every additional hour of pumping. They do not, for example, include depreciation and interest cost on capital invested in establishing the LIS because, once incurred, these costs do not vary with hours of pumping. In the case of diesel LISs, for example, incremental costs will mainly include three costs: cost of diesel consumed per hour constituting over 70-75 per cent of incremental costs; paid out or imputed cost of labour used in supplying and managing the flow of water; and the cost of wear and tear which, in diesel engines, is significant and varies with hours of pumping although not in a smooth, one-to-one manner as the costs of diesel fuel do. For a 5 hp diesel LIS, incremental costs have been estimated to range around Rs 6 per hour in 1986 in field conditions (Shah and Raju 1988). It is important to note that incremental costs per hour of pumping for diesel LISs of the same hp would remain largely unaffected by changes in the head; what will, however, be affected is the rate of discharge and the incremental cost per *unit* of water pumped.

In a highly competitive market where the sellers' bargaining power is low, the difference between water price and incremental cost will tend to be very small; as the bargaining power of water sellers increases, the difference between the price charged and incremental cost will increase. As a result, the ratio of water price to incremental pumping cost may often be a useful index of the bargaining power enjoyed by the sellers; low values of the ratio indicate limited bargaining power and high values indicate high bargaining power. Approximate values of this index in each of the seven locations from where we have field data on diesel LIS prices are set out in table 5.3.

This table shows the index of monopoly power enjoyed by sellers to be increasing from 1.25 in West Godavari to 3-3.5 in Madurai and Karimnagar districts. In the latter districts, after covering the full costs (including overheads), the sellers are earning a substantial profit from their water sales; but in West Godavari the present price is perhaps only marginally higher than the average cost and the sellers' profits from water sales are quite modest. The West Godavari sellers' main interest in selling water is to spread their overheads over a larger command area; in the absence of a market for their surplus capacity, they would have absorbed all the overheads themselves. Any surplus

Table 5.3: Price, incremental cost and the index of water sellers' bargaining power: Diesel LISs

Location	Water price (Rs/hour)	Ratio of water price to incremental pumping cost of Rs 6/hour
1. West Godavari +	Rs 7.23-7.7	1.23-1.32
2. Western UP and Punjab	Rs 8-10	1.3-1.7
3. Eastern and Central UP	Rs 10-12	1.7-2.0
4. Northern parts of Kheda district in canal command*	Rs 15	1.89
5. West Bengal	Rs 14	2.3
6. Panchmahals in Gujarat	Rs 16-18	2.7-3.0
7. Madurai and Karimnagar	Rs 16-21	2.6-3.4

Notes: *In Kheda, farmers use 10 hp engines. Diesel cost per hour was estimated to be Rs 6.75 and total incremental cost to be Rs 7.95 (Shah and Raju 1986).

+ In Pandalparru (West Godavari) average diesel cost per hour was estimated at Rs 4.70; however, the buyer was supposed to provide all the labour so that implicit cost of labour was low; but repair cost was higher at Rs 0.75/hour. Incremental cost/hour was estimated at around Rs 5.85.

over their *direct* costs that they generate by selling water would reduce their burden of overheads and would therefore be beneficial to them.

One advantage with the framework developed in these sections is that it is possible, indeed easy, to test the results with other sets of data from other locations (other than those included here). It also implies that one can predict, with some accuracy, how market prices are likely to respond to changes in various components of incremental costs. For example, one can infer that a 10 per cent increase in diesel price throughout the country would raise water prices in West Godavari by less than 15 per cent but in Madurai and Karimnagar and other areas with comparable conditions by 25-35 per cent.

5.9 Incremental Pumping Costs in Electric LISs: Flat versus Pro-rata Tariff

This same mode of analysis can be applied equally effectively and with interesting results to the prices charged by electric LIS owners in different regions. With electric LISs, the incremental cost of lifting water depends upon the method used by the State electricity board for pricing of power for lift irrigation. In States like Gujarat and West Bengal, where power supply to agricultural connections is metered and charged for on a pro-rata basis, power cost accounts for over 80-90 per cent of the incremental cost of pumping and, as in the case of diesel LISs, the water price ends up as a multiple of incremental cost, the multiple itself being a direct function of the bargaining power of the sellers. In Kheda district of Gujarat for example, owners of 21 hp electric LISs in the head reach of the Mahi-Kadana irrigation project (where the bargaining power of sellers is very low) charge only Rs 15 per hour; but in the tail (where their bargaining power is higher) sellers with 21 hp LISs charge Rs 25-27 per hour (Shah and Raju 1988).

In most States other than West Bengal, State electricity boards charge for power supplies to agricultural connections on flat rates linked to the hp of the LISs. These rates vary greatly across the States: from Rs 48 per hp per year in Andhra Pradesh and Tamil Nadu to over Rs 300 per hp per year in Uttar Pradesh. In all these States charging flat rates, however, the cost of power is delinked from the hours of LIS operation and is, therefore, excluded from the incremental cost of lifting water. The incremental pumping cost thus includes only the implicit cost of labour used by the seller and the cost of repair and maintenance. These labour, repair and maintenance costs are much lower for electric LISs than for diesel ones. Sellers with electric LISs and paying flat rates for power thus have a powerful incentive to sell water to other farmers even if the competition that so results pushes the water price down. Once they have paid the flat rates, the sale of water at any price higher than the implicit wage cost and maintenance cost per hour adds to the sellers' net profit.

Flat rates generate powerful incentives to sell water. This is suggested by the fact that all States which have switched from pro-rata to flat tariff system have experienced sharp and rapid increases in the hours of operation of electric tubewells. In Andhra Pradesh, the switch to flat tariff in 1982 increased average power consumption per electric LIS by 60 per cent (Shah 1986). A study by the Rural Electrification Corporation reported power consumption per electric LIS in Uttar Pradesh to have increased from 2,065 units in 1973-74 just before the introduction of flat tariff to 6,724 units in 1979-80 (REC 1980:2). Likewise, when the Maharashtra government offered farmers an option to pay a flat tariff, 64 per cent opted for it and expanded their use of power from 2,191 units per electric LIS in 1975-76 to 3,142 units in 1978-79. In 1979, those paying flat rates used an average of 1,983 units per LIS mostly for selling water; but those who opted for pro-rata tariff used only 1,112 units (REC 1980:3). Flat tariffs thus stimulate increased lift irrigation, sale of more water and expansion of area irrigated per electric LIS. Pro-rata tariffs in contrast, reduce the pressure to sell and lower the capacity utilisation of LISs. Increases in pro-rata power charges tend to reinforce these effects. Evidence from Andhra Pradesh and Gujarat shows that in the former, the average power use per electric LIS increased sharply upon the switch to flat tariffs in 1982; but in Gujarat, a sharp increase in the pro-rata tariff over the last decade was associated with declining hours of operation of electric LISs (table 5.4).

Table 5.4: Trends in power consumption per well and pricing of power: Andhra Pradesh and Gujarat

Period	kWH/LIS	Andhra Pradesh Power Price (Rs/kWH)	Year	Gujarat++ kWH/LIS	Power price+ (Rs kWH)
1969-70/ 1974-75	2186	0.12	1974-75/ 1978-79	6664	0.23
1975-76/ 1981-82	2232	0.16+ Fixed charges*	1978-79/ 1980-81	5790	0.28
1982-83/ 1985-86	3294	Fixed rate of Rs 50/hp per year	1981-82/ 1985-86	5205	0.56

* October 1975 - March 1977, fixed charge was Rs 3/hp/month. April 1977 - October 1982, fixed charge was reduced to Rs 2/hp/month.
+ Weighted averages prevailing during each period.
++ A good part of the difference between power consumption per LIS in the two states is explained by the higher average hp per LIS in Gujarat.
Source: Shah and Raju 1988:42.

5.10 Determinants of Water Market Performance

The evidence that we have reviewed thus indicates that stimulating equitable water markets is essentially a question of influencing the behaviour of water sellers through affecting incremental pumping costs or their bargaining power or both. In table 5.5, we summarise the major lessons from our analysis

Table 5.5: Determinants of water market performance

Areas where:	Low incremental cost (as for electric LISs paying flat tariffs)	High incremental cost (as for all diesel LISs and electric LISs paying pro-rata power tariffs in Gujarat)
	I	II
Sellers enjoy low bargaining power	Water price: very low Dependability: very high Adequacy: very high As for electric LIS owners in West Godavari Punjab, Haryana, UP	Water price: high Dependability: high Adequacy: high As for diesel LIS owners in West Godavari; electric LIS owners in Thasra, northern Kheda district
Sellers enjoy high bargaining power	Water price: moderately high Dependability: moderate Adequacy: high As for electric LIS owners in Madurai and Karimnagar districts.	Water price: very high Dependability: low Adequacy: low-moderate As for diesel LIS owners in Madurai and Karimnagar; electric LIS owners in Mehsana, Sabarkantha and Central Kheda districts in Gujarat
	III	IV

so far. The three main criteria used to assess water market performance are adequacy, reliability and price charged by sellers for irrigation service. The performance along adequacy and dependability scales has to be seen within the constraints facing the sellers. Where scarcity of water resource (as in Madurai or Karimnagar districts) and/or power (as in Bihar or West Bengal) is severe, the best efforts by sellers to provide an adequate and dependable service may not amount to much although we would rate the sellers' performance high.

A resource-poor water buyer is best off in a water market where sellers enjoy low bargaining power and face low incremental pumping costs (quarter I). In the sample of areas for which we have reviewed evidence here, this would be true of the buyers dealing with electric LIS owners in West Godavari and other coastal districts of Andhra Pradesh, and most areas in the Gangetic plains including parts of Bihar and Orissa where flat rates have resulted in low incremental pumping costs and rapid development of the ample groundwater resource has resulted in low bargaining power of sellers. In many backward areas in these regions, the simplest way to enable poor families to benefit from groundwater resource is to encourage the less poor to develop it rapidly.

In many of such areas where the bargaining power enjoyed by sellers is low, high incremental costs incurred by diesel LIS owners and electric LIS owners paying pro-rata tariffs result in relatively high water prices; however, the adequacy and reliability of the irrigation service tends to be high due to the competitive pressures among sellers.

Both quarters I and II typically represent WA areas; while situations described in quarters III and IV may, but not necessarily, occur in WS areas where incremental costs are low due to flat rates but the market structure is monopolistic (quarter III), as in Karimnagar and Madurai; electric LIS owners tend to charge moderately high prices and may not provide dependable and adequate irrigation service since the buyers are at their mercy.

The buyers of water are worst off in areas where both incremental costs and bargaining power are high. This has been true of most areas of Gujarat and buyers dependent on diesel LIS owners in all WS areas. Water prices typically charged are exorbitant and have no relationship with pumping costs; sellers can behave in an arbitrary manner; as a result the quality of irrigation service provided by sellers tends to be poor. The difference in the effect of water markets on buyers may be dramatic and can be best illustrated by comparing the condition of buyers in quarter I with those in quarter IV.

5.11 Effects of Equitable Water Markets

Well-developed water markets can have dramatic effects on a village community. In Anklav village of Kheda district in Gujarat, for example, an LIS owner sells water to a high average of 44 buyers. A sample of 26 LIS owners drawn out of a total of over 60, irrigated as much as 1,100 acres—over one-fifth of the village's farm land, by selling water (Shah and Raju 1988). In Midnapur district of West Bengal, the only two owners of diesel tubewells in Nepura village in 1986 sold water to 40 and 70 neighbouring farmers to irrigate *aman* rice and especially winter potato which has emerged as a lucrative new enterprise mainly on account of the emergence of opportunities for purchased irrigation (Shah 1987a). The Shah and Raju study (1988) of Pandalaparru village in West Godavari district showed the sample of 34 LIS owners irrigating nearly 300 acres of the buyers' land — again, about one-fifth of the total farm land in the village. In both Gujarat and Andhra Pradesh where land is very fragmented, water markets have enabled owners of LISs to irrigate their distant parcels of land with purchased water.

A buyers' water market helps to diffuse access to groundwater to all categories of farmers. Low water prices and high quality of irrigation service (as in quarter I) enable resource-poor farmers to derive the multiple benefits of irrigation without having to invest in their own LISs; high water prices

Table 5.6: Output and equity effects of groundwater markets: summary of results from two village studies

		Naglakuboolpur Dist: Meerut State: Uttar Pradesh (representing quarter I areas)	Untadi Dist: Panchmahal State: Gujarat (representing quarter IV areas)
1)	% of sample farmers with own LISs	Large 67 Medium 75 Small 8	100 57 38
2)	% of farm lands irrigated with own or purchased water	Large 100 Medium 100 Small 91	63 45 19
3)	% of small farmers growing *rabi* wheat	67	31.5
4)	% of small farmers' wheat area under purchased irrigation	87	36
5)	Average cost of irrigation per acre of wheat	Rs 133	Rs 685

Source: Shah 1985:15.

and low quality irrigation service (quarter IV) have the opposite effects. Table 5.6 summarises the findings of a comparative analysis of a village in Panch-mahals district of Gujarat with a monopolistic water market and a village in Meerut district of Uttar Pradesh where the water market was relatively competitive. Only 12 private tubewells in the Meerut village helped to achieve a 200 per cent cropping intensity in the entire village with low water sale prices. The intensity was only marginally lower for small farmers, 92 per cent of whom depended on purchased groundwater costing on an average Rs 133 per acre. The Panchmahals village had 50 diesel shallow tubewells but the price of water was high making the cost of purchased irrigation per acre of wheat Rs 685. Notably, since the water market was under-developed in the Panch-mahal village even large and medium farmers had to leave some of their fragments without borewells unirrigated. The cropping intensity achieved by small farmers was only 119 per cent while it was 163 per cent for the large farmers all of whom owned LISs.

Where water prices are very high, buyers tend to respond in two ways: where they are not used to irrigated farming and multiple cropping, as in the Panchmahals and other tribal districts of Gujarat, most continue rainfed farming; where resource-poor farmers are already used to irrigated farming, as in Kheda and Mehsana districts, they tend to switch to crops such as tobacco, summer *bajri* and groundnut which require less water. These crops typically generate lower and more uncertain returns and absorb less labour. Further, payment for water still takes away a substantial chunk of the gross output on buyers' land. The Shah and Raju study (1988) of Anklav village in

Table 5.7: Economics of irrigation with purchased groundwater: Pandalparru (West Godavari) and Anklav (Kheda)

		Pandalparru (c)		Anklav (d)	
		Sellers	Buyers	Sellers	Buyers
1.	Average value of output/acre (Rs)	7,986	7,302	5,428	2,620
2.	Average cost of irrigation	195 (a) (326) (b)	340	380 (619)	723
3.	Cost of irrigation as % value of output	2.4 (4.1)	4.7	7 (11.4)	27.6

(a) The costs are average pumping costs for sellers and purchase costs for buyers.
(b) Figures in brackets represent opportunity costs of water use on own farms as defined by sellers themselves.
(c) Approximating Quarter I conditions.
(d) Approximating Quarter IV conditions.
Source: Shah and Raju 1988:37

Kheda district and Pandalparru village in West Godavari district highlights these effects as summarised in table 5.7. In the West Godavari village with low water prices and a competitive water market, the value of gross output and cost of irrigation were similar for sellers as well as buyers, while in Anklav, the differences were substantial. Indeed, in West Godavari, resource-poor families were better off not owning LISs since the ruling water price was *lower* than the average full cost they themselves would incur if they established their own LISs. Some electric LIS owners were eager to supply water at as low as Re 0.50 per hour. And, as mentioned earlier, many owners of diesel LISs had decommissioned their diesel engines in favour of purchased water from electric LISs.

In Anklav, in contrast, the high water prices facing buyers meant that:

> "the average fertiliser use by the buyers is less than a fifth of the high amounts that the sellers use; their use of water (in kharif and annual crops) is 30% lower and the average yields that the buyers obtain are, in almost all cases, between 50-60% of the yields that the sellers obtain" (Shah and Raju 1988:36).

The low cost groundwater economy of Pandalaparru (West Godavari), in contrast, was intensive in both output as well as livelihoods. The aftermath of the introduction of flat power tariff in Andhra Pradesh in 1982 had seen considerably increased farm labour demand and wage rates in the village. Off season wage rates increased from Rs 8-10 in 1982 to Rs 15-20 in 1986 and peak season wage rates shot up from Rs 17-20 to Rs 25-30 per day. The 200 landless families of the village dependent solely on farm labour found it difficult to cope with expanded work opportunities; and, as a result, in the last two to three years, outside labour had been coming to the village for four to six months every year. The increased cropping intensities rendered farm work-

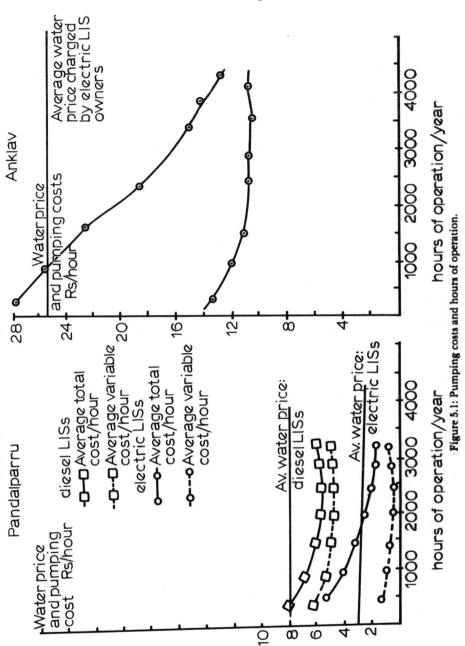

Figure 5.1: Pumping costs and hours of operation.

loads more continuous and reduced seasonal gaps in work opportunities for the landless (Shah and Raju 1988:35)

5.12 The Case for Flat Power Tariff and Recent Events in Gujarat

While several factors such as favourable aquifer conditions, rapid LI potential development and high LIS intensity, contribute to equitable water markets, flat power tariffs resulting in low incremental pumping costs for electric LISs are the most powerful means to stimulate water markets and to make them equitable. Three highly beneficial effects make a strong case for flat rates as a policy:

1) Flat tariffs reduce private water prices and create strong incentives for sellers to sell more water by improving the quality of irrigation service. This is true in both WA as well as WS areas. Flat tariffs thus operate both ways: they reduce both incremental pumping costs and sellers' bargaining power.

2) Increases in pro-rata tariff (or in diesel price) result in proportionate increases in water prices even though other components of pumping costs may remain unchanged. In Gujarat, for example, as the pro-rata power price increased from Rs 0.20 in 1975 to Rs 0.65 in 1985, the water price shot up from Rs 8-10 to Rs 23-27 per hour. In contrast, increases in flat rates have very slow effects on water prices. Uttar Pradesh charges five times as high flat rates as are charged in Andhra Pradesh and Tamil Nadu; but its water prices are only 20-30 per cent higher than in the latter States. In fact, raising flat rates from very low rates as in Andhra Pradesh and Tamil Nadu may, besides improving the viability of their electricity boards, make water markets more active and equitable by increasing the pressure on LIS owners to sell more water to share their higher fixed costs.

3) Since the prices that the electric LIS owners charge strongly affect those charged by diesel LIS owners, flat rates which result in low prices by electric LISs also help to lower the monopoly premia charged by diesel LIS owners especially in WA areas with high LIS density. The evidence supporting this thesis is presented in table 5.2. In brief, we have argued that the large differences in prices charged by diesel LISs in West Godavari and in most of Uttar Pradesh, Punjab etc, from those charged by diesel LIS owners in Madurai, Karimnagar, Panchmahals, Midnapur, and Northern Kheda has nothing to do with their pumping costs which are closely comparable. The only way these differences can be explained is by the fact that in the former areas, electric LISs paying flat rates and charging low water prices offer stiff competition to diesel LIS owners who are therefore obliged to keep their prices down.

The strongest and the most eloquent testimony in support of the case for flat tariffs has come recently from Gujarat where pro-rata power tariffs have a long history. In June 1987, the government of Gujarat announced the replacement of the pro-rata power tariff by a progressive flat rate in response to a major year-long farmer agitation in support, among other things, of flat tariffs. Under the new arrangements, LISs with different hp ratings were to pay different rates per hp. Those with a 10 hp or smaller pumpset were to pay only Rs 192 per hp per year; but those with 30 hp or bigger pumpset were to pay Rs 660 per hp per year.

While the wide-ranging effects that the new policy have begun to produce will take some time to work out fully, the evidence available by December 1987 (discussed in some detail in Shah 1987b) provides strong support to the hypotheses evolved in this chapter. The first important effect has been that many electric LIS owners who used oversized motors as a hedge against erratic power supply began to consider replacing them with smaller LISs. In just one of the rural offices of the Gujarat Electricity Board visited by Shah, over 15 applications were pending in November 1987 for replacing large motors by lower hp motors. In a quick survey of a dozen major suppliers of LIS equipment in Anand town of Gujarat, all pointed to a major increase in the off-take of 7.5 and 10 hp motors and almost stagnant demand for larger motors. In December 1987, however, the Gujarat government succumbed to the pressure from large LIS owners and agreed to reduce the maximum flat rate from Rs 660 per hp to Rs 500 per hp. This is expected to somewhat slow down this process of scaling down of the capacities of large LISs.

As would have been expected, the water prices charged by electric LIS owners all over the State began to fall soon after June 1st, 1987 when the flat rates came into force. Enquiries made in mid-November indicated that the fall in the price ranged between 25 and 60 per cent in different areas. Where water tables are deeper and motors used by LIS owners of larger capacity,

Table 5.8: The range of decline in water prices as a result of flat rates in Gujarat

	Region	Price ruling during		Per cent decline
		April-May 1987 (Rs/hour)	October-November 1987 (Rs/hour)	
a)	Mehsana dist: Vijapur Taluka, (25-35 hp)	29-35	20-25	28-30
b)	Sabarkantha dist: Prantij taluka, (20-35 hp)	22-32	16-23	27-28
c)	Ahmedabad dist: Dehgam taluka, (7.5-15 hp)	16-21	7-12	43-56
d)	Kheda dist: Anand and Borsad talukas (15-25 hp)	22-27	10-18	33-58
e)	Bharuch dist: Ankleshwar taluka, (7.5-15 hp)	11-18	7-12	33-45
f)	Bulsar dist: Bulsar taluka, (12.5-25 hp)	19-26	8-14	46-58

prices fell less than in central and southern districts of the State. Considering that in 1987, Gujarat saw one of the worst droughts of this century, the decline in water prices charged by the 300,000 electric LIS owners in the State have provided much-needed relief to the 1.5-2.0 million resource-poor water buyers. In Navli, a village surveyed in November 1987, 25 sellers who sold over 40,000 hours of water during 1986, slashed their prices down from an average of Rs 24.10 per hour to Rs 16.20 per hour. Even at the same level of water use, thus the buyers would save over Rs 3 lakhs or Rs 400 per acre every year in irrigation cost. More generally, estimates show that the flat rates will result in redistribution of some Rs 100 crores of irrigation surplus annually from LIS owners to water buyers throughout the State of Gujarat.

Even as the enormous social benefits of flat power rates are becoming increasingly evident, opposition is likely to grow especially amongst professional economists and decision makers in the power industry. Economists, used to marginal cost-pricing solutions to all problems of resource allocation, are understandably uncomfortable with the concept of flat tariffs which defy the marginal cost pricing principle. Power industry managers in States like Andhra Pradesh, Haryana and Punjab have been arguing for reverting to pro-rata tariffs. They have several reasons for apprehensions regarding flat tariffs—some of them quite unfounded; but some others quite valid. It is true that flat tariffs may not be an entirely unmixed blessing; however, we argue in the next chapter, that it is possible to minimise the adverse effects of flat tariffs without losing their substantial benefits.

CHAPTER SIX

Practical Policy

ABSTRACT

For rapid and regulated development of LI potential, interventions by State and public agencies have included State tubewells, institutional and credit support, subsidies to RPFs, spacing and licensing norms, rural electrification, and electricity pricing and management.

For putting poor people first, especially RPFs, field evidence points to electricity pricing and supply as powerful instruments. On pricing, pro-rata charging is bad for RPFs, with high water prices and arbitrary, exploitative and monopolistic water-selling, while flat tariffs are good, with low water prices, buyers' water markets, and a more dependable service from sellers. On supply, the management of electricity supply can increase productivity and equity, and more so with flat than pro-rata tariffs, with quality, including timeliness, predictability and convenience, substituting for quantity.

Policies to benefit the poorer in water-abundant (WA) areas include flat and preferably progressive tariffs; improved quality of power supply; an Intensive Groundwater Development Programme for rapid saturation with LI capacity; capital subsidies for RPFs for LISs; and abolition of spacing and licensing norms. For water-scarce (WS) areas they include NGO-induced groups, flat tariffs, priority or exemption for RPFs with spacing and licensing norms, and fine-tuned restrictions on a high quality power supply.

Policies vary in speed and scale of application: power tariff policies have quick, wide impacts; power supply management is slower and more localised; and other policy mixes need tailoring to local conditions. Action should assure early and large gains for the poorer while gathering experience for wider use of localised policies.

6.1 Current Thinking and Policy

At present, the participation by government agencies in LI development varies from State to State and may take some or all of the following forms:

— active involvement through State tubewell programmes
— assistance to private farmers through credit support by public sector banks and NABARD
— liberalised credit support and subsidies on capital costs to individuals or groups of RPFs under various poverty alleviation programmes

— monitoring changes in aquifer conditions through State-level ground-
    water boards or departments, continuing assessment of the water-
    resource position, and the categorisation of areas as dark, grey and white
— regulation of groundwater development in various regions through
    spacing and licensing norms enforced through electricity boards and
    public sector banks.

We have argued in chapters 3, 4 and 5 that the existing policy framework has
not done enough to encourage resource-poor farmers to gain more from LI
potential. We have also argued that the regulatory thrust of the current policy
framework and the manner of its implementation have failed to control
overexploitation of LI potential; where they have succeeded, the costs in
terms of adverse equity effects are unacceptably high. The vast beneficial
equity effects of flat tariffs used by most States for administrative convenience
have remained unrecognised and may be lost under increasing pressures to
revert to pro-rata tariffs.

In this chapter, we argue for a more powerful and sensitive mix of
instruments in a new policy framework for LI development. We then present
a broader mix of policies to stimulate LI development in WA areas and to
regulate it equitably in WS areas.

Four important instruments provide the framework for the policies we
recommend. These are: coordinated institutional support; power pricing;
power supply management; and support to groups of the resource-poor. The
importance and role of each will vary according to local conditions. The
objectives of policy vary according to resource potentials. In WA areas, the
major thrust is to stimulate equitable water markets. In WS areas, NGO-
induced groups have a role to play in the equitable distribution of scarce
water, but even in these areas, water markets need to be brought within the
influence of public policy.

6.2 Efficiency of Water and Energy Use

Much current research on LI in India concentrates on the low efficiencies in
the use of water and energy in LISs. As we discover later, the level of efficiency
in the use of these resources is closely linked with the kind of policies used
which affect economic returns from LI development.

Several indicators of efficiency are used; the most recent treatment of this
important subject is found in Feinerman 1988. A broad concept of efficiency
in this context is the proportion of water pumped that is actually used by
plants; the higher the proportion, the better the efficiency of the irrigation
system. This proportion has three components. First, the quantum of water
applied may be more than the plants need and use; sprinkler and drip
irrigation systems contribute to improving this "application efficiency".
Second, when a good deal of water pumped is lost through seepage while it is
conveyed between the well-head and the field being irrigated—the "conveyance efficiency" becomes low; this can be improved by lining the field

channels or by using underground pipelines. Third, there is the "pumping efficiency"; an LIS may use more energy than it needs to produce a given level of design discharge. Pumping efficiencies can be improved by better design, by better matching of pumps, engines, tubes, and groundwater conditions and by better maintenance of pumping plants.

Among these three components of LI efficiency, "pumping efficiency" has received most attention from researchers. Many studies indicate pumping efficiencies to be low. Pumping efficiencies are usually found in the range of 30-40 per cent when 60 per cent could easily be achieved. In field conditions, pumping efficiency can often be improved rather easily by simple, low-cost improvements and modifications such as replacing a foot valve or matching engine and pump capacity (often over-sized), the sizes of suction and delivery pipes, the required discharge rate, etc. or by the use of mono block pumps, low friction foot valves and pipes, and so on.

Improving "conveyance" and "application" efficiencies are not as easy. Both require substantial capital investments which farmers are not usually willing to make unless they improve the economics of an LIS substantially. Widescale use of water-saving "sprinkler" and "drip" technologies which have become popular in affluent WS regions in the world are still rare in India. However, lined water conveyance systems are widespread in some areas and becoming more common generally. This occurs through private initiative and there appears little scope for direct participation by the government or public/community organisations in building lined conveyance systems except by encouraging private effort through subsidies and cheaper credit.

Since improving the efficiency in the use of a resource is a relatively slow process, the search for alternative ways to do it will continue over a long period. Substantial efficiency gains will no doubt have their "trickle down" equity effects. However, in this book, our main concern is with exploring more direct and powerful ways of enabling the poor to gain more from groundwater. Therefore, unlike the 'normal' social science practice which treats "efficiency" as the objective function to be maximised with "equity" as a constraint, in this chapter, we examine policies that maximise "equity" effects with minimum adverse effects on "efficiency".

6.3 Pricing of Electricity for LI

1) EQUITY EFFECTS OF ELECTRICITY PRICING SYSTEMS

Decision makers in power industry as well as in groundwater bureaucracy have largely ignored the links between electricity pricing and supply policies, and equitable development of LI potential. A major finding from our analysis in chapter 5 was the various advantages of flat power tariffs. In particular, we noted that: (a) flat tariffs produce powerful incentives for LIS owners to sell water to others and result in the diffusion of access to water by stimulating active LI water markets; (b) flat rates produce low water prices, curtail the bargaining power of LIS owners and minimise the differences in real irrigation costs between LIS owners and buyers; (c) water prices respond slowly to increases in flat tariffs so that equity in groundwater development need not necessarily imply heavily subsidised power supply and an unviable power industry; (d) in WA areas, low prices charged by electric LIS owners oblige diesel LIS owners too to keep their prices low.

Pro-rata power tariffs produce opposite effects. They reduce the pressure to sell and thereby strengthen the sellers' monopoly power. They result in high water prices and monopoly premia charged by LIS owners. When pro-rata tariffs are increased, water prices tend to increase in the *same proportion* (and not by the amount of increase in power cost). LIS owners paying pro-rata power charges use the increasing power cost as an excuse to put up their premia; and such behaviour has been observed even in areas like the Kheda district of Gujarat where water markets are quite competitive. Figure 6.1, for example, traces the successive increases in water prices over the

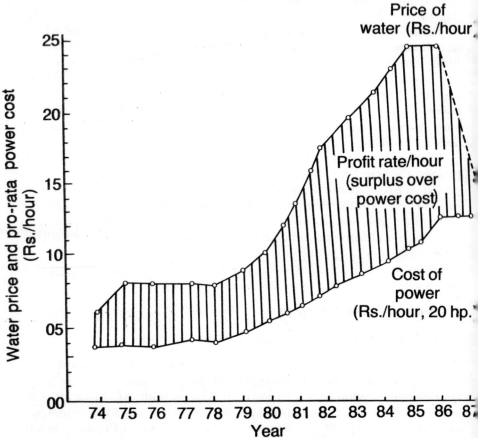

Figure 6.1: Exploitation of water buyers under pro-rata power pricing: Anklav area, Kheda district, Gujarat.

last 12 years in response to the rising pro-rata power charge in a region of Kheda district. What is notable is that water prices have increased only when the power price has been raised; that in absolute terms, water prices have risen much faster than power prices, although percentage increase in water price each time is comparable to increase in power cost per hour; and that the surplus over power cost from sale of water has increased by 300 per cent over the entire period.

For equitable development of groundwater, flat rates offer several crucial advantages. Resistance to flat tariffs, however, may persist or increase on account of two apprehensions, namely that flat rates will: (a) impair the viability of State electricity boards, and (b) reduce the efficiency of water and power use. These apprehensions are important though not necessarily valid.

2) FLAT RATES AND THE VIABILITY OF ELECTRICITY BOARDS

Electricity board managers have a general impression that flat rates undermine their viability and pro-rata tariffs promote it. One common effect of introducing flat rates, as we have noted, is to increase the hours of pumping, and so electricity consumption, sometimes by as much as 40 to 60 per cent over the previous level. With pro-rata rates, managers feel that higher power consumption will automatically be compensated by higher revenue. With flat rates, revenue is largely fixed, being determined by the recorded horsepower installed, and the levels of collection of dues. The negative view is reinforced by the experience of States with flat rates that are known to supply power to agriculture at a loss.

This view overlooks two crucial points about flat rates. The first is that those States with flat rates that operate at a loss do so not so much because the rates are flat as because they are too low. Increasing flat rates to four or five times their present (1988) levels in States like Andhra Pradesh and Tamil Nadu would leave their water markets largely unaffected but greatly improve the viability of their electricity boards.

The second point concerns costs and losses with pro-rata tariffs. The clamour by electricity boards for a switch to pro-rata tariffs on viability grounds, as in Haryana and Andhra Pradesh, is likely to prove infructuous and, in fact, self-defeating. Pro-rata tariffs impose massive costs of metering, policing and revenue collection which are saved under flat rates. Further, pilferage of power tends to rise sharply as pro-rata tariffs increase. In Gujarat, for example, only around 10 per cent of the power supplied by the Gujarat Electricity Board used to constitute transmission losses in the early 1960s when the pro-rata charge was low; but in more recent times, as the pro-rata tariff sharply increased, the proportion of power lost and pilferred rose to 28 to 30 per cent (GEB 1985:2). To contain such pilferage is more difficult than to minimise the fewer, simpler and more easily detected malpractices associated with the flat tariff system. Flat rates have, in fact, the potential to be more profitable for State electricity boards than pro-rata tariffs. Sanghal (1984), for example, argued that at 700 hours of LIS operation per year, the

UP Electricity Board earned more under the flat rate system than under the earlier pro-rata system. The REC study (1980: 7–9) of the switch from pro-rata to (subsidised) flat tariffs in Uttar Pradesh and Maharashtra showed that a good part of the reduced revenue under the flat rate system was made good by savings in costs. It also showed that a mere 10–20 per cent increase in flat rates would increase net revenue beyond the level under the pro-rata system. In particular, the study noted that "since metered system of tariff requires elaborate managerial and other infrastructural arrangement, notwithstanding the losses on gross revenue account, the flat rate system can subsist on less expensive management for the supply of energy and realisation of revenue" (REC 1980: 6). Notably, the REC analysis does not include the positive effect of flat rates in terms of reducing pilferage of power which has been an important contributor to Gujarat Electricity Board's economic unviability.

When these points are taken into account, flat rates set at appropriate levels should not undermine viability of the electricity boards; on the contrary, they should strengthen it.

3) EFFECTS OF FLAT RATES ON EFFICIENCY OF WATER AND POWER USE

Flat rates reduce the incremental cost of power and water to close to zero and provide no incentive for judicious use of power and water. In WA areas, they may result in inefficiency; in WS areas, they may result in over-exploitation of the aquifer. Empirical evidence in this regard is mixed and does not help to arrive at a firm conclusion. High pro-rata power charges levied in Gujarat made substantial investments in piped water conveyance systems appear sensible. A group of students of the Institute of Rural Management, Anand (Gupta et al. 1986:11) working in Kheda district found investments in underground pipelines profitable even at 20 per cent discount rate; and they also found that at the prevailing pro-rata power price, private·investment in piped distribution was profitable for LIS owners even if seepage losses were as low as 5.2 per cent whereas actual seepage losses were well in excess of 25 per cent. In Madurai, Copestake (1986) found the social rate of return on investment in pipelines as high as 40 per cent; however, farmers paying flat rates failed to see any gain in making investments in lined conveyance. Interestingly, diesel LIS owners who also incur a high incremental cost are rarely found to invest in pipelines, perhaps because they are mobile and therefore can deliver water at closer distances from the nearest well.

It is also commonly argued that high water prices in many parts of Gujarat have been a blessing in disguise in that they have forced economy in water use and reduced the incidence of diseconomies of aquifer over-exploitation. While this reasoning is persuasive and plausible, empirical evidence is conflicting. Among all the Indian States, Gujarat has been among those with the most serious problems in containing over-exploitation. A high pro-rata tariff has not prevented a progressive lowering of the water table in Mehsana and Sabarkantha districts and in coastal areas of Saurashtra where it has created an acute problem of saline ingress (Shukla 1985). Further, even if the high pro-rata charge does contain over-exploitation, it is highly unequitable since it is mostly the resource-poor buyers who are forced to "economise" on water since to them the price per unit of water is substantially greater than its incremental cost to sellers. There is therefore a need to examine whether high water prices through high pro-rata power tariffs is the only way of preventing overexploitation of aquifers. We believe it is not necessarily so.

In theory, likewise, the high incremental costs implied by pro-rata tariffs would also encourage efficiency in power use. Low pumping efficiencies are caused, among other things, by the choice of oversized motors in relation to suction and delivery pipes, discharge required and well yield and by lack of proper maintenance. Patel's work with 1600 electric LISs in Gujarat showed that, in spite of a high pro-rata tariff, pumping efficiencies were extremely low. Farmers apparently use oversized motors because a pro-rata charge related to actual consumption does not penalise the use of over-capacity motors; flat power tariffs however, do, especially if they are progressive. With some extension effort, Patel could persuade several hundred farmers to make power saving investments such as in low friction foot valves, replacement of coupled motor and pumps by monoblock pumps, and of GI pipes by rigid PVC pipes, because he could demonstrate the effects of such improvements on their power bills. Where flat rates are levied, farmers making such investments would not save on their power bills, but would increase their well discharge.

As far as power use efficiency is concerned, thus both flat rates and pro-rata tariffs have merits and demerits. To the extent that use of oversized motors results in inefficient power use, flat rates too have a positive impact of increasing the efficiency. When power supply is restricted and erratic, farmers tend to prefer larger motors and pro-rata power tariff does little to discourage such practices (Shah 1985). But a flat tariff linked to the hp of the LIS does, especially when progressive, because it imposes a higher cost on those using (unnecessarily) high capacity motors. In fact, an important trend that the REC study (1980:2) detected in Uttar Pradesh and Maharashtra was a sharp increase in the use of 3 hp and 5 hp motors and a decline in 7.5 hp motors when they switched to flat rates. They found the average load per LIS to have declined from 6.71 kw in 1973-74 to 5.03 kw in 1979–80 in Uttar Pradesh. A similar trend began in Gujarat after the government changed to a progressive flat rate in June 1987 (Shah 1987b).

As water markets develop and become more refined, the process stimulates investment in efficiency. A detailed study of private investments by LIS owners in pipeline networks in Gujarat disproved the notion that high pro-rata power cost was the prime motivator for such investments. Many LIS owners had invested in pipelines 20 to 30 years ago when pro-rata power costs were very low. The main motive behind such investments was to maintain competitive edge. Early investors aimed at achieving a monopoly position over a large command, at times over two or three villages, by taking water to distant farmers. By doing so, they drove several sellers out of business; many others followed suit by making similar investments.

In many areas of Gujarat, water markets have thus assumed a highly advanced and sophisticated form. A study of Navli village in Kheda district found that 24 LIS owners had between them laid 60 km of underground pipelines to serve an irrigated area of nearly 4 square km. Most parcels could get water from three or four different outlets each from a different pipeline network attached to a private LIS (Shah 1987b); as a result, seepage losses were negligible. It is unlikely that the adoption of flat tariff in Gujarat will reduce incentives to invest in pipelines in such markets since the pro-rata power charge was not the main driving force behind the original investment.

Ensuring efficiency of resource use is a particularly complex problem in this context since two precious resources—water and energy—are involved, and they have different relative values in different contexts. Hydel power is cheap and abundant in the Punjab; but most power used in Gujarat is thermal and more expensive. Likewise, water is more abundant in the Gangetic plains where the need to make efficient use of it is less pressing than in some of the WS areas of the hard-rock south where water is more valuable at the margin. As water markets in different areas develop to more advanced stages, the key to a more efficient and equitable regulating mechanism may lie less in the choice of tariff system and more in the sensitive management of the power supply.

6.4 Management of Power Supply

1) QUANTITY VERSUS QUALITY OF POWER SUPPLY

The quantity, reliability and predictability of power supplies for LISs may have a crucial impact on the extent of monopoly power enjoyed by water sellers. An abundant and regular power supply as in Andhra Pradesh and Punjab helps to improve the performance of the water markets on dependability and adequacy grounds while also helping to keep the price charged by electric LIS owners low through the flat tariff. Where diesel engines are used in electrified areas to beat the irregularity and inadequacy of power supplies, an abundant power supply would tend to reduce the "rent" extracted by diesel LIS owners too.

Despite increased outlays, the power supply situation in India is unlikely to change drastically in the near future. Arguing for abundant or unlimited power to be supplied to LISs may therefore be unrealistic. It may also be unnecessary. For the problem with power supply for LI may not be one of sufficiency as much as of regularity, convenience and timing. Field studies indicate that the actual number of hours that power is supplied in a year is often three to four times the number of hours that an average LIS is operated. Shankar (1986), for instance, reports the following information for a sample of 140 private LISs in Allahabad district of Uttar Pradesh for the year 1985–86.

Table 6.1: Hours of power supply and operation of LISs in Allahabad district of Uttar Pradesh

	Power supplied (hours)				Total	Average hours of operation of LISs	Average area irri- gated per LIS (ha)
	per day	day night	per day	season night			
Kharif	3.5	3.06	431	376	807	223	7.99
Rabi	3.91	4.58	500	586	1086	353	14.78
Zaid	2.77	3.66	144	190	330	87	2.15
Total	3.55	3.8	1075	1153	2228	653	24.92

Average number of hours that an LIS was operated was only a third of the hours for which power was available. The reasons why pumps operated for so few hours were to be sought elsewhere: too little power was available in summer when irrigation is needed most; all loadshedding in summer hit agriculture first; only 52 summer days had power against 128 days in rabi and 123 days in *kharif*; there was no certainty or advance information about the likely power supply position; and, most importantly, over half of the power was supplied during the night when irrigation entails increased transmission losses and less effective field application. Irrigation at night is inconvenient to buyers as well as sellers, involves more labour and increases the hassle of management. At times, higher wages are paid for night irrigation and more labour is required, which may be its only spillover benefit to the landless.

Indeed, there is a growing belief, often supported by evidence, that increasing unreliability of power supply in some northern States has resulted in a substantial shift to diesel LISs; most new capital investment has substituted for old rather than adding new capacity. The practice of keeping a diesel set as a standby has grown especially amongst the wealthy; and the poor are switching outright to diesel sets which are costlier to install and operate. Sharma (1988:15) thus found that diesel sets as a proportion of total LIS in Uttar Pradesh in general went up from 70 per cent in 1980–81 to 73 per cent in 1983–84 but in eastern Uttar Pradesh where power supply is particularly problematic, from 66 per cent to 71 per cent over the same period.

Even when limited, power supplied to farmers at times of the day convenient to them, during the peak irrigation periods of rabi and summer, and on a schedule which is widely known and dependable, may have stronger positive effects on water markets than increased but undependable and unreliable power supplied through an infrastructure prone to frequent disruption. If the voltage drops suddenly, the coil of a pump burns out, involving loss of continuity in irrigation and expensive repair. Electric power lines can be stolen, as is common in parts of Bihar, causing an entire zone of electric pumpsets to fail for an indefinite period. More common and serious than either of these are the "trips" and breakdowns especially in the critical periods of rabi and summer irrigation. These are times when irrigators are vulnerable as water tables drop, requiring more power to lift a given quantum of water, and as hydel power is cut back for lack of water. The setting is right for the "rent seekers" to have a field day. The vulnerability of the farmers during such times often encourages "the field staff responsible for the maintenance of the supply lines to deliberately cut off supply in order that the tubewell owners are obliged propitiate them" (Singh 1988a).

In making the water markets more efficient and equitable, the amount or hours of power supplied to agriculture during a year are of less crucial importance than its quality represented by reliability, predictability, convenience, timeliness and adequacy during periods of peak irrigation demand. In fact, it is likely that with improved *quality* of power supply, judicious restrictions on the *quantity* of power supplied can be used to nullify most of the ill effects of flat rates without reducing their benefits.

2) RESTRICTED POWER SUPPLY AND EFFICIENCY IN WATER USE

Abundant power supply under a flat tariff may in fact increase the difference between the opportunity cost of water to the seller and the buyer; in such a situation, even after meeting the buyers' demand, a typical seller would have time left to irrigate water-intensive crops on his own land since the incremental cost of water would be close to zero. As the power supply gets restricted, however, the seller has to choose between irrigating a water-intensive crop on his own land or selling water to others. The profits foregone by selling less water become the opportunity cost of growing water-intensive crops on the sellers' own land. A judiciously restricted power supply can thus encourage the LIS owners also to economise on water use as much as buyers do since the perceived cost of water to both buyer and seller will tend to be equal to the sale price of water.

It is also natural that under a restricted and predictable power supply regime, and as water markets become more advanced and sophisticated, sellers who want to make the most of their limited power supply will begin to see seepage losses caused by unlined channels as a cost. incentives to minimise such loss would make investment in a lined distribution system profitable under a restricted power supply regime and would help sellers to increase their profits without the buyers necessarily losing. Public policy support through credit or subsidies would encourage LIS owners to invest in lined water conveyance systems, with positive equity and efficiency effects. The pay-offs in terms of livelihood gains by RPF water buyers from a better knit LI grid through underground pipelines can be gauged only by the extreme monopolistic features of the water markets in many regions where unlined field channels are predominantly in use. Singh (1988a) describes how, in an eastern Uttar Pradesh village, right of way for water has become an important instrument of monopoly power; whereas Shah's studies of Gujarat have shown that piped conveyance systems have made right of the way a non-issue there. Thus encouraging private investments in piped water distribution through subsidy programmes will be desirable not only for efficient use of power and water but also for the livelihood of poor people.

3) Restricted Power Supply and Over-exploitation of Groundwater

At present, in many areas, spacing and licensing regulations are used to restrain well interference and over-exploitation of groundwater. We examined in chapter 3 how such norms hit the RPFs hard because they depend, much more than the affluent, on institutional financial agencies and electricity boards through which the norms have traditionally been enforced. Spacing and licensing norms have thus systematically prevented the resource-poor from claiming their due share of groundwater and instead have helped the less poor rapidly to preempt it. Against this, these norms offer no promise of effective control on mining and over-exploitation in WS areas, since their enforcement is not based upon a proper and exhaustive monitoring of LIS construction activity. There is no practical way yet devised of preventing those who can raise their own finance and are willing to bear the higher cost of diesel engines from establishing LISs and pumping water at will. As happens so often, such restrictions penalise the poorer and give a comparative advantage to the less poor.

Restrictions on power supplies can be a more effective and equitable method of controlling over-exploitation of aquifers in water stress areas. Less power means less water extracted by electric LISs. How much power should be supplied can be gauged by deducting the water extraction by diesel LISs from the safe yield of the aquifer during a given period. Restrictions on power supply to a given number of hours which are known to users would raise the monopoly power of electric LISs but would have only marginal impact on prices charged by them under a flat tariff which renders the incremental cost of lifting water close to zero. The effect produced would be similar to what Copestake (1986) observed in the highly water-stressed areas of Madurai, and Shah (1986) observed in Karimnagar district. In both these regions with low aquifer potential, low well yields limited the amount of water that electric LIS owners could sell just as restricted power supplies would do. The monopoly power of LIS owners was high as was evident from the exceedingly high (two to three times the incremental cost) rent extracted by diesel LIS owners; however, the sellers using electric LISs who also enjoyed high monopoly power but paid low flat rates still charged water prices to buyers as low as between a third and a fourth of those charged by diesel LIS owners. Limited water is thus shared more widely and sellers are not able to skim off the increased income from irrigation as diesel LIS owners do.

The capacity of public policy to effectively control over-exploitation in WS areas through restrictions on power supply will depend on the farmers' preference for electric versus diesel LIS. Although there will always be situations where diesel engines will score over electric motors, the choice of electric motors can be influenced by power pricing and power supply policies. High power prices as in Gujarat largely nullify the cost advantage that electric LISs would otherwise enjoy; on the other hand, an erratic, unreliable and frequently interrupted power supply as in Uttar Pradesh and

Bihar will encourage farmers to choose diesel LISs in spite of their higher operating còsts. Shah and Raju (1986) found a large number of diesel LIS owners decommissioning their LISs to use purchased irrigation from electric LISs when Andhra Pradesh switched to low flat rates in 1982. In balance thus, encouraging the use of electric LISs through attractive power pricing and power supply policies with judicious restrictions on a high quality power supply, may well be a more effective method of regulating the rate of ground water withdrawal in WS areas than the spacing and licensing norms used at present.

4) RESTRICTED POWER SUPPLY AND ECONOMIC VIABILITY OF FLAT RATES

A change from pre-rata to flat tariffs normally causes an immediate increase of 40 to 60 per cent in the power use per LIS. This is mainly as a response to the powerful incentive to sell water under flat rates. Even when flat rates are set high enough to cover the actual cost of generating the amount of power used per LIS under a pro-rata tariff, the increased power consumption resulting from flat rates remains unpaid for. Since very high flat rates may be politically unpopular, restricting the power supply to agriculture can be an effective method of minimising the losses to the electricity boards too. Two caveats, however, must be stressed.

First, every unit of power supplied to agriculture may, on the margin, generate four to six times as great a value as the cost to the society of generating that unit of power. A bulk of this value reaches poor people as water buyers who tend to use water more productively than LIS owners (see, e.g., Satya Sai 1987). These equity and productivity effects therefore need to be weighed against the economics of the electricity boards in evaluating decisions relating to power tariffs and power supplies. Second, very high flat rates accompanied by stringent restrictions on power supplies will have a disincentive effect on private investment in electric LISs. The implications are as follows: for a given level of flat rate, predictable hours of power supply should only be restricted to a level at which the average cost of LIS operation is lower than the prevailing water price in the region. Alternatively, if power supplies have to be restricted to a certain level, then flat rates should be reduced if that is necessary so that the average cost remains lower than the price.

Restricted power supplies with strong institutional support to the resource-poor will tend to increase the relative importance of small holder LIS owners as sellers in water markets. This is because the LIS owners with large holdings will need to use the bulk of the power supply for irrigating their own fields. The trend currently noticed in many regions for large farmers to use water to increase income from their own land *and* extracting "water rent" through sale will be checked through power supply restrictions. Further, a progressive levy of flat rates will have desirable equity effects in such a context. In a restricted power supply regime where smaller farmer sellers will have more surplus water to sell than larger farmers, a progressive flat rate will provide a further economic advantage of lower average cost. This advantage will be further strengthened if institutional support gives resource-poor farmers priority in power connections, increasing the dependence of the more affluent on diesel LISs and on purchase of water from electric LIS owners.

In summary, then, power pricing and power supply policies can be more important in equitable development of lift irrigation potential than most decision makers in groundwater departments and electricity boards have imagined. This is especially so when they are supported by strengthened institutional back up. Flat rates can produce strong positive equity effects but may undermine incentives for efficiency. Pro-rata tariffs reduce benefits of LI development to poor people without necessarily encouraging efficiency and viability. These effects are summarised in table 6.2.

Table 6.2: Desirable and undesirable effects of flat versus pro-rata tariffs

	Flat tariff	Pro-rata tariff
A *Water market*		
1. Water price	Low	High
2. Premia charged by diesel LISs	Low	High
3. Dependability	High	Low
4. Adequacy	High*	Low
5. Overall productivity and equity effects	Very positive	Negative
B. *Viability of electricity boards*		
1. Power demand	Sharp increase[+0]	Decrease
2. Metering cost	Zero	Substantial
3. Collection Cost	Very low	Very high
4. Incentive to pilfer power	Disappears	Very strong
C. *Efficiency of power use*		
1. Incentive for power saving investment	Low or nil	High
2. Use of over-capacity motors	Strongly discouraged[0]	Encouraged
D. *Efficiency of water use*		
1. Danger of over-exploitation	High[+0]	Low
2. Incentive to invest in pipelines	Low[+]	High
3. Difference in water use efficiency of buyers and sellers	High[+]	High

* Subject, of course, to the availability of water.
0 Progressive flat tariffs will have further positive impact on these
+ All the four major undesirable effects of flat rates—B1, D1, D2 and D3—can be minimised through judicious restrictions on "high quality" power supply to irrigation. C1 will however remain a drawback of flat tariff just as C2 will remain as a drawback of pro-rata tariff.

6.5 Water Abundant Areas: Institutional Support for Saturation

In all WA areas, the emergence of equitable water markets can be facilitated by increasing LIS density and by removing the constraints that impede participation by the resource poor in the development of LI potential. Such constraints usually take the form of the "hassle" involved in obtaining institutional credit. The degree of "hassle" involved has a strong scale bias; for the resource-poor with less clout and contact, less creditworthiness and little to offer as collateral find it more difficult to overcome bureaucratic "hassle" than the affluent elite. Spacing norms and licensing regulations exacerbate the "hassle" factor. For poor people to obtain the subsidies and other benefits that they are entitled to involves even more bureaucratic red tape. There are psychic and financial costs involved in approaching banks, government departments and other institutions which deter and discourage poor people. A loan application involves collecting a variety of documents; getting subsidies involves even more. After all these, there is the risk of rejection. Often, substantial unofficial payments have to be made. These hassle factors not only slow down the saturation process but also reduce poor people's share in the benefits of saturation.

The limited development of groundwater potential in regions with some of the highest concentrations of rural poverty is associated with their low rates of rural electrification. While the national average for coverage of villages under rural electrification programmes was over 64 per cent in 1984, in the eastern region this figure was lower: 49 per cent for Bihar, 51 per cent for Orissa, and 50 per cent for West Bengal (NIRD 1985:353). Rapid rural electrification can stimulate the pace of groundwater development in these regions. It will lower the cost of purchased water and improve its supply, as competition increases between sellers. As we noted earlier (sec. 6.3), the normally lower operating costs of electric LISs tend to depress the prices charged by diesel LIS owners. Priority allocation of power connections to resource-poor families or their groups would help to augment their direct command over groundwater in this process of saturation.

Strengthening institutional support for LI development and targeting it to the resource-poor is important in this context and would stress: rapid rural electrification in areas like eastern Uttar Pradesh, Bihar, Orissa, and West Bengal which have large and concentrated groundwater potential not yet fully developed; and improved access for resource-poor families to institutional credit and the subsidies and benefits available under various anti-poverty programmes.

NGOs have played a useful role in minimising the "hassle" by acting as sympathetic intermediaries for poor people. Most NGOs, however, operate on too small a scale to be able to step up substantially the pace of saturation. Where they do, the impact is dramatic, as is evident in the role played by the Deen Dayal Research Institute in Gonda district of eastern Uttar Pradesh (DDRI 1981; Chambers and Joshi 1983). This district, like others in eastern

Uttar Pradesh, has substantial aquifers close to the ground surface and also highly fragmented landholdings. Between 1978 and 1980, DDRI posted two graduate fieldworkers in each of the district's 30 blocks. These fieldworkers assumed the role of honest brokers between farmers, bankers and government. In two years, 31,000 shallow tubewells were sunk and 16,000 pumpsets (mostly diesel) were bought. The cost to the farmer of an engine and a pumpset was brought down from Rs 6,500 to Rs 5,000 by eliminating unofficial payments of Rs 1,550 believed necessary to secure cooperation from the bank and government staff. A substantial lease market emerged for diesel engines since the number of tubewells far exceeded the number of pumpsets available and the lease transactions were carried out at surprisingly uniform prices throughout the area. The overall effect was evidently sharp increases in land productivity and total output, good access to irrigation for small and marginal farmers, a rise in real wages especially where wages were paid in kind and of women involved in transplanting, weeding and harvesting (Chambers and Joshi 1983:3–4).

What the DDRI accomplished in Gonda district appears more easily replicable than the experiments of many other NGOs. Such replication would have dramatic effects in all WA regions which are not yet saturated. The idea itself has nothing new about it; for the government does, from time to time, keep announcing such programmes. In 1988, for example, the Minister for Agriculture announced a million tubewell programme while the Finance Minister, in his budget speech, announced Jal Dhara, to supply pumpsets to marginal farmers (Padmanabhan 1988). The Gonda experience of DDRI makes a strong case for an Intensive Groundwater Development Programme (IGDP) in these regions which would invite villages to volunteer or bid for saturation. These villages would have camps by senior well-qualified government and bank staff to complete all formalities through streamlined procedures minimising the hassle for the poorer. The camps could usefully include functionaries from the electricity boards too. For often, electrification of a village does not automatically imply electrification of tubewells. In fact, there are substantial scalar economies and lumpiness involved in supplying power connections. As a result, an electricity board would normally not be willing to provide power connections except to a cluster of tubewells to which it would be cost effective to draw a cable. For electricity boards, it might be a wiser strategy to use such IGDP camps to electrify groups of tubewells rather than to relax the viability norms and draw cables for individual farmers as the West Bengal government has seemed keen to do.

6.6 Groups and Markets: Equitable Regulation in WS Areas

WS areas constitute the bulk of the hardrock areas of the southern peninsula where recharge available for withdrawal is low, capital costs of establishing LISs are high and the risk of well failure is substantial. They also include WA areas where water tables are falling, and coastal areas where lowering water tables may lead to salinity ingress.

In such areas, the main question is of regulating the rate of groundwater withdrawal and of ensuring equitable distribution of the limited water that is available. Where it is not as yet fully appropriated, the question is how the resource-poor can capture their share of the remaining potential; where it is already developed, the task is to devise ways in which the poor can gain more from it.

In Chapter 4, (sec. 4.4) while reviewing the experience of NGO-induced group efforts to own and manage LISs, we concluded that LI groups can add little to equitable access in WA areas over and above what equitable markets can achieve; and that groups are more likely to fail in WA areas because of the difficulty they face in competing with private sellers. Since private sellers are willing to offer the same—often better—terms than group LISs can offer to their members, the logic of group formation itself comes into question.

In WS areas, however, the logic behind group action is stronger. Capital costs of LISs are substantial and risks of failure are high; private sellers are not as numerous as in WA areas, nor can they offer as reliable and adequate an irrigation service as private sellers do in WA areas. Because of these factors, groups tend to be more numerous and successful in WS areas; they also help to achieve a more equitable distribution of access to LI potential. Public policy should actively encourage groups of the resource-poor to establish, own and operate LISs in WA areas by supporting NGOs involved in promoting and helping such groups; and by according them priority in licensing, electricity connections, credit support, subsidies and exemption from spacing norms.

We have earlier explored the powerful equity effects of flat electricity tariffs—particularly when progressive—on the working of the private groundwater markets. An important exception to our argument favouring progressive flat tariffs occurs in case of groups of RPFs. In some areas of Gujarat, RPF LI groups promoted by Sadguru Seva Sangh in Panchmahal district and by Aga Khan Rural Support Programme in Bharuch district faced serious problems of economic viability after the imposition of progressive flat rates. In each of these cases, many RPF families formed the group and used large capacity motors for lifting of water. The new policy imposed on them a power cost per hp (Rs 660/hp/year) three times higher than for an individual LIS owning RPF with less than 7.5 hp motor (Rs 195/hp/year). Many groups became unviable particularly in areas with scarce water. NGOs supporting LI groups of RPFs, such as the Aga Khan Rural Support Programme, whose groups in Bharuch and elsewhere had suffered a serious blow, took up the matter with the authorities. Happily, an enlightened Gujarat government readily, in October 1988 evolved a special, equitable formula for LI groups. Under this the total installed H.P. will be divided by the number of members of the group to obtain the ratio of installed H.P. per member. The rate applicable to RPF lift irrigation groups will be comparable to twice the value of this ratio. Thus, all RPF groups with installed H.P. per member of 3.53 or less will pay H.P. rates chargeable to individual farmers owning LIS of 7.5 H.P. or less. A group of 80 RPFs using a 40 hp LIS will be charged as if each owns a 1 hp LIS.

Initial reaction of NGOs as well as LI groups to this modified flat rate for LI groups has been favourable. It is likely that the new policy will encourage the formation of LI groups, not necessarily of RPFs alone. Indeed, some of the water companies operating in many parts of the State will want to change to the cooperative format to benefit from the new policy. Only time will tell the ultimate overall effect.

Even in the most supportive policy environment, however, groups are unlikely to dominate the LI scenario in WS areas. Private LIS owners will continue to play a dominant role. In many such WS areas, as in Karnataka or in the Telangana region where a taboo on selling water prevents the emergence of markets, access to LI potential will be highly unequal and largely appropriated by resourceful LIS owners. Creating an environment which encourages LIS owners to begin to sell water to their neighbours, even at high prices, will result in significant equity gains. For, the resource-poor in WS Madurai who can buy water, albeit at high prices, from diesel LIS owners, are better off than the resource-poor in other WS areas who just cannot buy water at any price. In many southern areas, electricity boards actively discourage water selling by electric LIS owners; this makes sense from their own limited viewpoint but from the viewpoint of the poor people, it may be disastrous.

Flat rates can stimulate water selling in such areas. Steeply progressive flat rates may achieve several good results: they can encourage small holders to invest in LISs; improve small LIS owners' share in the water market; heavily penalise use of high capacity motors; and encourage large land owners to buy water from small holder LIS owners with greater surplus irrigation capacity. These effects will be further augmented and total withdrawal regulated to safe levels if "high quality" power supply is restricted but not so much as to undermine the viability of private LISs.

6.7 Equitable LI Development: The Overall Strategy

The instruments available to a public policy committed to targetting more of the gains from LI development to the poor are many and powerful; and the likely effects of these instruments are diverse and conflicting. The trick seems to lie in understanding the various relationships and in striking the right balance, with a mix of instruments that optimise productivity and equity benefits without imposing unduly high costs in terms of lowering water tables, depleting aquifers or creating an unviable power industry. The mix will differ between WS and WA regions and even within these regions, according to the level of resource development.

Table 6.3 provides an illustrative summary of policy mixes which, in our

Table 6.3: Optimal mix of policies for different regions

Groundwater potential	Extent of groundwater development	Macro policy intervention	Technological interventions	Institutional support
High	High	*High flat tariff, preferably progressive *Restricted but high quality power supply *Abolition of spacing and licensing norms	*Encourage small pumps *Encourage investments in power saving devices	*Landless groups for lift irrigation
High and waterlogged areas in canal commands	Low	*Low or progressive flat tariff *Less restricted power supply *Well managed State tubewells *Abolition of spacing and licensing norms	*Encourage small pumps and tubes	*Rapid rural electrification *Landless irrigation groups *Intensive Groundwater Development Program *Priority to RPFs in power connections
Low and areas prone to salinity ingress	High	*High but progressive flat rates *Restricted power supply *Spacing and licensing norms with spacing exemptions for RPF groups	*Augment recharge *Subsidised pipelines *Encourage drip-irrigation *Develop surface water irrigation systems	*Ground water surveys *Priority to RPF groups in power connections *Encourage NGO experiments in equitable water allocation

Low	Low			
	*Steeply progressive flat rates *Less restricted power supply *Ban big pumps except by RPF groups *Spacing and licensing norms with spacing exemptions for RPF groups	*Encourage small pumps *Subsidise pipelines *Promote drip-irrigation *Develop surface irrigation-cum-aquifer recharge systems	*Groundwater surveys *Priority access to RPFs *RPF groups where big pumps are necessary *Encourage NGO action	

view, can form the basis of a more equitable lift irrigation development strategy in India. In all the four situations characterised by differing potentials and development, flat tariffs would produce highly equitable results. We believe that, because of the infeasibility of controlling diesel LISs, spacing norms and licensing policies, far from providing an effective check on over-exploitation, will only strengthen the monopoly access of the less poor and render private water markets inequitable. Therefore, spacing and licensing norms should be stringently enforced only in areas like Mehsana district in Gujarat and Coimbatore district in Tamil Nadu where the lowering of the aquifer has assumed frightening proportions, and in coastal strips such as in Saurashtra region in Gujarat and the Minjur aquifer of Tamil Nadu where overexploitation has led to saline ingress. Restricted but regular and predictable power supplies are the most equitable method of regulating the rate of groundwater withdrawal.

We might stress here that proper monitoring and management of the relationship between the level of flat rates and restrictions on "high quality" power supply are crucial for equity as well as for a check on over-exploitation.

Differential flat rates and power supply policies in different parts of the same State are also implied. In waterlogged areas commanded by a canal irrigation project, for instance, high inducements to farmers to use groundwater irrigation through very low flat rates and plenty of power supply are indicated. In other parts of the same State, however, a fragile groundwater balance may necessitate punitive flat rates and restricted power supplies. This may raise difficult questions of interregional discrimination, though less in the case of canal irrigation encouraging those near the head reaches to use groundwater irrigation can help spread available surface water to larger areas.

In WA areas with very meagre development of the potential, an Integrated Groundwater Development Programme on the pattern of the Deen Dayal Research Institute's experiment in Gonda district would increase the pace of saturation and poor people's share in the newly developed groundwater resource. In such areas where the water table is close to the ground, development and popularisation of small pump technology and low cost tubes would further reinforce the equity effect. Progressive flat rates can give small farmers with small hp pumpsets an economic advantage, while also encouraging larger farmers to buy water from them. NGOs and government could play an important role by enabling small groups of landless families to sell water as a source of livelihood and employment.

In WS areas, the main questions are how to prevent the affluent from pre-empting the resource and how to minimise over-exploitation. While licensing and spacing norms based on continuous monitoring of electric as well as diesel LISs may have some role to play in WS areas with a high degree of exploitation, here too, progressive flat rates can be useful to discourage high discharge pumpsets and to give a comparative advantage to small farmers. Equity can be enhanced in two ways in such areas: by encouraging groups of small farmers and NGOs seeking to establish equitable allocation of water, and by providing the poor priority access to new power connections. In water stress areas, small farmer groups and NGO interventions for equitable allocation are likely to yield far more positive results than in the water-abundant areas where the cost of securing direct access is low and the scope for purchasing water at fair prices is high.

There remains the pervasive problem in WS areas of the wasteful and inequitable cultivation by LIS owners of water-loving crops such as paddy, sugar cane and banana. We have not come across any successful efforts by the government to deter such wasteful use of water, but it will be important to learn from the experience of Maharashtra's prohibition of sugar cane introduced in 1986. If effective deterrents can be found, they should be vigorously enforced. Market mechanisms can also play a part. A well-developed private water market may over time discourage such inefficient water use by equalising the cost of water to buyers and sellers. Some evidence of this has been observed in WA areas of Kheda district in Gujarat where LIS owners have reduced banana cultivation with lifted water because selling water to others has become more profitable (Shah and Raju 1986). In WS areas, a restricted but dependable power supply might provide conditions for similar development of water markets, and encourage investment by LIS owners in conveyance systems to minimise transmission losses. With a more dependable, if restricted, supply of water, RPFs in WS areas would have an incentive to grow water-sparing crops. These would be socially more desirable because of their higher value to water ratios and higher labour requirements. The outcome would then be more productive, more equitable, and more livelihood intensive uses of the scarce water.

In both WA as well as WS areas, encouraging private investments in underground pipeline systems should get high priority on efficiency as well as equity grounds. This could be done in several ways such as: (a) direct subsidy from either the electricity board or the anti-poverty programmes to pipeline costs, (b) use of underground pipelines by State tubewells, and (c) making pipeline investment with subsidy a condition for institutional finance for private LISs.

Some of the policies which follow from our analysis require different combinations of instruments in different areas. With these, discrimination is needed, between WA and WS areas, and within each, between those that are more developed and those which are less. Both the roles of organisations and the rules of government have to differ from one area to another. Of these, the roles of organisations are the easier: NGOs can adapt their actions to local needs, for example in promoting LI groups in WS areas, and government can mount task forces where necessary, for example for the Intensive Ground-water Development Programme in WA areas. Differentiating the rules of government is more difficult, involving as it does choices of who gets what, and being open to local pressures. Here a progressive approach will be best, starting with those zones where there is the most obvious collective interest in localised controls. These will usually be areas of groundwater over-exploitation, of saline ingress, and of waterlogging. Experience gained with localised and experimental treatment of problem zones such as these can help identify appropriate sets of measures for wider application. In this way, as experience and confidence are acquired, early gains for the poorer can provide a foundation on which later gains can be built.

The case for zonal policies for problem areas should not obscure the priority of those measures which are quick-acting and reliable on a much wider scale. As we have seen, major gains for the poorer can come from changes made for whole States, as with Andhra Pradesh's and Gujarat's switches from pro-rata to flat rates for electricity. The scope for such massive and immediate impacts should be fully explored and exploited without delay.

PART THREE

Trees and the Poor

CHAPTER SEVEN

Forestry for Livelihoods

ABSTRACT

Traditionally, people have depended upon forests and revenue lands for the collection of livelihood goods such as food, fruit, fuelwood, fodder and fibres. Their access, consumption and income have been affected by deforestation, plantations replacing mixed forests, diversion of artisan's raw materials to industry, and management neglect of revenue lands. Those who gather minor forest products (MFPs) from forests receive extremely low prices because of monopoly controls and exploitation, whether of contractors or of government following nationalisation.

On forest lands, social security plantation schemes to afforest degraded lands have provided little or no participation beyond wage employment. Elsewhere, when species selection has been right, and benefits assured and direct, people have looked after forests and have cooperated with the Forest Department, as in Sukhomajri and Arabari, although clear rights and prompt payments can remain problems.

On revenue lands, traditional community management has been better in upland and tribal areas with smaller, more cohesive villages than in the plains with larger, more socially differentiated villages. Community forestry on these lands has a bad record for participation: the Forest Department has tended to treat community forestry as an extension of the forest, planting species for the market not villagers' needs, not sharing funds and management with village bodies, and not clarifying rights or procedures for allocating benefits.

To realise the vast potential of forests and village lands to support the livelihoods of the poor requires putting their priorities first, pointing away from single products like timber and poles, and towards a diversity of labour-intensive products, with open competition between public and private buyers and good market information.

In chapter 1 (sec. 1.6) we argued that trees can support the livelihoods of rural people in three ways: by providing recurrent subsistence needs—of fodder, fuel, food, fibre, and many non-timber products; as sources of income, especially in otherwise slack seasons; and as capital stocks or savings banks to be cut and cashed to meet contingencies. In chapter 2 (sec. 2.6), we showed that while the area under actual tree cover has declined and continues to decline, those lands especially suitable for growing trees because they are degraded are vast and increasing. Of these, degraded forest lands account for 36 m ha, degraded revenue, panchayat, and other government or village lands for 13 m ha, and degraded private lands for 35 m ha.

In analysing conditions and trends, and seeking to support and augment the subsistence, security and self-respect of the poor through trees, the various categories of land fall into two major classes: public and private. In this chapter we examine rights and access of the poor on public, that is, forest and revenue lands, and in chapter 8 we examine the potential for helping the poor on private lands through farm forestry.

7.1 Forest Lands

Except in the Himalayan region, India's forests have generally speaking not been uninhabited wildernesses. Even in the remote forests people have either been living traditionally or were brought by the Forest Department and settled there for cheap labour. These are called forest villages. Although many have now been given the same status as that of other revenue villages, around 5,000 are still classified as forest villages. In all there are about 48 million forest dwellers living within or in the vicinity of forests for whom forests have been basis of their livelihoods and means of survival (NCHSE 1987:30).

Besides fuelwood and other wood products, forests provide what are misleadingly termed "minor" forest products (MFPs). Most MFPs come from forests, although some trees yielding MFPs occur on private fields, and also provide valuable assets and flows for subsistence and cash. Seventy per cent of MFPs are collected from the five States of Maharashtra, Madhya Pradesh, Bihar, Orissa, and Andhra Pradesh where 65 per cent of the tribal population live (Guha 1983:1890). MFPs include fodder and grasses; raw materials like bamboo, canes and bhabbar grass for artisan-based activities of the poor; leaves, gums, waxes, dyes and resins; and many forms of food, including nuts, wild fruits, honey, and game (See table 2.15 for a list). These often play a vital part in the livelihood strategies of the poor. Collection has the advantage of requiring skills which can be taught and passed on by the poor themselves, and much of it is done in the lean agricultural months of March-July when other activities are not available, as shown in table 7.1.

For tribals and others who live in or near forests, MFPs provide both subsistence and income. As already stated, they are the source of a major portion of their food, fodder, fruits, medicines, and other subsistence and consumption items. Then, the collection of MFPs is a source of cash income, especially because of their increasing commercial importance. A survey done in forest regions of Gujarat revealed that nearly 22 to 27 per cent of the adults and 70 to 72 per cent of children go to forests for collection (GOI 1982:19). Thirty-five per cent of the earnings of tribals in a district of Gujarat and up to 38 per cent in Madhya Pradesh have been found to come from these items (GOI 1982:21). Women's contribution to cash income of the household is higher in villages close to forests than in commercialised villages (ILO 1986). Such gathering by women can improve their status in the family.

Table 7.1: Collection period for various minor forest products

Commodity	Potential of production in lakh tonnes	J	F	M	A	M	J	J	A	S	O	N	D
						Months of collection							
Grasses	5.3	x	x	x	x							x	x
Fibres and flosses	1.3				x	x	x	x					
Bamboo & canes	43.1	x	x	x	x	x	x	x	x	x	x	x	x
Mahua	4.9			x	x	x	x						
Neem	4.2				x	x	x						
Karanj	1.1					x	x	x	x	x			
Kusum	0.9					x	x						
Sal seeds	55.0			x	x	x							
Khakan seeds	0.5				x	x							
Gums & resins	1.8			x	x	x	x						
Myrobalans	1.5	x	x	x									
Tendu leaves	4.8				x	x	x						
Tamarind	2.5	x	x	x	x								x
Lac	0.3				x	x	x	x					
Tasar	0.3								x	x	x	x	x
Wild fruits	Not estimated but considered enormous	x	x	x	x	x	x	x	x	x	x	x	x

(IIST 1987; Gupta and Guleria 1982a:133)

As regards fuelwood, which provides 69 per cent of fuel for cooking in rural areas (only 5 per cent comes from commercial fuels, the rest from cowdung and agriculture residues), the importance of collection from public lands can be judged from the fact that only 15 per cent of fuelwood is purchased, 62 per cent is collected from forest and public lands, and the remaining 23 per cent is collected from private lands (see table 2.17). There is much evidence to show that peoples' access to forests for meeting their basic subsistence needs has deteriorated, and that this is fairly widespread. A few examples were given in chapter 3 (sec. 3.3). Some of the processes which have caused this are:

— deforestation
— priority to man-made plantations in place of mixed species
— lack of people's awareness about their rights and privileges
— falling production and payments, and the nationalisation of MFPs
— diversion of MFPs to industries
— exploitation by government agencies and contractors in marketing of MFPs
— lack of programmes to regenerate sources of MFPs
— non-involvement of the people in forest management

We shall discuss these briefly in turn.

DEFORESTATION

Poverty in India is generally considered to be linked with lack of private land, or its low productivity. Changes in collection of free items from forests go largely unnoticed, and are not accounted for in GNP. However, much of the misery of tribals and forest dwellers is due to deforestation which removes the resources on which much of their livelihood has been based (Dasgupta 1988:7). For instance, earlier tribals in Koraput district of Orissa used to depend for eight months of the year on forest products, but now (1988) with depleted forest resources, their survival is threatened. (*Indian Express*, April 3, 1988). Loss of forests has also increased the pace of migration of tribals to the towns where they become low paid wage labourers (DN 1988).

Deforestation has increased the drudgery of rural women who generally collect forest produce, as they have to go further. Two decades ago, when the Orissa forests were lush and abundant, collection of forest products took only 1.7 hours. This had increased to seven hours by 1986 (see table 3.4) due to receding forest line. In semi-arid areas of Sabarkantha women spend up to six hours a day in collecting dead branches of trees (Nagbrahman and Sambrani 1983). A study described the working conditions of women in South Bihar as follows:

> Everyday some 300 women firewood pickers disappear into the forests. They cut timber and greenwood, which is illegal. 68 per cent of them have been hurt either by the axe or by wild animals while collecting wood. They earn around Rs 120 a month, and half of them are always in debt. They have a two-day cycle, walking as much as 12 km to collect fuelwood and then travel by train to the town for sale—along the way others make money off them; the railway man who allows them free on trains, the village headman who takes a cut, and the forest guard who looks the other way when forests are being axed. (Ninan 1981)

The receding tree line means that only adult members can now go to forests to collect. Diminished supplies forces them to cut down on their consumption of MFPs, as they must market a greater proportion of their collection (Fernandes et al. 1988:116, 124).

A study (Agarwal and Narain 1985:189) of 170 households in nine villages of district Ranchi (Bihar) showed that headloading (fuelwood collection by the poor from public lands and carrying it on their heads to the nearest market) had emerged as an important profession in the previous 15 years; and more than a fifth of the households in the surveyed villages reported headloading as their major occupation. Another study (Agarwal 1987:181) estimated that at least three to four million people were involved in this profession, making it India's biggest source of employment in the energy sector. In Rajasthan alone four lakh families are reported (NWDB 1988a:15) to be engaged in extraction of firewood from forests. From the forests of

Madhya Pradesh 6 million tonnes of firewood are taken out every year for sale in towns and cities (exclusive of wood collected for domestic use). It is a low paid and a high risk occupation, as pilfering wood from reserved forests for sale is an offence (collecting wood for self-consumption from protected forests is permitted on paper, but frowned upon by the forest staff in actual practice). The study commented that it was ironic that tribals, who for centuries lived in harmony with forests, were today forced to eke out a living by further destroying their forests.

This brings us to the general question of causes of deforestation. The relative contribution of the two categories of consumers, people and industry, has been a subject of controversy in India, which has blurred its objective analysis. A study done by a voluntary agency (PRIA 1984:35) showed that one-third of rapid deforestation in Himachal Pradesh was due to excessive exploitation by the forest-dwellers, and the rest due to commercial interests. It also observed that forest dwellers' over-exploitation is a recent phenomenon, caused by two factors. First, increasing marginalisation of small land owners has forced them to seek new avenues of income, like head-loading and second, the indiscriminate tree felling by the contractor-official-politician nexus has had a corrupting influence on the forest dwellers, who also wish to "make hay while the sun shines". Another study (Reddy 1987) found that degradation of forests was caused by demand from both wood-based industries and fuelwood-collecting households living close to forests. As these examples indicate, local patterns of deforestation vary and it is never a simple matter of numbers outstripping environment (Westoby 1985).

In any case, the debate on who is responsible can hardly lead to feasible solutions, as demand from both sectors, household and commercial, is continually increasing. Controls proposed by foresters to curb headloading or the number of livestock are hardly practical in the Indian political environment. The remedy lies in enhancing supplies through reforestation rather than in demand management.

MAN-MADE PLANTATIONS

Scientific forestry in India has meant raising trees in order to get sustained yield of timber for markets in perpetuity. Right from the First Plan in 1952, emphasis was laid on the conversion of "low" value mixed forests into "high" value plantations of commercial species like teak, eucalyptus and bamboo. Separate corporations have been set up with specific targets to convert mixed forests to man-made plantations. An estimated one million ha of forest has thus been cleared for growing industrial raw material in the last decade (Dogra 1987), depriving millions of poor of the livelihood goods that they used to get from mixed forests.

RIGHTS AND PRIVILEGES

The colonial forest policy provided that declaration of an area as forest should not abridge or affect any existing rights or practices of individuals and communities. These rights, of collecting firewood, timber and other products, are fairly extensive, well documented in Forest Settlement Reports and have not been curtailed by the successive State governments. Yet, in actual practice the poor may not be able to derive much benefit for three reasons.

First, government has created new rights of industrialists through long-term agreements to supply forest products at a low price. An ex-Forest Secretary of Madhya Pradesh writes, "This is clearly discriminatory. The rights of a huge section of society cannot be wiped out in order to benefit a few industrialists. For instance, the Orient Paper Mills was promised a lakh tonne of bamboo per year from four districts of the State. This eliminated all bamboo from Rewa, Panna, Satna and Shahdol. When such a situation arises the F.D. tells the villagers to fend for themselves because there is nothing in the forests for them" (NCHSE 1987:iv). One wonders whether such unilateral abrogation of people's rights is not illegal.

Second, forests "burdened" with people's rights are generally more degraded, and have little to offer. Third, people are far from fully informed about what they can legally collect from forests, and what is prohibited. A government evaluation of tribal districts (GOI 1987a) revealed that out of 767 tribals interviewed only 145 said that they had the right to the collection of timber from forests for making agriculture implements, 222 could send their cattle for grazing, 143 said that they had no rights in forests and the rest did not know the precise position for sure in this regard. There has hardly been any attempt by the F.D. to publicise peoples rights: partly due to the fear that it would aggravate degradation, and partly due to the administrative culture of the F.D. of keeping the people in dark. It suits traders and petty officials if tribals are not aware that they were entitled to collect MFPs. Dapubai, a tribal woman in Udaipur got only Rs 7 for 10 kg of gum, which took her 10–12 days to collect (Bhatt 1988:v), although its market price was Rs 250. When asked to comment on the low price, she said, "How can I demand a higher price? The trader's man threatens me to report to the Forest authorities for entering forest area. Then we will get nothing."

The ability of tribal people to enjoy their rights in forests is insecure when they are so uncertain what they are. But informing them is not considered politically desirable, whereas keeping the poor ignorant of their rights and leaving them to the mercy of the low-paid forest staff is perceived as politically neutral. Such is the irony of the Indian political system!

7.2 Minor Forest Produce

As already shown in table 2.15 a vast potential exists for doubling employment opportunities through collection of MFPs from 2 million personyears to 4.5 million personyears. But in reality, although government revenues from MFPs have increased substantially in the past two decades, total employment and incomes have at best remained stagnant, and have quite often fallen; the quantities collected and the payments to collectors have rarely risen and often fallen. Thus not only has the potential of helping the poor through MFPs remained largely untapped, but their subsistence and incomes have often deteriorated.

FALLING PRODUCTION AND NATIONALISATION

The nationalisation of these MFP commodities, done in different States in various years from 1960s to the end of 1970s, presumably with the intention of helping the poor, has affected their interests adversely.

Tendu leaves, as one of the most important MFPs, are a case in point. In Madhya Pradesh the production of tendu leaves fell from 5.10 million bags in 1981-82 to 3.9 million bags in 1985-86 (GOMP 1987:33). In Orissa, and despite nationalisation, production of tendu leaves over a longer period has remained stagnant, as may be seen from table 7.2.

Table 7.2: Average annual production of tendu leaves in Orissa

Average during the period	Production (M.T.s)
1967-68 to 1972-73	36000
1973-74 to 1978-79	37700
1979-80 to 1984-85	35200

(Gupta and Guleria 1982b:82 and GOO 1988:8)

After nationalisation the collection of sal seeds fell in India from 2 lakh tonnes in 1979 to only 60,000 tonnes in 1987 (GOI 1988c). Production of lac, another nationalised item, had gone down from an average of 32,000 tonnes per year during 1961-70 to 16,000 tonnes during 1981-86 (GOI 1988c).

Nationalisation reduces the number of legal buyers, chokes the free flow of goods, and delays payment to the gatherers, as government agencies find it difficult to make prompt payment. This results in contractors entering from the back door, but they must now operate with higher margins required to cover uncertain and delayed payments by government agencies, as well as to make the police and other authorities ignore their illegal activities. This all reduces tribals' collection and incomes.

From the point of view of the poor, it is not just volume but remuneration that matters. After meeting all expenses and profits, tribals should be paid Rs 1.31 a kg for collection of Sal seeds in Madhya Pradesh, but the government pays them only 55 paise a kg (GOI 1988c:55). In the case of tendu leaves in Orissa, during the twelve years 1967-79, increases in the unit price led to a twelvefold increase of gross revenue per tonne (5.5 times at constant prices), from Rs 297 to Rs 3,514 (Gupta and Guleria 1982b); but over the second half of the period, from 1973-79, workers' wages per quintal collected remained stagnant at current prices at Rs 35-36 (ibid: 84), which was a drop in real terms of 50 per cent.

Nor was remuneration anywhere near equivalent to the minimum statutory wage: during 1979–80 the average daily wage obtained by workers for eight hours of work in Orissa came to Rs 1.61, whereas minimum statutory wages were Rs 4 (ibid: pp. 85–86). It increased to Rs 5.25 in 1984, (Fernandes et al. 1988:141) but was still only a little over half of the minimum wage.

Before nationalisation, the tribals could sell the produce of their own trees to anybody, but under the new system produce from trees on private land has to be sold to the Forest Department only. In almost all cases the Forest Department has appointed agents formally or informally (GOI 1987b). This has put the tribals at the mercy of two different sets of people, the contractor as well as the government department, and whatever payment that tribals get has to be routed through both of them. A Government Commission was told (Bhatt, 1988:xxv) by the tribal women in Madhya Pradesh that when they walked a long distance to the office of the Forest Corporation to sell their produce, they often found it closed, or were told to come the next day. This forced the tribals to sell to the traders at only 20 per cent of the government price. Private trade in Sal seeds is illegal in Madhya Pradesh, but shopkeepers manage to exchange it with tribals for daily necessities at a low price. They then sell it to government bodies, thus defeating the very purpose of nationalisation (GOI 1988c). This results in delay, and makes tribals indifferent to trees on their own private land. This is evident from the following conversation (Dogra 1987:2).

INTERVIEW WITH SUNDERLAL GOND, KESLA, MP

Q. Sunderlalji, can you tell us whether the nationalisation of the tendu leaf trade has benefited the adivasis in any way?

A. The loss and gain in short is that the money which we used to get from the output of the fields before nationalisation, we don't get any more. That is to say the contractor who used to buy the leaf of our plants used to pay us. Now he does not give us any money.

Q. Why don't you get money now?

A. I don't know what orders have been issued by the government, but we don't get the money. You see in our own fields we have some trees. Some of these have been planted by us. Earlier, in the *malguzari* system we could sell the produce of these trees to anybody and it used to be our income. Now, under the new system, all trees, whether they are on forest land, or on our fields, are under the control of the Forest Department—I may still be the owner of the trees, but I cannot sell their produce. I cannot collect any leaf, branch or fruits. These will be sold by the Forest Department.

Q. Can you collect minor forest produce like—*mahua*, Achar, firewood etc. from forest for your own use and/or sale?

A. Yes, we can still do and we have to do otherwise we cannot survive. But a lot of new restrictions have been imposed on collection. In the *mahua* season no Adivasi can collect and sell more than 25 kg of *mahua* at a time. Now this is creating a lot of difficulty for us. The season is very short. One has to collect as much as one can get. If you do not take it somebody else will take it. If no one takes it then it will go waste. It is our one major source of income. Now the market is far off. It is not possible for us to go to the market everyday to sell only 25 kg. To go to the market means a whole day is gone. This is hurting us a lot as our income has gone down. Again they have imposed restrictions on storage of dried *mahua* in our houses. No family is allowed to store more than two quintals. It is very little for our domestic consumption. It is one of our major sources of food in the rainy season, as well as a source of cash. Now we are being denied this source of survival.

DIVERSION OF MFP TO INDUSTRIES

Some MFP items, like sal seeds, have become important for industrialists. This reduces the consumption of MFP as a staple food and medicine for the tribals, especially when the total supply from forests has declined because of deforestation (Fernandes et al. 1988: 105). As their consumption declines they are forced to borrow more and at a high rate of interest from moneylenders for buying grain. Then even if they would like to consume minor forest produce they are not able to do so as pressure from moneylenders forces them to sell.

Sometimes industries, in order to maximise the collection of MFPs, use methods which are destructive to these plants. An obvious example is extraction of resin from pine trees. In tendu tree areas, contractors slash all undergrowth to promote a better growth of tendu leaves. In the process, many fruits, roots and medicinal plants get destroyed. Besides, it causes soil erosion (Dasgupta 1986). Where industries hold leases of forest land for extraction of bamboo they utilise even the better quality bamboo for pulp, although according to rules only inferior quality bamboo should be used as pulp, and the better quality should be sold to artisans. Furer-Haimendorf (1985) describes how a particular paper mill exploited bamboo in a tribal region by bringing in hundreds of labourers from different States and used methods of extraction which endangered future regeneration.

EXPLOITATION IN MARKETING

Products collected by tribals and others from forest lands are sold to businessmen or government corporations. The terms of the transactions are often severely to the disadvantage of the sellers. In Sarguja (M.P.) tribals get only 50 paise for every kg of *mahua* that they sell, but to buy the same *mahua* flowers during the lean season they have to pay Rs 3 per kg (Fernandes et al. 1985:105). In Madhya Pradesh and Orissa the price which tribals get for tamarind is as low as Rs 1.40 to 1.75 per kg whereas it sells for Rs 9–11 per kg in the Bombay market. Sometime the traders follow a barter system by offering 1 kg of sweet potato costing less than a rupee for 1 kg of tamarind (GOI 1988c:40).

Nor do government interventions appear to have been generally successful. This has been admitted in a number of government reports (GOI 1981b:42; GOI 1982; GOI 1987b), and has been well documented in six volumes of evaluation studies undertaken for the Department of Tribal Development, Government of India (GOI 1988c). In 50 out of 68 villages of Orissa it was found (Fernandes et al. 1988:140) that government agencies had not managed to eliminate middlemen. On the other hand, the same middlemen who till recently exploited the tribals as moneylenders and merchants continue their work in the garb of agents of government bodies.

The result is that the price tribals get for their produce is very low, when compared with its price in the neighbouring markets. As table 7.3 indicates, it

Table 7.3: Pricing pattern of some important forest produce in 1983–84 (in Rs)

A	B	C	D	E	F
Produce	Sold to	Unit	Price to producer/ collector	Price in nearest town/outlet	D as % of E
Firewood	Businessmen	Bundle	3.5	6.00-9.00	39 to 58
Bamboo					
Industrial	Forest Dept	Tonne	130	380-500	26 to 34
Commercial	Forest Dept	1,000	1,300	3,070-3,780	34 to 42
Leaves					
Sal	TDCC	Quintal	40	75	53
Kendu	OFC	Quintal	70	780	9
Sal Plates	Businessmen	Bundle	0.5	3	17
Fruits					
Mango	Businessmen	Kg	0.50-1	3-5	10 to 33
Kendu	Businessmen	Kg	0.50-0.75	1-1.50	33 to 50
Jackfruit	Businessmen	One	0.50-2	3-5	10 to 60
Tamarind					
(Deseeded)	Businessmen/ TDCC	Quintal	150-200	350-500	30 to 55
Seeds					
Mahua	Businessmen/ TDCC	Quintal	90	250	46
Sal	TDCC/OFC	Quintal	90	1,200-1,500	6 to 7.5
Others					
Lac	Businessmen	Quintal	70	1,400	5

(Fernandes et al. 1988:140)

Note:

TDCC = Tribal Development Cooperative Corporation of Orissa Ltd.

OFC = Orissa Forest Corporation

GCC = Girijan (means tribal) Corporation

    (All are government organisations)

is rare for them to receive even half the subsequent sale value, and for some of the major items—kendu (called tendu in other States) leaves, Sal seeds, and lac—which have great significance for the poor in terms of volume and opportunity, the proportion is astonishingly low, in most cases less than 10 per cent. It may be pointed out that sometimes the price quoted in column E includes several overheads like State royalty (see table 3.5 for the example of Sal seeds), transport and handling, and therefore is not always comparable. Still it illustrates the fact of exploitation at the hands of procuring organisations.

A workshop on marketing of MFP held in May 1979 at Hyderabad recommended that there should be competitive procurement and marketing by public, cooperative and private agencies. This would generate healthy competition. The reverse seems to be happening. Government agencies like to deal only in commodities where they have a monopoly and profit margins are assured. Ten years back, the number of items handled by GCC (AP) and TDCC (Orissa) was more than twenty. Now it has come down to the two or three most profitable ones (GOI 1988c). Where government alone does marketing it is inefficient; and where it is left to private trade, it is exploitative.

LACK OF PROGRAMMES FOR MFP REGENERATION

Regeneration of MFP has attracted only a token effort so far. There has been little or no place for MFP in social forestry schemes. The Seventh Plan target for MFP planting is only 85,000 ha, as against a total afforestation target of 9 m ha for the five-year period. In Orissa, where dependence of the tribals on MFPs is quite high, only 4 per cent of the trees planted during 1986–87 were MFP species (GOO 1988). Large-scale propagation techniques for important MFP like tendu and *mahua* are still to be developed. Many MFP require a period of 18 months to two years at the seedling stage, as opposed to three to four months for eucalyptus and *Acacia nilotica,* which are the main social forestry species. This discourages the social forestry staff burdened with targets to achieve, from promoting MFP species.

Government of India and the State governments spend millions of rupees in the name of tribal upliftment. However, tribal policy and forest policy, despite the rhetoric, have never been integrated so far. They run on parallel tracks. Whereas the policy in Tribal Development is to give new skills and assets to the tribals, forest policy tends to reduce the access to and value of the existing assets for the tribals. One lesser known reason for this isolation and contradiction is that development and planning in India are associated with spending of money. As in the case of forests, changes in policy or nature of species or laws, are not seen as an integral part of the development process because these have no direct financial implications. The Indian planner unfortunately has still to understand the difference between planning and budgeting.

7.3 Forest Management and the People

In much of the 95 per cent of forests in India which are owned by the government, the Forest Department's control and domain are highly fragmented. Given the ease of access to forests it has been impossible, in practical terms, for the Forest Department to enforce its property rights. Forest lands too, like revenue lands, have been a victim of the "tragedy of the commons" phenomenon where community rights and management have not existed or have broken down. Therefore, any effort towards reforestation can yield results only if it involves local people in planting and protecting trees. Sharing of management or usufruct or both with the people, if properly implemented, could have wide-ranging implication on forest regeneration and welfare of the poor. Some experiences will be discussed.

SOCIAL SECURITY SCHEMES

Even if forest lands are not leased to poor individuals, there is a good potential for helping the poor by enabling them to raise trees on forest lands and then giving them a share in the intermediate products and final produce. Thus F.D. retains control, but people too develop an interest in protection.

In Maharashtra, the poor were engaged in afforestation of 2 to 4 hectares of barren forest lands. The poor family was provided material worth Rs 200 per beneficiary to construct a hut on the land in question. For their labour contribution they were paid Rs 150 per month for the first five years. They were also entitled to fruits from the trees planted by them. From the sale of the final product, half of the net realisation would go to the family.

Several States like Gujarat, Rajasthan, Madhya Pradesh and Karnataka have social security schemes similar to the Maharashtra scheme. Experiences may differ, but the two sets of evidence available indicate a lack of success.

One of the authors, Saxena visited in 1988 a number of sites in Andhra Pradesh to find the reasons. First, nowhere had any agreement been executed, or any letter given to the poor establishing their claims to usufruct. We were told that the agreement deed was pending with the Law Department. However, informally many officers feared that signing a written agreement may be against the spirit of the Forest Conservation Act. Second, there was no continuity in wage employment. Although the scheme started in 1984, very few of the workers were at the site from the beginning. Third, each year the workers were shifted to a new site. They did not work on a sequence of contiguous plots as was envisaged in the scheme. Fourth, discrepancies existed from district to district on what was told to the beneficiaries, and the degree of effort made to accommodate local needs. Some DFOs permitted cultivation of legumes as an inter-crop but some did not, although the State government scheme specifically permitted this. Fifth, species were selected such as eucalyptus and *Acacia auriculiformis,* which did not produce any intermediate goods of substantial benefit to the poor. On the other hand, people were so poor that women were forced to use leaves of these trees for cooking, though the fumes harmed their eyes. This also removed litter from the ground, thus increasing the possibility of soil erosion. Their sense of identification with the planted trees would have been stronger had socially more useful trees been planted. The result of all this was that the beneficiaries saw themselves as wage employees working for less than minimum wages. The part of the deal concerning share in the final produce meant little to them.

The other evidence comes from a study (Hiralal 1986) of the Maharashtra scheme in a village. The following facts came to light:

i) All chosen beneficiaries, except one, were found to be working on the private fields of the Forest Guard.

ii) The beneficiaries considered themselves to be temporary paid employees of the Forest Department. They were hoping to become permanent in due course. They had no knowledge of the scheme of sharing the final income or of their right over intermediate products.

iii) More than 80 per cent of the trees planted were of Teak, a commercial species, which would not yield any benefits in the short run.

iv) Twenty-four workers had applied to the Divisional Forest Officer for getting the benefits of this scheme but almost a year had passed with no satisfactory reply, despite meeting the concerned authorities several times. At the same time, the Forest Department recommended to the government that the scheme should be discontinued as people were not taking an interest in it.

That social security forestry has provided wage employment is evident; but the other planned elements appear problematical.

LESSONS OF SUCCESS

On the other hand where benefits are unambiguous, and species are what people want themselves, they have on their own taken initiative to look after forests, or to cooperate with the Forest Department. Three instances will be discussed below.

i) *Sukhomajri*

The success of the Sukhomajri project in Haryana in achieving peoples cooperation is well known, but merits being recalled. No brief account can do justice to the history of the project, for which the reader is referred to other sources (Seckler and Joshi 1980; SPWD 1986; Chowdhry 1986; Mishra and Sarin 1987b; Chopra et al. 1988; and IEG 1988). Due to over grazing and consequent soil erosion in the catchment area, the lake Sukhna in Chandigarh was silting up. To control this, a number of earthen dams were built, from which each household (*chula*) was assured an equal amount of water, irrespective of whether it owned land or not. In their own self-interest the village people sold their goats, and kept their grazing animals away from forest lands which provided the catchment for the dams. The area sprang back to life, and is now full of grasses, shrubs and trees.

Several critics argued that what was possible in Sukhomajri was not easily replicable, as unlike other villages Sukhomajri was a homogeneous village, being practically a one-caste village of Gujjars (only two out of 59 families are Jats). Also land distribution was not too unequal and this made it an atypical, non-conflict situation. To explore the viability of the model the project was extended to several neighbouring villages. Here we describe what happened in the village Nada, which consisted of four hamlets, including a Harijan hamlet of 17 families out of which five were landless.

Three dams were constructed in this village, out of which one was exclusively for Harijans. Whereas the other two provided only supplemental irrigation to the fields of caste Hindus, the Harijan dam provided enough irrigation for four crops in a year. This led to a repeated demand from the hamlets of caste Hindus to amalgamate the water of all dams. This was rightly rejected by the project's advisors.

But since only 12 of the Harijan families owned in all less than 2 ha of cultivated land, and five families were landless, the promise of irrigation could not serve as a sufficient incentive to stop them grazing their animals in the hills. Protecting the hills was therefore linked with production of bhabbar grass, to be utilised in rope making. Earlier, due to overgazing and lack of consensus over protection, the annual yield of natural grass from barren hills was barely 40 kg per ha. This could be increased to 7,000 kg of bhabbar grass per ha with adequate protection. The market value of air-dry bhabbar grass was 60 paise/kg but if processed into rope, it sold for Rs 2-3 per kg. Thus one ha of denuded hilly land brought under bhabbar could then generate an income of Rs 20,000 in a year! But the poor would invest their labour in protection only if their benefits were secure.

The land belonged to the Forest Department, which was not prepared to lease it to the community. However, the department agreed to designate the plantation a research project, and contract the village society to harvest grasses. Thus Harijans got usufructuary rights on forest lands on a sharing basis. Despite problems, the yield of bhabbar in 1986 was almost 8 tonnes to a hectare!

Although the Harijans' society is continuing to harvest bhabbar, natural grass, firewood, and fodder and poles from subabul trees, in lieu of grazing and protection as was agreed, yet there has been no written long-term agreement so far (1988). Absence of legal and secure rights could have wiped out the achievements in no time, if Sukhomajri and Nada had not received tremendous publicity, both national and international. The plaques in the local school plantation naming those who planted trees reads like a Who's Who of India's rural development. This helped the villages to resolve conflicts within the community and with the Forest Department.

Despite the fact that the Haryana F.D. has tried to duplicate this model in about 50 villages in a less exacting form, it must be admitted that committed leadership which guided Sukhomajri is a resource which is difficult to reproduce in the government system. On the other hand several NGOs like BCT (Andhra Pradesh). Anthyodhya Sangh (Tamil Nadu), Gram Gaurav

Pratisthan (Maharashtra), Gram Vikas (Orissa), and Ubeshwar Vikas Mandal (Rajasthan) have achieved excellent results in wasteland development (Vohra 1986) because of strong and committed leadership. This often makes such projects "beautiful but non-replicable". This is not to denigrate outstanding achievement, at least it helps in evolving new models, which then can be tried in other places. But even without the help of outside committed leaders it is possible to achieve harmonious collective action, as the next two examples of community protection show.

ii) *Village committees in Orissa* (ORG 1985)

The rehabilitation and reforestation of degraded forests is an important component of the social forestry project in Orissa, although so far it has remained a departmental activity with little peoples' participation (SIDA 1987: 70). However, there are villages, where people had been actively involved in protecting forests even before the project started. In some cases initiative for doing so was taken by forest officers; in others it was local.

In village Jugal, district Mayurbanj, 3,000 ha of forest land has been protected for the last 25 years. The main motivation and leadership was provided by a Forest Ranger and by a respected leader of the village. Fairly elaborate arrangements were worked out by a committee regarding protection and harvesting as three different villages were involved in joint protection.

In village Badajiuli, district Keonjhar, a village committee had been functioning since 1971, although its meetings are not held regularly. The people seem confident that no systematic working is required. The reason was that they have their cultivable lands around the forest area. Hence any sound of chopping of trees can be clearly heard by the people working in the field. This makes detection of pilferage easy.

A protection committee consisting of members from several villages has been functioning well in Kesarpur village of the same district. The situation had become quite acute in the late sixties as afforestation led to soil erosion and gully formation. As the hill became barren a perennial stream became dry. A heavy landslide in a neighbouring village frightened the villagers and made them think that immediate steps had to be taken to check erosion. In 1974, they started protecting trees from biotic intervention. In 1978, the F.D. agreed to introduce plantation on the hills provided people sold their goats. This was also agreed and a couple of households who initially did not do so were fined by the community and forced to follow suit. Today 13 villages around Kesarpur having 2,000 families jointly protect about 1000 acres of forest. In addition plantation has been undertaken over an area of 120 acres. The hill now looks green with a variety of forest species and good undergrowth. Gully formation has been checked and the stream has again started flowing.

In the villages where the scheme had been successful one noticed the existence of a strong local leadership. Even when there were factions within such villages, they did not seem to influence their faith in the leadership.

There was a good deal of convergence of opinion, evidence of community involvement, and enthusiasm on the part of the people to project a good image of themselves, which indicated strong social cohesion. Villagers took great pride in their efforts and liked to show their achievements to outsiders. Group solidarity bolstered the self-esteem of the villagers, both as individuals and as a community.

However there is as yet no official policy giving people harvesting rights or share in produce from territories protected by them. This has apparently affected involvement of the people. In the absence of clear rights, their initial enthusiasm may decline.

iii) *Arabari, West Bengal* (GOWB 1988a)

Vast areas of forests of the southern lateritic tracts of West Bengal have been virtually unproductive on account of commercial exploitation, unregulated fuelwood collection by poverty-stricken people and grazing by village cattle. In the year 1972, Divisional Forest Officer, Midnapore, West Bengal, took over a block of 1,272 ha of denuded forest for rehabilitation. Until then, the stumps left in the area had thrown up vegetative shoots every year which local poor people used to cut down and sell in the nearby market for subsistence. The value of the forest in terms of commercial timber in 1972 was nil.

The rehabilitation scheme focussed on generating sustained productive employment in the forest area, so that people did not have to sell fuelwood in the market. The project also grew fuelwood so that people could get it on a token fee, at cost price and arranged cattle grazing on a rotational basis. The project permitted the people to raise paddy on forest lands, which was sold to the same people at cost price. Thus all immediate requirements of the people were taken care of. It was also promised that people would get 25 per cent of the final produce if the scheme succeeded. In the period 1972-1985, people's cooperation was nearly complete. Productive employment was created by maintenance of shoots that grew on stumps over 700 ha, and plantation of *Acacia auriculiformis*, eucalyptus hybrid, cashew nut, sabai grass and sisal over about 560 ha. People received their fuelwood and plough pieces at cost price and rotational grazing areas for their cattle. The government of West Bengal approved in March, 1987, the distribution of 25 per cent of the usufruct to 618 beneficiary families in view of their exceptional cooperation in the maintenance and protection of these forests.

An erstwhile totally degraded government forest has now become a luxuriant forest, better than any found in the area. The commercial value of the standing crop, which was nil in 1972, has been calculated at Rs 90 million in 1988. The beneficiary share thus stands at around Rs 22 million, out of which each family is likely to earn about Rs 4,195 annually at present value in perpetuity. Although payment has still not been made (till September, 1988 because of a court case) to the families, the success of the Arabari experiment has led elsewhere in West Bengal to the formation of 659 voluntary village committees, each promising to look after the forests on similar terms. By October 1988 it was estimated that over 68,000 ha of forest land was being protected by village groups (Poffenberger 1988). The Government of West Bengal has (Sept., 1988) formulated an ambitious scheme costing Rs 330 million based on the Arabari philosophy for rehabilitation of 2.5 lakh ha of degraded forests. The thrust of the project is on micro planning at the grassroot level and intensive communication between the forest personnel and village committees. Income during the period of coppice regrowth of Sal will be generated through development of horticulture, tasar and lac cultivation, kendu leaf pruning/collection, and soil and water conservation works which will recharge groundwater for minor irrigation through wells.

Even in these three success stories we find that rights which should accrue to the people — to forest lands in Nada, harvesting rights in Orissa villages, and share of produce in Arabari—were delayed, or not well defined, or agreement was not executed with the people, or not well publicised. Even in Arabari, the government order of giving a share of 25 per cent was issued only 15 years after the verbal promise, and 18 months passed from the date of the order without payment being made to the families. No wonder such success stories of collective endeavour on forest land are so few.

7.4 Revenue Lands

Revenue lands comprise two categories: government wastes which are owned by the government but used by the community; and grazing lands which are vested in village bodies. There is little *de facto* distinction between the two categories, as both are used for grazing, and are generally considered degraded. These are also referred to as common or community lands. As we saw in chapter 2, the total area available for vegetation is around 12 m ha. With some 6 lakh villages in the country, the average is about 20 ha per village, but there is much regional variation as well as variation between neighbouring villages. In villages of intensive cultivation, common lands are of marginal importance, but in hilly and unirrigated villages common lands still offer livelihood possibilities for the poor. These "CPR-limited" and "CPR-dependent" villages (Blaikie, Harriss and Pain 1986: 484) correspond roughly to the A and B category of villages defined in sec. 2.1.

Concerning these lands, we will examine two key issues: first, to what extent have communities been managing common lands as opposed to only using them as an open access resource; second, to what extent has afforestation of common lands by the Forest Department been a viable programme and of help to the poor.

The philosophy of afforestation of common lands is that after the initial investment by the government, the trees would be handed over to the village communities for protection and management. The capabilities of village communities, whether represented by the Panchayat (consisting of several villages) or by the village hamlet consisting of 50-200 families only, to manage the land and tree resource then determines the long-term physical viability of the programme, as well as the social effectiveness in flows of benefits to the poorer.

As often in rural development, there are polarised views. One social science view of an Indian village is "an atomised mass, composed of individuals who are not in any organised fold except the family and extended kin-groups which form the sub-caste" (Gaikwad 1981: 331). According to this view, rigid stratification of village society inhibits development of institutions representing a common will. Grossly unequal land tenure and access to markets ensure that only a powerful minority gains in the name of the community (Eckholm 1979).

Bandyopadhyay (1983), however, disputes that social and economic inequalities have hindered the possibility of community ownership, participation and control in India. Management of village commons has been a historical reality for two reasons. First, whereas private resources in India were governed by individualistic and class dominated norms, there have been communally shared norms when it comes to community resources. Second, the self-sufficient nature of the traditional village economy guided the exploitation of common resources through a system of self-control. He therefore concludes that there are no structural barriers to achieving community participation in social forestry projects.

It is difficult to settle this controversy. We can at best cite a few cases and take note of trends.

TRAGEDY OF THE COMMONS?

On the negative side, several studies (e. g., Gadgil 1987) have shown a lack of control and management of commons by communities. Jodha's (1986, 1987) study of 82 villages in dry regions of the country revealed that at that time not a single village was using control measures such as grazing taxes or penalities for violation of norms on the use of common lands. Only eight out of 82 resorted to rotational grazing or provided for a watchman to protect them from unauthorised use. And only 12 undertook measures such as fencing or trenching towards the upkeep of common lands.

Another study (Gupta 1985: 313), of a World Bank assisted project of developing pastoral lands in Western Rajasthan, showed that wherever management of projects had been handed over to the people, fences had broken down and resources were getting degraded. Or again, in many semi-arid tracts, for example in Junagadh district in Gujarat, it is common for people to appropriate top soil from the common grazing land and cart it to their own farms, sometimes continuing even until land is reduced to rocks (Shah 1987).

A field study (Saxena 1988) of four villages in the States of Uttar Pradesh, Himachal Pradesh, Madhya Pradesh and Tamil Nadu respectively observed that village organisations are weak, are not trusted, have no experience of forestry programmes, and are dominated by the rich. They are also not keen to take over plantations unless funds for protection are provided, and their rights are settled. People seemed to have more faith in the coercive authority of the State than in their own participative institutions. They wanted opportunities for family-based enterprises, and seemed indifferent to the fate of non-private lands. It also appeared that these villages had no history of providing management to the commons, since in the past this had been the responsibility of either the landlord or government.

SUCCESS OF COMMUNITY ACTION

On the positive side, there are regions in India where communities have shown a capacity for managing their land resources. For instance, studies of forest panchayats of the Uttar Pradesh hills (Saxena 1987b; Ballabh and Singh 1988), observed that panchayat lands were better protected than revenue or forest lands, which are under the control of the government. The 70 Cooperative Forest Societies founded in the forties in the hilly Kangra area of Himachal Pradesh functioned well (USAID 1988), but these were suspended in the seventies and their areas transferred to the Forest Department.

Why does collective action succeed in some cases and not in others? Some tentative hypotheses may be arrived at by comparing the small-sized Uttar Pradesh hill villages (several tribal villages have similar characteristics) with the larger villages found in peninsular India and studied by Jodha.

First, as a panchayat in the plains controls several villages, common land belonging to one village may be under the control of a Sarpanch who is not from the same village. This breeds distrust. The forest panchayat in the hills is typically an actual user association, managing its own small area with clearly defined boundaries. There is evidence from other Third World countries too (Odell 1982) that the most effective local institutions develop in those small communities where most people know each other.

Second, the topography of the upland villages makes their common lands visible from most of the dwellings, so that any unauthorised felling cannot escape notice. In contrast, the area of a flat village in Central-South India may well be spread over 5-10 km in one direction, which makes it easy for "free riders" to escape undetected.

Third, hill and upland villages usually have better land resources. This attracts better management from the people, as its protection is more vital for their survival. On the other hand, once degradation sets in, people become indifferent to protection. In district Kheda in Gujarat, grazing lands are so degraded that the dependence of an average milk producer on the grazing lands—and hence his or her stake in their preservation is low (Shah 1987c). There are thus two syndromes: a valuable resource well-managed because it is worth managing well; and a degraded resource neglected because it is degraded.

Fourth, remoteness from roads and markets further helps in retaining mutual obligations in the hills, and discourages poaching by outsiders.

Fifth, in the hills, fear of reprisals from village elders deters too frequent abuse of common resources. In contrast, the old system of authority in the plains villages has been undermined without being replaced effectively by a new one, resulting in a hiatus of confidence (Wade 1987).

Sixth, the hill settlements are more homogeneous in caste, with one caste usually dominating both in land and number, whereas villages in the plains tend to be multi-caste, which makes social control more difficult.

Finally, in the hills, all families including the rich are highly dependent on forests for their survival needs of fodder and fuelwood. Elsewhere, the village elite and the poor are typically not so equally dependent on the common lands. In the plains, the rich often have more cattle whereas the poor have more sheep and goats (Gupta 1984). As the productivity of the commons declines, the rich shift to privately grown fodder on their own land, while the poor still use the commons for their sheep and goats. The rich then lose interest in the upkeep of commons, while the poor lack the power and organisation to manage the commons themselves. This may be one reason why in Gujarat, the Indian State best known for community endeavour, only 60 out of 18,000 villages have come forward to start community fodder farms whereas many times more villages have opted for income generating eucalyptus plantation on grazing lands (Shah 1987c).

Table 7.4 describes some of the major contrasts between the two types of villages.

Table 7.4: Upland/tribal villages compared with villages in the plains

Characteristics	Upland/tribal villages	Villages in the plains
Topography	undulating	flat
Population	50-100 families	500-1000 families
Type of wastelands	mainly owned by F.D.	mainly revenue and private
Used by	one village	several villages
Dependence on wastelands	very high	alternatives available
Authority of village elders	still intact	only within caste group
Market and State penetration	weak	fairly strong
Caste homogeneity	one caste dominant	multi-caste
Minimum requirement for regeneration	protection only	funds required because of degradation
Users within a village	all families	mainly the poor

The personal interests of village elites in management of the commons appears a crucial element. Even a market dominated village may develop collective action, if it is in the interest of all, including the powerful people of the village.

An example in the context of fodder is a study of 41 villages in district Kurnool, Andhra Pradesh (Wade 1985, 1988) which found four institutions commonly at work in these villages: an informal village council (distinct from the statutory panchayat); a standing fund for paying wages for protection; a work group of field guards to regulate grazing; and common irrigators to regulate supply and distribution of canal irrigation water. Field guards patrolled the village area and made sure that no animal grazed a standing crop. After a crop was harvested, the stubble was put to common use, being let out to nomads with sheep and goats, who wanted grazing, for which they paid to a village fund about Rs 5,000 in a space of six weeks. Field guards were paid from the sums raised.

A study of fodder farms on common lands in Gujarat (Shah 1987c) found that some panchayat leaders took a great deal of personal interest in setting up and running such farms. They seemed to work for non-economic rewards, such as power, reputation, and social status. Once established, the successful farms were run on business lines, with the interaction between a farmer and the fodder farm similar to that between a buyer and a private seller. An average farmer did not show any interest in running the farm. In fact its success was due more to the initiative of the leader than to community spirit. This makes such enterprises precariously dependent upon quality and integrity of leaders, willing to work for extra-economic rewards.

We can conclude, then, that community control and management can work in three circumstances. First, in villages which share the characteristics of the left half of the table 7.4. Second, where gains from organisation are high, for both, the village elite and the commoners. And third, where a leader is willing to run the show for non-monetary gains. Analysing the success of sugar cooperatives in Maharashtra, Attwood (1988:69-87) reached similar conclusions: cooperatives succeed not because there are no classes in the village society, but because an alliance between the rich and poor farmers for the successful running of the cooperative sugar factory is in the economic interest of both the classes.

GOVERNMENT LAND TENURIAL POLICY

Structural barriers to community action would have been less insurmountable, had government policy favoured communal tenure and village organisations. Unfortunately, both the land distribution policy of the 1970s and the community forestry of the 1980s seem to have been influenced by Hardin's ideas (1968, 1971) that there are only two sustainable policies: either the commons should be privatised, or they should be brought under the control of a coercive authority.

Policies can be understood against a historical perspective. A study (Singh 1986) has observed that in the 19th century up to two-thirds of the land in India was under community hegemony. Privatisation and government appropriation have been the two main processes which have reduced this proportion. Although there was much regional and local variation, even at independence large areas remained under community control, especially in tribal areas. However, since independence, survey and settlement operations have diminished these areas. Land settlements carried out in the last 40 years have recognised communal tenure only in the Northeast Indian States. In parts of Bihar there is a dispute between the Revenue and the Forest Departments regarding the exact status of tribal forests, called Khuntkatti forests; the former regards it as communal land owned by the Munda tribe whereas the latter considers it now to be forest property. In other tribal areas communal ownership, control and management may exist in practice but it has not been recognised by the formal legal system (Burman 1987: 2). There is no provision under the Indian Forest Act for recognition of community rights. The Act recognises rights of individuals alone. This undermines community competence and control. Or again, in Andhra Pradesh despite orders from the Panchayat Raj department, the transfer of non-forest government land to the Panchayats has not taken place. In Orissa rights of the beneficiaries and formulations of joint management plans under the new Village Forest Rules, 1985, have been made entirely a prerogative of the Forest Department. The village forest committee there is not, as might be supposed, a vehicle of people's initiative for managing their community resources, drawing upon funds from the government in support. Instead, it is an instrument of the government to induce the local population to cooperate in the implementation of a programme of the Forest Department.

Transition in land rights from communal to private ownership has affected women adversely. So long as land was commonly owned, women had a voice in its management, but with private owning of land, their control has got diluted. The result is that both extension programmes and credit services are geared to men, which helps them to get into the "cash" sector leaving women behind in the subsistence sector.

7.5 Community Forestry

The community woodlot programme, which aims at raising trees on village lands has not been as successful in sheer quantitative terms as the farm forestry component. There have been shortfalls in achievement of targets, as in West Bengal (GOWB 1988b), Orissa (SIDA 1987), Madhya Pradesh (USAID 1985b) and Uttar Pradesh (GOUP 1984). Evaluation reports of community afforestation schemes in India, such as those of Tamil Nadu (SIDA 1988), Orissa (SIDA 1987), Uttar Pradesh, Rajasthan, Gujarat and Himachal Pradesh (USAID 1988), and Andhra Pradesh (CIDA 1988), have in general found little evidence of communal interest or of management capabilities of the panchayats. Benefits to the poor beyond wage employment seem to be in doubt. We referred to the evaluation of Tamil Nadu and Karnataka S.F. projects in chapter 3 (sec. 3.3). Some other findings are discussed below.

The community forestry programme of a few villages in Madhya Pradesh was studied by an independent agency, CENDIT (1985a). It was observed that there was factionalism in the village on caste and political lines and the poor were hardly consulted about social forestry activities. The interests of villages other than the main village of the panchayat were ignored. There was no tradition of democratic decision making. Government officers were mainly interested in fulfilling targets, and often adopted the line of least resistance. The panchayats were not keen to take over plantations. Often community land was handed over to the F.D. to avoid encroachment by the poor, or its allotment to the scheduled castes by the government. The practice of the panchayat auctioning grass from such plantations reduced the availability of fodder for the poor.

The mid-term review of Madhya Pradesh social forestry project (USAID 1985b) commented that the principal aim of social forestry to build up institutional capacity of panchayats had fallen by the wayside because of the existing political economy of the panchayats. It concluded that short-term political motivation of the leaders and cattle pressure would not allow community managed plantations to last very long.

The mid-term review of Andhra Pradesh Social Forestry Project (CIDA 1988:50) stated that, "In most villages visited, the landless and weaker sections are unaware of their intended role as members of the village community, nor are they convinced that the panchayat best represents their interests. It is doubtful whether they could have any say in the final decision about how to use the community's share after the final harvest."

The mid-term review (ODA 1986) for Karnataka in 1986 was more forthright, "The project has failed to achieve the intended priority to the landless, and to develop a policy for the distribution of benefits."

In Maharashtra several village woodlots were to be handed over to the panchayats. The mid-term review for the State in 1985 went into the reasons for their reluctance (USAID 1985a: 22-23) to take over responsibility for management. It attributed this to people's lack of self-help attitudes, sarpanches' worries about theft and encroachment, the time-consuming nature of legal action against encroachers, and lack of income to meet protection costs.

7.6 Reasons for Poor Performance

The generally poor performance of community plantations can be attributed to many factors, but seven stand out.

i) MISDIAGNOSIS

There appears to have been a misdiagnosis that given access to land and funds, communities and the poor would prefer fuelwood plantations to trees for food, fodder, and incomes. Urban fuelwood shortages have been projected onto rural areas. Middle class perceptions have also played their part. This is not to deny the hardships of many of the rural poor in collecting fuelwood. But the poor were not consulted about their priorities. Fuelwood was rarely their most acutely felt need: for one thing, in many parts of India the spontaneous spread since the 1960s of *Prosopis juliflora* has provided a vast new fuelwood resource for the poor. The USAID/World Bank Report (1988: 27) too called for a reappraisal of the original premises, as "fuelwood is a lesser priority for rural households than increased income." Moreover, the poor face many other shortages and have many other concerns besides fuelwood including food, employment and cash. "For rural communities, woodfuel is only one useful product of trees, trees are only one form of woody biomass, and woody biomass is only one aspect of much broader farming or landuse systems. Woodfuel problems must therefore be tackled indirectly." (Leach 1987: 92). It was a mistake to assume that fuelwood shortages faced by the poor could or should be solved in isolation from other aspects of poverty, or that fuelwood would necessarily be their preferred priority benefit from trees.

ii) BUREAUCRATIC IMPOSITIONS

Community plantations in fact, whatever the theory, have usually been bureaucratic impositions on villages. Participation has been limited, at best confined to a few members of a village elite. Forestry staff have tended to perpetuate the myth that plantation management is a complex undertaking beyond the abilities of villagers (USAID 1985a:24) and which they should therefore not manage. Community members, especially the poor, have not accepted these plantations as their own. People's involvement has been limited to the handing over of common lands to the Department and to wage employment (ILO 1987:64-65). They have otherwise remained passive spectators of the raising of trees on their land (NCAER 1988:96).

iii) CONTROL OF FUNDS

Had village organisations been able to control and spend funds right from the beginning of community forestry projects, there would have been better chances of their taking an active part in decision-making and management. The role of the Forest Department would then have been mainly extension and technical support. As it was, in all cases funds have been controlled by the Forest Department, not the village organisation.

iv) SMALL AREAS

Often only small areas of say 2 to 4 ha have been available in villages. The entire area has then been taken up for afforestation in a single year. This has then caused hardship to those whose livestock depended on the commons for grazing. Such a small area is liable neither to satisfy the fuelwood needs of the village, nor to promise sufficient non-monetary returns to village leaders who are expected to devote their time and energy to raising the woodlots. Of the 30 community woodlots in Gujarat, set up between 1974 and 1976, only eight had a plot size greater than 4 ha (USAID 1988).

v) THE POOR AS LOSERS

The poor have often been losers or have not gained where they might have done. The concentration on trees for urban fuel, poles or pulp rather than for fodder, MFP, rural fuel or low value fruit is understandable because unpalatable trees are so much easier to protect; but they do not provide any substitute feed for the grass lost, nor do they improve the gathering of produce by the poor. Most social forestry projects did not list helping the "gatherers" as an objective. Foresters' perception, that unplanned entry into plantations for "gathering" is against scientific forestry, has also played its part in this, limiting the benefits to the poor.

vi) SPECIES SELECTION

Species have been based on convenience of staff rather than needs of people. People have not been asked what trees they prefer, least of all the poor and women. Socially useful species producing fruit, fodder and other MFPs have had little place. Market oriented species like *Acacia nilotica, Acacia auriculi-formis,* and eucalyptus have been preferred (CIDA 1988:52), as they are nonbrowsable, can grow fast, and require little management. Possible use of other species either in overhead mixture or as understorey has not been seriously considered. Spacing has often been reduced to avoid intermediate management operations, to reduce plantation cost, and to cut down on staff supervision time. In Gujarat, the density of plantation per ha on village woodlots was as high as 2,554 (IIPO 1988:xvi). As a consequence, spacing, thinning and pruning which could have produced intermediate yields of grass and tree products for the people have not been made use of (Banerji 1986). Coppicing or clear felling after seven to ten years may produce income to the panchayat or to government but village consumption of tree products is little increased. Technology with which the foresters were familiar for large-scale plantations for markets within forest areas was applied to small-scale village woodlots, where the need was more for fodder and subsistence than for timber. These issues will be further discussed in chapter 9.

vii) RIGHTS AND DISTRIBUTION POLICY

The last and most serious reason for the poor performance of community plantations has been the failure to define, establish and publicise the rights to the trees and the procedures for marketing and allocating benefits (NCAER 1988:104). This could be illustrated by examples from almost anywhere in India where community plantations have been undertaken. A few examples can serve for illustration here.

In West Bengal, an order was issued in 1986 that only 25 per cent of the total produce was to be given to the panchayats, provided they assisted in protection, maintenance and raising of community plantations. This proviso brings uncertainty as "assistance" is likely to be decided by the field level officers in a subjective manner. Further this share of 25 per cent was to be given to the economically backward people to be selected by the panchayat. But it was not clear from the order whether the poor would get it free or at a subsidised price. Similarly the mode of disposal of the balance of 75 per cent by the Department was not clarified. An official evaluation (GOWB 1988b) admitted that till September 1988, nowhere has the 25 per cent share been given to panchayats.

In Karnataka several villagers, when asked by a World Bank team about distribution as late as in 1988 (Brokensha 1988) said, "We know nothing about this". Even forestry officials disagreed with each other about the rules. The shares which would go to the individuals, village, mandal panchayat and the Forest Department were still (1988) to be clearly laid down in Karnataka.

In Uttar Pradesh, 80 per cent of the auction proceeds from community forestry are to go to the village panchayat, but the expenses incurred by the F.D. in raising plantations are first to be deducted. But since the expenses are unknown, it is difficult for the panchayat to know what the benefits of participation will be. Moreover, the costs incurred by the Forest Department will be known only to the Accountant General. The time taken to determine costs may mean that the actual accrual of funds to the panchayat's coffers will be delayed for several years.

Wide variation in the pattern of disposal of grass, an early output of social forestry projects, was seen in the Madhya Pradesh villages (USAID 1985b). In some villages grass was rationed to every household, in others to those only with cattle, in others only to landless and backward classes. In a few cases chowkidars had been beaten and politically powerful villagers had grazed their cattle on the community plantations.

A government evaluation of Orissa S.F. Project (GOO 1987) indicated that 82 per cent of the villages did not know how the produce from village woodlots would be distributed. Most of the people did not expect any share from the final output. They looked upon such woodlots as another category of reserved forests.

The mid-term evaluation report (CIDA 1988:51) of Andhra Pradesh observed, "Final benefit sharing agreements are neither finalised nor formalised, which obviously causes uncertainties in the minds of beneficiaries."

During field visits in Maharashtra, Karnataka and Andhra Pradesh by one of the authors it was found that even where a Government Order existed on distribution, field staff had little knowledge about it. Their interpretation of Government Orders varied from place to place. The villagers considered social forestry trees as government property, and were generally reluctant to get involved in their maintenance. In our judgement, uncertainty about the distribution of benefits and who will gain and how is the most important factor in explaining the poor response of the people in community forestry.

Rights to trees and distribution policy are not official preoccupations in the early stages of tree planting, but are very important for the people. Unless they are clearly defined and credible from the start, the chances are high that benefits will be unfairly distributed later.

Thus, peoples' participation has hardly ever been achieved in Indian village forestry projects initiated by the government (ILO 1988:41-50). Despite the theory and superficial appearances, field investigations and evaluations suggest that community woodlot programmes in which communities raise tree plantations for their own use on community or government lands have not been tried by government at all! Instead, government control has been extended and what has been raised on common lands has been departmental plantations of commercial crops (Gadgil 1985:318).

Community forestry is in the ultimate analysis a programme for community action for the benefit of the community. Precisely because community woodlots are difficult to manage, with the twin dangers of tragedy of the commons if no control is exercised, and of appropriation by a few if protection and survival are good, it is vital that the positive lessons of experience should be learnt. Effective community forestry needs not only funds and the right kind of policies but also political support. Unfortunately there has been little evidence of political commitment to strengthening community control and management. Without such commitment, there is a danger that even schemes which are good on paper will fail.

7.7 Conclusions

To sum up this chapter, there exists a vast potential for helping the poor through forest and village lands. The major lesson of experience is that any attempt to realise that potential must start with the priorities not of officials and other professionals, but of the rural people, and especially the poorer, themselves. To date, this has been very much the exception rather than the rule. This requires that field staff find out and identify with the needs of the people, and that policy makers share that commitment. Again and again in practice, the priorities of the poor are found to be subsistence and income to provide adequate and secure livelihoods. For forest and village lands to help meet these livelihood needs points away from single products mainly for the market, like timber and poles for sale obtained through felling, and more towards a sustainable diversity of products obtained from living trees through the labour-intensive process of gathering. According to local needs and opportunities, these may include fodders, fuelwood, fibres, fruits, mulch and others of the many minor forest products. These conclusions have major policy implications which will be analysed and developed further in chapter 9.

CHAPTER EIGHT

Why Small Farmers Don't Plant Trees

ABSTRACT

In a range of climates from arid to humid, on soils varying from degraded to fertile, and where their rights are secure, small and marginal farmers plant trees to diversify and reduce risk in their livelihood strategies, and to complement other enterprises. Some 5 to 6 m ha of degraded lands, mostly suitable for trees, have been allocated to the poor, but the potential on this and other RPFs' land is still largely unexploited.

Several factors deter RPFs from planting and protecting trees. Insecure land tenure, especially in tribal areas and on allotted degraded land, inhibits long-term investment in trees. Restrictions on harvesting, transit and sale of trees and tree products discourage planting, invite rent-seeking by officials and contractors, and make farmers' benefits uncertain and small. Largely in consequence, most prices paid to farmers and MFP collectors are scandalously low, often less than 20 per cent of the market sale price, and sometimes derisory. Environmentalists and officials often err in urging and implementing restrictions which are self-defeating. RPFs with their small lots and lack of influence are at a disadvantage in market access. Forest Department extension has often been inappropriately standardised and overconcerned with targets. Finally, tree *patta* (allotted) schemes contain many "catches" which mean hassle and disincentives for the poor.

Lessons from NGOs' successes show the importance of staff continuity and commitment, and of secure rights and returns for RPFs. For RPFs to plant and protect trees requires secure land tenure, free choice of species, unrestricted rights of usufruct including felling, unrestricted rights of transit to markets, competitive markets, and good market information. For RPFs to gain their full share of benefits from trees, their rights must be secure, their priorities must come first, and they must be free from restrictions and hassle.

8.1 Farm Forestry and the Poor

Where people have been encouraged to raise trees on their own land and where their title to the trees they raise has been undisputed and clear, tree cultivation by private households has surpassed expectations. This is indicated by the manner in which farm forestry targets in State after State in India have been exceeded, especially in the first phase of the Social Forestry Programme, when all other components like block plantation on community lands have done less well.

The reported growth of the farm forestry programme in the country over the past years is shown in table 8.1.

Table 8.1: Progress of farm forestry in India

1 Year of plantation	2 Total no of trees planted in millions in that year	3 No of trees planted on private lands	4 3 as % of col 2
1981-82	1320	440	33
1982-83	2080	900	43
1983-84	2420	1190	49
1984-85	2640	1280	48
1985-86	3020	1390	46
1986-87	3520	1600	46
1987-88	3420	1750	49
1988-89	4000 (target)	2000 (target)	50

(NWDB 1988c)

It may be noted that by 1987-88 the popularity of farm forestry seemed to have reached a plateau. This was partly because of drought in some States, but largely due to the unpopularity of eucalyptus with farmers in the very States where it had been extremely sought after a few years earlier. For instance, in Haryana only 4 million plants could be sold in 1988, a year of very good rainfall, against a peak distribution of 43 million in 1984 (*Indian Express,* 1.11. 1988). Although the data in table 8.1 indicate that the share of private plantation has been steady at slightly less than half of the total, yet it is believed that bogus reporting in the farm forestry sector has been on the increase to show fulfilment of unrealisable targets. An evaluation report (SIDA 1987:24) of Orissa observed, " . . . the mission encountered some instances where nursery registers were not consistent with farmers' accounts of what they had received, it may be that the recorded data overstated what has actually been distributed. It is notable that a very high proportion of the reported 1984/85 beneficiaries sampled had no trees provided by the project on their farms when surveyed in 1987."

The participation by small and marginal farmers in the farm forestry programme has been low so far. We gave two examples in chapter 3 (sec. 3.3). A few more are illustrated below.

The FAO/SIDA study on Gujarat (FAO 1985) revealed that farmers with more than 5 hectares of land planted on an average roughly twice as many trees as those with under 5 hectares. Even when the small and marginal farmers planted trees the survival percentage was rather low. Many non-participating farmers counted lack of land, shortage of capital and non-availability of water as the main factors responsible for their not planting trees. Obviously, they would be largely poor farmers.

Skutsch (1986) visited a number of villages in Gujarat and found that only in the village of Nanajalundwa had small farmers planted eucalyptus under the influence of one particular Range Officer. On the other hand, in the villages of Khanpur, Jetalpur and Nanisarsen very few participating marginal and small farmers could be found. However, in many places large farmers got classified as small farmers to get benefit of government subsidy.

Another case study (Wilson and Trivedi 1988) of two Talukas of Gujarat showed that less than 5 per cent of plantations were carried out by small and marginal land holders.

The interim review of Andhra Pradesh Social Forestry Project (CIDA 1986) observed that the social objective of the project to assist the weaker sections of society had hardly been approached.

The Orissa evaluation (SIDA 1987:89) observed that in the farm forestry programme, the project did not target the landless (i.e. those with only homestead lands), small and marginal farmers, despite the provision for this in the Appraised Project Document (APD). Nor, it appeared, had there been contact persons, preferably landless/small/marginal farmers(s), to help with this programme as provided for in the APD.

Why have small farmers not benefited from tree planting opportunities on their own lands? Are there structural barriers to their participation, or has it been due to sheer neglect by the programme implementing agencies? This we consider now.

8.2 When Small Farmers Do Plant Trees

Lack of tree planting by resource-poor farmers is generally attributed to their poverty and short-time horizons. It is believed that they have to give absolute priority to their immediate subsistence needs and cannot undertake long-term investment. The gestation periods of trees before they yield income or capital value, in this view, makes them unattractive to poor farm families. As we shall show, however, while this diagnosis has some truth for some of the very poor, it misleads, diverts attention from other crucial factors, and often leads to policies which are self-defeating.

In the Indian context, four situations stand out in which small farmers plant and protect trees. The first is in semi-arid regions where trees are a part of the farming system, and increase soil productivity and land sustainability by providing fodder, mulch, and shade for crops, and hence complement agricultural production. The second is in regions of high rainfall and good soil where trees on homesteads and on small plots increase income. The third, is where uncertain agriculture neither gives enough income, nor enables the farmer to seek work outside the village; in such conditions, even small farmers may be keen to shift their lands to trees which demand less labour, and to concentrate on wage labour for meeting their immediate consumption needs. And the fourth is on land which cannot support agriculture, but will produce a tree crop. We will illustrate these with an example from each of four different combinations of ecological and socio-economic conditions.

1) ARID AND SEMI-ARID LANDS

A study (Gupta 1984) of 24 villages of district Mahendragarh in Haryana suggested that in that semi-arid region small and marginal farmers had a higher density of trees per hectare of land, but as irrigation increased, tree density on their land declined. The distribution of trees in the three irrigation zones was as shown in table 8.2.

Table 8.2: Distribution of trees in three irrigation zones (based on a survey of 662 farmers in 24 villages)

Farmer category	Per ha number of trees with irrigation being		
	low	medium	high
Marginal	8.8	8.5	3.8
Small	7.3	5.5	4.0
Medium	8.3	5.3	5.7
Big	4.3	5.7	5.2

(Gupta 1984)

The seasonally dry tropical regions present farm households with a major problem of inter-year and intra-year variability of rainfall (Jodha et al. 1987). Farmers adapt to this by building diversity and flexibility into their farming systems and household economies. Trees and livestock often play an important part in this. Thus in semi-arid villages of Mahendragarh multi-purpose trees like Jat (*Prosopis cineraria*) and Kikar (*Acacia* sp) help in reducing risk caused by uncertain rainfall. With their access to moisture deep in the soil profile, trees can photosynthesise and produce foliage in years and seasons when annual crops fail (Singh 1987:125). In drought years farmers can then fall back on livestock and artisan-based activities, which require leaves, fodder and raw material obtained from these trees. Their strategies include activities which use wild grass like moonj, the hair, wool, and skin of livestock, and the labour of women and children (as men migrate in search of work) to sustain craft activities like rope-making and weaving.

But with the introduction of irrigation in semi-arid zones, trees are less important and even a nuisance. Chemical fertilisers tend to reduce the need for nutrients from trees. Irrigation provides some of the counterseasonal security previously provided by trees and tree products. Trees also impede cultivation, and so are cut, and saplings are not protected. Hence tree density on the irrigated land of small farmers tends to be low.

2) FERTILE LAND WITH HIGH RAINFALL

In regions of high fertility and good rainfall like West Bengal and Kerala, small farmers usually maximise returns from land through multi-storeyed cropping, where perennial crops such as coconut, arecanut, rubber and pepper are inter-cropped with seasonal and annual crops like tapioca, bananas, pulses and vegetables. Trees are preferred which have multiple uses, especially yielding fruit, fodder and mulch and being suitable as supporting structures for the cultivation of pepper, betels and various climbers. This diversity also reduces risks from pests and adverse weather as they tend to affect different crops differently (Singh and Usman 1986:110).

In two villages in district Trichur, Kerala, the number of trees per ha was higher in the small holdings, as shown by table 8.3.

Table 8.3: Tree density in homesteads in Kerala

Size of holding	Mean number of trees/hectare (rounded)
Small	620
Medium	276
Large	211
Very large	121

(Nair and Sreedharan 1986)

An extension of cultivation of tall perennial crops such as coconut and arecanut, permits a judicious combination of a number of tree crops leading to better utilisation of vertical space. Thus, a multi-tier cropping system can intensify cultivation of both tree and agricultural crops.

The study also observed that with rising land prices and greater penetration of market processes there was a tendency to increase commercial cultivation of cash crops, relying heavily on purchased inputs. Rather than grow trees as a complement to agriculture, the tree crops were then of shorter duration and aimed at meeting specific market demands (Arnold 1987:177). Other trees were being replaced with coconut, which did not provide fodder and green manure.

3) UNCERTAIN CROPS AND SECURE NON-AGRICULTURAL INCOME

The third set of conditions where small farmers plant trees on agricultural land is when returns from cropping are uncertain and farmers have a stable income from sources other than their own private land.

In village Kovilur, Trichurapalli (T.N.), many resource-poor farmers have diverted their dry lands from groundnut to cashew and eucalyptus plantations (Malmer 1987). The groundnut crop fails every two or three years. Fluctuations in output prices also affect the farmers. On the other hand, wage employment is available in the neighbouring district of Thanjavur but this requires long absences from the village. Therefore, by planting long gestation tree crops, poor farmers are free to concentrate on improving their income through wage labour. In a sample of 27 small and marginal farmers it was found that 18 had planted blocks of trees on their lands. The loss of ground crops did not hurt them financially as they could gain more from work outside the village. Adoption of farm forestry is therefore a search for a safe source of capital and income. Rather than produce for their subsistence needs, farmers channel their energies to more profitable agricultural labour and off-farm activities, while using their lands for tree crops requiring little labour or management.

4) TREES ON DEGRADED LAND UNSUITABLE FOR AGRICULTURE

A fourth set of conditions is where poor people own degraded land, or have such land allotted to them which is unsuitable for crops, but suitable for trees. Benefits from trees are then additional to their other sources of income, which may allow them to wait while the trees mature.

These conditions are illustrated by experience (Sen and Das 1988) with the Group Farm Forestry Programme in West Bengal. Ceiling land was allotted to the landless or near landless, but it produced little except grass to which all had access. Then, under a new scheme, the allottees were persuaded to plant these degraded lands with eucalyptus, which belonged to the allottees. In one complex at Nepura village in Midnapore district, a study (Shah 1987a:6) found that the area planted with trees had increased from 13 acres in 1981 to 510 acres in 1986. Ninety per cent of the area planted consisted of *patta* land. For the poor families of these villages, who continue to depend upon farm and forest labour even after the assignment of land *pattas* to them, tree cultivation on *patta* land has proved to be a major source of additional income. Over 70 families in Nepura complex who harvested their 1981 farm forest plantations in 1985 and 1986 earned an average of Rs 5,900 each. Amongst these, many Santhal (name of the tribe) families, and other poor, who were entirely dependent on labour for their livelihoods, promptly invested their revenue from the sale of trees to buy small plots of paddy land which was then used to take three crops with purchased irrigation water; a few other families dug shallow tubewells themselves; many used the money to tide over contingencies, pay off old debts, repair or build houses and to marry their daughters. The main lesson, however, is that for most of these families, trees had become a major instrument for capital accumulation; and, for those who deployed this capital judiciously, livelihoods would be for the rest of their lives more secure.

Two important factors at the heart of the success of this West Bengal Group Farm Forestry Programme are: (a) effective implementation of a land distribution programme through participation of grass-root level institutions; this ensured that the title as well as possession of the land actively went to the intended beneficiary family; a 99-year *patta* also enabled the holder to enjoy virtual ownership rights; and (b) early and effective initiatives by the F.D. to give technical advice and assure the *patta* holders that their right to do whatever they wished with their trees would not be infringed or curtailed at any stage. These factors do not exist in most other States; more so in the tree *patta* schemes (see table 8.7) devised for tree cultivation by RPFs on wastelands.

8.3 Land Ownership and the Poor

Two points as regards land ownership and the poor need to be noted. First, the poor in India can be broadly classified in two groups. Poverty in wet areas is generally associated with landlessness, as even a small farmer is able to rise above the poverty line because of higher productivity through multiple cropping. The situation is different in dry areas where even a farmer with 4 hectares may be quite poor, with land which hardly produces enough to sustain the family. Here landed farmers often undertake wage labour to supplement their incomes. In such areas poverty is linked with low productivity, rather than with landlessness. In the whole of rural Maharashtra, for instance, 63 per cent of the landless and 60 per cent of farmers owning less than 1 ha were below the poverty line, while the situation of those with between 4 and 8 ha was not so very different, with still 48 per cent below the poverty line (Blair 1986).

Second, much degraded land has been allotted to the rural poor in the last two decades. About 2 lakh hectares of culturable wasteland was distributed to the poor during the third and fourth Plans under a centrally sponsored scheme (GOI 1988a). Much more significantly, other land allotted includes 1.78 million ha of ceiling surplus land (GOI 1985a:133), and perhaps an equal amount of government wasteland. The allotment of government wasteland in some of the States is as given in table 8.4.

Table 8.4: Allotment of wastelands to the poor in some States

State 1	Area (hectares) 2	Beneficiaries (Nos.) 3
Uttar Pradesh	8,33,459	23,87,870
Andhra	4,27,200	5,99,273
Gujarat	2,40,194	1,29,301
Himachal Pradesh	NA	55,606
Orissa	2,60,576	3,96,326
Tamil Nadu	22,013	NA
Bihar	3,61,600	9,78,006
Total	21,45,042	45,46,382

(GOI 1988a)

In addition, 1.87 million ha of Bhoodan land was taken possession of by the State governments, out of which 0.9 mh has been distributed, mostly in Bihar, Orissa, Uttar Pradesh and Madhya Pradesh (GOI 1986a:126), making the total allotment of degraded lands of the order of 5 to 6 million ha. These degraded lands often have a potential for growing trees and shrubs through agro-forestry to give more income than the alternative of a feeble or non-existent agriculture.

The enormous potential for helping the poor through trees on their own lands has scarcely begun to be exploited. To blame their weak economy or their inability to wait while trees mature are not convincing explanations of this neglect, given the evidence of West Bengal Group Farm Forestry Project, of the Vansda Tribal Tree Growing Project (sec. 8.7) and of peasant behaviour in other parts of the world e.g., Haiti (Murray 1986; Conway 1987). Other explanations have to be sought.

We suggest that the main reasons why the poor have not planted more trees on degraded lands are:

1) Insecurity of land tenure.
2) Legal problems in harvesting and sale of trees.
3) Market imperfections.
4) Non-existent extension services.
5) Various hassles in Tree *Patta* Schemes.

We shall discuss these in turn.

8.4 Insecurity of Land Tenure

Security of land tenure and a sound base of land records are necessary preconditions for the poor to take to tree plantation. Any doubt in their minds about their land rights or the recording of these rights would obviously inhibit them from investing their labour and meagre capital resources in a crop which yields benefits only after several years.

Unfortunately land records are in a bad shape, especially where share cropping is widely prevalent and tenants are unable to assert their rights, or where land has been recently allotted by the government.

On the whole, it has been the poor and especially the tribals who have suffered. In Central India, communications were poor, shifting cultivation was practised, and the identification of individuals with particular plots was weak. These factors worked against proper establishment and maintenance of land records. Lands under the possession of tribals got recorded as government lands and were often transferred to the Forest Department. Thus the poor tribals have become defined as encroachers even on lands which were cultivated by their ancestors.

The importance of security of land tenure as a precondition for planting trees is illustrated by evidence from the southern part of Mirzapur district (U.P.), which has a substantial population of tribals living below the poverty line. The tract is dry, drought-prone, rocky, undulating with poor tree cover, and highly susceptible to soil erosion. The existing vegetation is not sufficient to prevent run-off of the soil during the monsoons, which further depletes the soil and exposes the bare rock underneath. Any programme to improve the economic lot of the people in this area should, therefore, first try to check the flow of water and conserve soil. This could be done if a massive programme of tree plantation were undertaken.

Unfortunately, no such programme can be successful unless tenurial problems are sorted out and people are sure about their land ownership rights.

During the pre-independence period no settlement or recording operation was ever done in this area. Land records were also not maintained. As the soils were inferior and pressure on land was low, people practised shifting cultivation without ever bothering about getting their rights recorded. Therefore, when the Zamindari abolition took place in Uttar Pradesh in 1952, the people in this area got no rights, and most land of the two tehsils in South Mirzapur was recorded as government land, which was, in 1953, transferred to the F.D., ignoring the existing land rights of the people. The maps of the villages of the tehsil show that land declared as reserved forest under Section 4 of the Forest Act is interspersed with lands owned or occupied by the people in such a manner that contiguous plots of forest land over a large area cannot be formed (GOUP 1983b).

Insecurity of tenure and pendency of thousands of criminal cases and eviction notices filed by the F.D. against the local people are getting in the way of promotion of people's movement in afforestation. This is supported by the experience of the Banwasi Sewa Ashram, a reputed NGO working with the tribals in that area, which, despite having received funds from the NWDB, could not get people interested in planting trees, as there was no incentive to undertake any long-term investment, whether planting trees, or soil and water conservation on "encroached" lands (p.c.; Prem Bhai 1987).

This is not an isolated example, but typical of a widespread condition. According to the Report of Task Force on Shifting Cultivation (FRI 1984:10) the estimated total area under shifting cultivation in Orissa was 3.7 m ha. The entire area is now under forest domain (total forest area in Orissa is 6.0 m ha), but tribals had been practising shifting cultivation on those lands from times immemorial. If that was so, why were these lands not declared as under private cultivation? How could agricultural lands be declared government lands? Why were these assumed to be unoccupied lands with no private interests, and declared as forest lands?

In India as a whole, over 2 lakh tribal families live in about 5,000 forest villages (see sec. 7.1 for definition) but possess no rights to the lands they cultivate (GOI 1984:129). The Ministry of Agriculture, vide their circular dated 23rd March, 1984 advised the States to confer on them heritable but inalienable rights, but no progress has been achieved. The guiding principle still seems to be the old decision of the Central Board of Forestry that, "No occupancy or permanent right should be conferred upon the forest villagers settled in the forests" (GOI 1976:45).

The lack of respect for the entitlements of land rightholders is illustrated by the example of 21,200 ha of community forest (called Khuntkatti forests) in 253 villages of Chota Nagpur division of Bihar. These forests belong to the Munda tribe but the Forest Department has taken over their management. It should pay 10 paise per acre per annum as rental to the tenure holders. Yet in the last 30 years compensation has been paid only to seven of those entitled. The official reason given is that the tenure holders have not filed their claims! (Singh 1980:17-18). Non-fulfilment of guarantees weakens the claim of the community over their lands, and in the years to come it will not be surprising if F.D. establishes *de jure* as well as *de facto* rights over these Khuntkatti forests too.

The participation of rural women in farm forestry programmes is also discouraged by tenure arrangements, since in several States they cannot inherit agricultural land, and hence do not own trees in their own rights. Thus, according to land laws in Uttar Pradesh (Saxena 1987a) after a land owner's death his land will devolve only to the male issues in equal shares. A married daughter can claim a share only if the land owner had no son, widow, mother, father, unmarried daughter, brother or unmarried sister. One wonders if such unfair provisions of law are not violating the equality provisions of the Constitution. They certainly reduce the incentives to women to plant and protect trees.

Another category of cases where insecurity of tenure is widespread is where land has been recently allotted. There has been no proper demarcation of plots in such cases, possession and land deeds have not been given to the beneficiaries, and records have not been corrected. Sometimes, not delivering a written deed is the policy of the government, as in the Social Security Plantation in Andhra Pradesh, (sec. 7.3) and in the Forest Farming for the Rural Poor (FFRP) programme in Orissa.

The FFRP enables the rural poor to practise both forestry and agriculture on degraded government lands on a usufruct basis. The poor are assisted with seedlings, fertilisers, and wages. All capital expenditure is borne by the government but produce is to be used by the person.

An evaluation (Niswass 1986) revealed that there was a good response to the scheme which could be tried on a larger scale. The biggest drawback was that the scheme did not give any secure title over land to the poor, and therefore their interest in it was short-term, limited to immediate benefits. Wherever the staff took interest in keeping the beneficiary's motivation high the scheme succeeded, but elsewhere success was only modest.

Another evaluation (SIDA 1987) of this scheme reiterated that there was no written contract or document safeguarding the rights of the selected beneficiaries, and they had to rely on the assurances of the project officers. What was worse, the State government has not yet (1988) clarified what kind of rights to land or trees are to be conferred to the persons identified under the FFRP scheme.

The conditions of insecure land tenure found in these examples—in Mirzapur district of Uttar Pradesh, forest villages, shifting cultivation in Orissa, Khuntkatti community forests of Bihar, and the FFRP scheme of the Orissa Social Forestry Project—deter the poor from long-term investment. It would be irrational for them to plant trees when they cannot be sure of their possession of the land ten years later. They are naturally tempted to take a quick agricultural crop—meagre and marginal though it be—rather than wait for a tree crop to mature. If land is too degraded for a crop, it is liable to be left fallow, without trees being planted, thus defeating the very purpose of land distribution in the first place. The provision of permitting utilisation of NREP/RLEGP funds for planting trees on private land of the poor (GOI 1986c) will remain largely unimplemented if the security of their rights is not assured. It is significant that private tree plantation is more successful in the erstwhile Mahalwari and Ryotwari areas of India—areas with better traditions of owner cultivation and secure land rights—than in the Zamindari areas, though the latter are better endowed with natural advantages of good soil and adequate rainfall. Only secure tenure encourages long-term investment.

8.5 Legal Problems in Harvesting and Sale of Trees

As in the example of *casuarina* trees in Tamil Nadu (sec. 1.6) trees can be good investments as savings banks for the poor, enabling them to accumulate capital. But trees would become poor people's banks only when their right to ownership of trees is not disputed and impeded by law or bureaucratic regulations. Quite often this is not the case. Rights which people have over trees planted on private lands are often ambiguous. There is a widespread impression in the villages that if trees are planted on private lands, not only would the trees belong to the government but land on which such plantation takes place would also revert to government. In contrast to Africa (Riddell 1987:6), where trees are often planted to establish tenure rights, in India they are often removed to demonstrate claims to land. Even as late as 1987 a SIDA team touring in South Bihar encountered tribals' fears that if they planted trees their lands would be taken away by the government (GOB 1987). The fear is not baseless as the Bihar Private Forest Act and similar other enactments did precisely this in the past, by "nationalising" private trees.

In most States people can cut trees only after going through a laborious process of getting a permit from designated minor functionaries—with consequences easy to imagine. There are three different sets of laws: a farmer cannot harvest trees without permission; a permit is required to transport them; and lastly some trees can be sold only to the F.D. What is the effect of these laws and how do they operate in practice?

Such forest laws leave villagers in doubt whether any wood they produce will belong to them. Perversely, the immediate impact of such legislation is always more destruction of private trees as people wish to cash their assets before the government machinery to enforce laws is set up. For instance, in Maharashtra just before the Private Forest Acquisition Act, 1975 was enacted the holders of private forests cut and sold all the trees on their lands (p.c., Collector Dhule 1987). Besides, such laws make people indifferent to tree growing, depress their margins when they wish to sell trees, and encourage corruption and middlemen's profits. They also discriminate against poor farmers, as they are less likely to be able to obtain permissions at the time of need. The mid-term review of Andhra Pradesh Social Forestry Project (CIDA 1988:82) rightly observed, "Majority of small and marginal farmers are not aware of the market value of their products. Intermediaries are already starting to reap the lion's share from the purchase and sale of such products.''

A study of Pahela village in district Bhandara, Maharashtra (CENDIT 1985b) showed that although transport of wood within the village was not prohibited, in practice people were often harassed by officials. A poor farmer complained, "The contractors from Delhi, Hyderabad and Bombay come here and take away all the wood. ... The F.D. officers go out of their way to be helpful to the contractors. And what happens to us? I can't cut even a branch of a tree on my field without the forest guard bullying me. ... If I go to the DFO to get permission to cut a tree growing on my own land, 'come back tomorrow', I am told every time.''

A District Collector in Uttar Pradesh conducted an enquiry into this problem. He obtained from the forest office the list of those who had received permits to sell their private trees. He then checked up in the field.

He discovered that the list of 17 names contained three which were either fictitious or of people who had not applied for permits. Clearly these were cases where permits had been obtained fraudulently by the contractors. Out of the remaining 14, two were marginal farmers who had obtained the permits on their own, without involving an intermediary. But when they took their permits to the local police station, they were asked to pay illegal gratification. On their inability to do so their permits were confiscated, and they were not allowed to fell their trees.

The remaining 12 admitted that they obtained the permit through the services of a middleman who "dealt" with the forest and police bureaucracy. The district Collector concluded in his report, "The consideration for these services rendered was adjusted in the sale price.'' He also observed, "It will not be an exaggeration to say that the marginal farmers and the poor tree *patta* holders will never be able to obtain a permit on their own from the forest department. Even if they do, they might not be able to 'convince' the local police. They will have to seek the protection of the local contractors.''

In Moradabad, a prosperous district of western Uttar Pradesh enquiries made by the Chief Development Officer (Kumar 1987) revealed that in all cases except one, farmers applied for permission through intermediaries. In the isolated case, where a big farmer tried to do it himself, it took him 14 months to get permission as against a normal period of two to three months for contractors. He complained of harassment from F.D. as he had to spend more than Rs 600 in travelling from his village to the forest office a number of times. In other cases trees were sold on as-is-where-is basis, and expenditure on felling and transport was borne by the middlemen. As shown in table 8.5, the price obtained by the farmers was only about two-fifths of that prevailing in the local market.

In Himachal Pradesh farmers cannot sell their commercial trees in the open market. All such trees have to be sold to the Forest Corporation, and that too only once in 10 years. Payment is made by the Corporation in four instalments spread over a couple of years. The logic is that as the Corporation is working on behalf of the farmers, it cannot, by definition, make losses; therefore all overheads of the Corporation must be fully met before the last instalment is paid to the contractor. This results in low and delayed payments to the contractors, who in turn exploit farmers.

In one prosperous village in Himachal Pradesh (Saxena 1988) farmers had a number of Khair (*Acacia catechu*) trees on their private lands. In 1983-84 this village was selected for felling of trees, according to the 10-year rule. A contractor on behalf of the farmers got permission for felling from the Forest Department, and moved an application in January 1984 to the Revenue and Forest Departments for joint demarcation of the trees. This took a long time, and ultimately the contractor could obtain the export permit only after 30 months, in July 1986. The whole process took about three years to complete. During the several months between the felling and getting permission to transport the trees, the wood must also have deteriorated. The farmers were only paid at the time of felling, in April 1986, which was almost two years after the settlement of the price. They got only 15 to 30 per cent of the estimated value of standing trees at farm site, as calculated by the Forest Department itself. The rest was lost because of long delays, uncertainty about payment by the Forest Corporation, the way farmers were kept in the dark about laws and procedures, poor publicity of market information, lack of competition leading to monopoly, and bureaucratic rents at various levels.

The rules concerning sandalwood trees present a striking instance of self-defeating regulation. Sandalwood is considered to be very auspicious for all religious ceremonies. Sandalwood and its oil are also used in perfumery and medicine. Despite increasing demand, sandalwood production in Karnataka has been declining. Its price of Rs 12.50 a tonne in 1955 has now risen to Rs 80,000 a tonne in the open market (Roy 1988). One reason for low production is absolute State control over sandal trees even on private lands. This means that an individual can derive no economic benefit from a sandalwood tree as he can neither cut it nor sell it. At the same time, due to the high price there is a lot of illegal felling of sandal trees from forest land. Thus a vicious circle has been established leading to a price spiral. "Supply increases as the price increases", is the old law of economics. In this case a price increase of 6,000 times (600 times in real terms) has actually led to a decline in production! In the present scheme of things there are incentives only to the smugglers.

Such restrictions are based on assumptions about the behaviour of rural people which are widely shared by bureaucracies all over the world. They believe that farmers cannot be trusted with a resource which only yields income after a gap of several years. Such a prejudiced view has, however, no empirical basis. Besides, such controls act as self-fulfilling prophecies: they deter protection and promote irresponsible felling. To effect a change in the people's behaviour one should start by trusting them with trees, at least those on their own lands. Some decades back, similar apprehensions were expressed regarding giving poor people land and security of tenure: it was said that they would only produce for consumption and not for the markets, and that more land would make them lazy. Experience from all over the world has shown that once assured of security of rights, peasants have proved themselves worthy of trust through their hard work, rationality and market orientation.

Excessive regulations lead to corruption. A study of north Indian fuel markets (Chatterjee 1987) found that transporters carrying fuelwood to Delhi have to pay Rs 500 per truck as "on-road considerations", a euphemistic phrase for bribes. These laws also keep the over-burdened bureaucracy busy in pursuits which (from the social point of view at least) are totally unproductive. Even when an officer is not corrupt, he is judged not on the basis of his help to small farmers, but whether he has been able to contain complaints of illegal fellings within "manageable" proportions. Yardsticks of performance get distorted, doing immense harm to social forestry programmes.

Awareness of laws and rules in India outside the bureaucracy is limited. They are generally shrouded in secrecy or in mystifying language. The cardinal principle governing the working of a government office is that "a good decision is better than a quick one". Therefore movement of papers takes a lot of time, which is often independent of bribes involved. This has two implications for a tree farmer. First, because of lack of knowledge, he cannot on his own negotiate a permission; he needs a middleman to help him. Second, even the middleman does not know how much time the entire process is going to take; he therefore charges excessive margins. In the study of Delhi markets it was seen that taking all costs into consideration, including on-road bribes (which were generally Rs 50 a tonne) and profits, fuelwood should be sold in the town of Delhi for Rs 505 a tonne, whereas the actual retail price (less taxes) averaged around Rs 800. The rest covered the risk or the uncertainty margin.

A political scientist may wonder, why large farmers have not been able to use their political clout with the State governments to get these laws changed in their favour? This may sometimes have happened. In Gujarat, all restrictions have been removed from the harvesting, transport and marketing of the three most popular species—eucalyptus, subabul, and *casuarina*—but whether this was the outcome of political activity or given as a present to the farmers by a benevolent bureaucrat is not known. Exemptions from harvesting restrictions exist in Uttar Pradesh too for 27 species, but as farmers still require permission under the Transit Rules the exemption makes little difference to the costs and uncertainties they face. In any case, such exemptions are not very well known, as admitted in the USAID/World Bank Report (1988), thus defeating its intention.

The farmers are pitted here against two powerful lobbies. One is that of government servants who have got accustomed to using controls as the only means to regulate economic activities. Even where legal powers do not exist these are often assumed. For instance, the Uttar Pradesh Tree Protection Act does not apply to the towns, and yet even in Allahabad, which is famous for its legal luminaries, the city police checks all trucks carrying timber, and harasses those who do not "behave".

Government officers and the public see implementation differently. Thus according to the collector in Dhule, a tribal district of Maharashtra, the Tahsildars give too many permissions under the guise that trees are obstructing agricultural activities, although he thought the Act called for more stringent action (p.c. 1987). On the other hand, the Academy of Development Science, a voluntary organisation working in the same State, felt that because of these restrictions a poor tribal could be forced to sell a teak tree on his private land to a contractor for just 15-20 rupees although its market value was at least Rs 2,000 (p.c. ADS 1987).

The other lobby is those environmentalists, academics and members of the press who tend to see planting trees for economic gain in capital and cash as moral sin. Peoples' participation, according to them, should mean planting trees for the next generation, or for meeting fuelwood and fodder needs of the people, or for supplementing agricultural production. A market orientation, in their view, harms the poor, as they are vulnerable to exploitation by middle-men, have little control over markets, and are likely to sell their trees for a song long before their optimal silvicultural and economic stage is reached. Peoples' participation is also equated with arousing collective spirit among the community, which alone will ensure that the new wealth being created through the programme reaches the poor.

The influence of this lobby of mainly town-bred environmentalists on policy making in India should not be underrated. Their views have an aura of respectability and are readily accepted as defining desirable objectives. The standards set by them for evaluating the results of a programme become the accepted norms, and a contrary viewpoint is easily branded as an anti-poor stance.

The two lobbies, of officials and of environmentalists, agree in seeing rules and controls as solutions. In the climate of opinion they have created, it makes good headlines if a Chief Minister announces that all tree cutting has been banned in a State; in contrast, a decision to liberalise tree cutting would be condemned as retrograde. But as we have seen, the tragic irony is that the rules and controls are self-defeating. They discourage tree planting and protection, and they discriminate against the poorer farmers, especially in marketing and prices.

Table 8.5 gives striking evidence of these low prices.

In none of the 12 cases did farmers receive even half the market outlet price, while in eight of the 12 they received less than 20 per cent! The best price was obtained in Uttar Pradesh, where the green revolution has increased farmers' familiarity with the markets. Areas listed from (a) to (e) in the above table were tribal pockets, which were the worst sufferers of over-regulation and control.

Table 8.5: Comparative prices of forest produce obtained by farmers and prevailing in market outlets

A Village/district	B Species/produce	C Payment obtained by farmer	D Sale price in markets	E C as % of D
Chotanagpur, Bihar (a)	Tendu leaves	Rs 15 per qtl	Rs 200 to 600 per qtl	2.5 to 7.5
Betul, MP (b)	Chiranji seeds	Rs 3-5 per kg	Rs 50 per kg	6 to 10
Shankargarh, Sarguja, MP (c)	Tendu leaves	Rs 4.50 per 100 bundles	Rs 40 per 100 bundles	12.5
Raigad, (d) Maharashtra	Teak & mixed wood	Rs 300-350 per truck	Rs 2,000-3,500 per truck	9 to 17
Suleswar, Phulbani Orissa (e)	*Mahua* flower	Rs 0.40	Rs 2.50	16
Hyderabad AP (f)	Firewood	Rs 61 per tonne	Rs. 347 per tonne	18
Shakruri, HP (g)	Khair	Rs 46 per tree	248 per tree	18
Sarguja, MP (h)	Sal seeds	0.41 Rs per kg	2.2 Rs per kg	19
Allahabad, UP (i)	*Mahua* tree	Rs 600 per tree	Rs 2,000	30
Kharot, Mathura, UP (j)	*Prosopis juliflora* (fuelwood)	Rs 20 per qtl	Rs 60 per qtl	33
West UP (k)	Fuelwood from eucalyptus	Rs 300 per tonne	Rs 800 per tonne	37.5
Moradabad UP (l)	Local mango age 60 years	Rs 860 per tree (av of 255 trees)	Rs 2,000 per tree	43

Sources: (a) Fernandes and Menon 1988.
    (b) , (c) Guha 1983.
    (d) Amrit Bazaar Patrika, 2.11.1988.
    (e) Bhattacharjee 1987: 13.
    (f) Alam & Dunkerley 1985: 88.
    (g) Saxena 1988.

    (h) Dasgupta 1986.
    (i) Shankar 1987b.
    (j) Saxena 1988.
    (k) Chatterjee 1987.
    (l) Kumar 1987.

Several factors are involved in determining farm gate prices; but the evidence accumulated, some of it presented above, leaves no doubt that the uncertainties, bribes, difficulties and delays involved in selling trees are linked with rules and controls, and are a major reason why farmers, and especially those who are poorer and weaker, often get such scandalously low prices for their trees and tree products.

The objectives of the environmental moralist lobby are not in dispute. Preventing environmental degradation and satisfying the consumption needs of the poor are certainly laudable national objectives. Where we differ is not in the objectives but in the means. It is unrealistic as well as inequitable to thrust collective social objectives upon resource-poor farmers if they see no private gains from what is being advocated. Beyond quite narrow limits, resource-poor farmers cannot be expected to forego private gain or to accept private loss for social gain. A realistic policy will seek ways in which ecological and social benefits are the byproducts of tree growing. And tree-growing will be adopted because farmers see enhanced capital assets and cash incomes as the main benefits. For resource-poor farmers, even more than for the resource-rich, this requires freedom from any legal restriction which gives officials or others the power to extract rents.

For many resource-poor farmers, trees are like savings banks (Chambers and Leach 1987) but with the advantage that they often appreciate in capital value much more rapidly than bank deposits. They provide reserves which can be cashed to deal with contingencies, such as costs of medical treatment, marriage expenses, a large purchase, or any sudden or large need for money. Where a good market exists for tree products, they can provide an alternative to taking loans and indebtedness. They are also often a source of income from their produce. When resource-poor farmers are prohibited from felling trees on their own land, it is like a bank manager refusing a depositor permission to withdraw money from an account. A banker interested in net deposits does not tell a new account holder that he can only deposit money and not withdraw it. Bankers who acted in such a manner would not last long. When the movement of timber and other tree products is restricted, it is like prohibiting people from taking money from one part of the country to another. Political leaders and officials who tried to introduce such a regulation would quickly find themselves in trouble.

Fortunately, there is much evidence that with the removal of restrictions, and with assurance of rights to trees and of freedom to market them, both environmental and social objectives can be achieved simultaneously. To take just one example, in Haiti (Conway 1987; Murray 1986), once poor farmers were convinced that they could harvest and market their trees free from controls, they surprised pessimists by both planting far more and by cutting fewer trees than had been anticipated. When harvesting trees is accepted as legitimate, poor farmers tend to postpone it and use trees as savings. On the other hand controls and uncertainty about their ownership, rights and marketing promote "irresponsible" felling, by converting trees into cash and other assets which are more secure.

8.6 Market Imperfections

For farmers in general, and for resource-poor farmers in particular, marketing is a weak link in the chain. To understand the reasons for this, we will start with an historical perspective.

During the colonial period in India timber supplies to the markets were mostly from government forests. This was not because private and common lands did not have trees on them, but because these were supposed to meet domestic rural demand for fuelwood, fodder and small timber. The market price was low, roads were few and extraction costs were high. It seems reasonable to suppose that peasants often believed, in zamindari areas at least, that all trees belonged to the State or the zamindar, just as land did, and that sale of neither land nor trees by the peasants was permitted.

It was perhaps during the Second World War that for the first time timber supplies from private lands became a significant source for the markets. As the war pushed prices up, contractors approached zamindars and superior tenants and bought their trees at throw-away prices. Then as zamindars feared losing land rights after independence, they hurried to sell off their trees in order to make as much money as possible before it was too late. Since then private trees have been a substantial source for timber supplies.

It has, however, only been in the eighties that markets for trees grown on private land have attracted much attention. Although a market for *casuarina* has long existed in Tamil Nadu, it has been the market for eucalyptus in west and northwest India that has been most remarked upon. With the "tree revolution" of the eighties, many large farmers and absentee owners converted agricultural holdings into commercial plantations, and smaller farmers followed, planting on borders and bunds as well as in small blocks. The early adopters made impressive profits because of the scarcity and high prices of poles. But by 1987 the market showed signs of saturation and prices dropped. As so often, the smaller and poorer farmers planted later and suffered most.

Small and poor farmers are also victims of market imperfections. Although surveys predict huge gaps between demand and supply of forest products at least till 2000 A.D., tree farmers in some parts of the country find it difficult to sell their produce (Das 1988), and typically, small farmers with small lots find it hardest of all (FAO 1988; ILO 1988:8).

Market imperfections can be illustrated by a study of the experience of farmers in two talukas of districts Mehsana and Bhavnagar in Gujarat, both areas of intense farm forestry (Wilson and Trivedi 1988). Prices (all figures are in rupees) per hectare received by the farmers in these talukas for eucalyptus poles showed great variation, ranging from 3,300 to 202,500 (both these extremes representing producers who sold directly in the market). The mean price per hectare for the sample of 38 farmers was 20,575, but the standard deviation was 19,385. Of the 45 producers who sold trees, only nine made a relative profit; 36 would have been better off sticking to agriculture. The consensus in the village was that farmers 'cannot make money out of trees. Since 1984 no farmer in the two talukas had planted eucalyptus. Further, in 1987 none of the producers who had already felled their trees was taking a second rotation. They were planning to return the land to agriculture. Many producers felt bitter towards the Forest Department for their advocacy for eucalyptus. The study concluded by stating that government's credibility suffered a great deal as it had promised unrealistic returns.

The easy and obvious explanation is the overproduction of eucalyptus poles which saturated the market. In Haryana, of all the private trees planted till 1986, 95 per cent were of eucalyptus (NCAER 1987:153). In Uttar Pradesh it was 94 per cent (IIPO 1988:39), and in Tamil Nadu 79 per cent in 1985-86 (GOTN 1988:24). In Punjab, a seven to eight year-old tree in 1988 was reported to be unsaleable at even Rs 25 whereas the Forest Department had earlier hinted at a price of Rs 100 and some of those who were in early on the market got Rs 150 (Das 1988). In Gujarat, the price of a four-to-five inch eucalyptus fell from Rs 60 in 1986 to Rs 23 in 1988 (Bhattacharjee 1988b). The worst hit were tribals who were finding it impossible to find buyers even at the reduced price.

But Wilson and Trivedi's (1988) study in two districts in Gujarat shows that there was much more to it than just the imbalance in supply and demand. Marketing in the area was an arbitrary and uneven business. Those who got good prices through direct sales tended to be the well-known, well-respected members of the community. Some producers received good offers from merchants through relatives, while others were unable to get any offers at all. The merchants from large towns, Gandhinagar and Ahmedabad, appeared to give better prices than local merchants and commission agents, although because of the costs of transport, they were less ready to buy. Selling to commission agents also involved the hazard of underpayment or non-payment: four farmers from different villages sold on contract, but three of them got only half the agreed sum and the fourth got nothing although his trees were cut by the contractor. In such conditions, small and weak farmers appeared especially vulnerable. An ILO study came to similar conclusions (1988:26-29).

Other factors may also have contributed to market imperfections. In Gujarat, restrictions on the harvesting and transport of eucalyptus had only recently been lifted, and might not have been well enough known to have affected the price. The market was dominated by contractors who did most of their business in forest auctions and were little interested in picking up small lots from dispersed producers. Eucalyptus lacked a major alternative market: it is not much used as timber, and pulp mills receive their supplies from liberal imports and subsidised pulpwood from the Forest Department. The pulp mills therefore lack incentives to buy from farmers, and anyway lack the infrastructure to purchase and collect from large numers of scattered small producers. Factors and imperfections such as these may be found in other tree-product markets, each of which deserves to be examined in its own right.

The response of rich farmers has been to lobby for pulp mills. In the Punjab in 1988, they succeeded in persuading the government to set up a mill at the cost of Rs 300 crores (*Tribune*, 28 March 1988). But with the capacity utilisation of pulp mills in India running at less than 60 per cent (*Financial Express*, 20.8.88 and Gupta and Shah 1987:iii), and with competition from imported and subsidised pulp, this seems unlikely to boost demand for eucalyptus from farmers. Solutions have to be sought in lifting legal restrictions on cutting and sale of trees, and in sorting out marketing imperfections, so that small farmers get a fair price for their produce. We shall further discuss these solutions in chapter 9 (sec. 9.10).

8.7 Non-existent Extension Services

Even with legal hassles removed and market infrastructure created, poor farmers will still require extension and support concerning the value of trees, technical questions and their rights. After all, tree farming for profit is often a new economic activity, especially where exotics are concerned. A few examples will illustrate how the approach to small farmers is crucial in deciding their response.

A comparison (Sen et al. 1985) of three group farm forestry schemes on *patta* land in West Bengal in three ecologically similar villages is enlightening: in the first village, extension evoked a strong response; in the second, tree planting seemed to be imposed by a political leader; and in the third village, tree planting failed to take off.

The main reason for the differences was the approach of the Forest Department. In the first village the forest Range Officer established dialogue with the selected local progressive and innovative persons, including a school teacher. A number of meetings were organised in the village where the initial experimenters talked of their experience. This helped others to gain confidence.

In the second village the Range Officer contacted a local political leader. This alienated villagers belonging to the rival political faction. A plantation of 40 ha was raised involving 150 *patta* holders but it was seen as a departmental work, and the allottees made no arrangements for protection. They migrated to distant places during the lean agricultural period and non-participants from adjoining villages damaged the tender plants, giving as their excuse their need for pathways to other villages.

In the third village the situation was worse. The Forest Range Officer found that the local leadership was not able to persuade the *patta* holders to plant eucalyptus, as they wanted traditional plants like *neem* and *mahua*. Recourse was then taken to planting eucalyptus departmentally on *patta*

lands and the *patta* holders were promised wages. They were also assured of
cash assistance on the basis of survival of seedlings. As the people worked for
wages, and had not chosen the species, they did not identify with the plants or
feel they owned them. Also, the plots were not demarcated so farmers did not
know which were their individual plots of trees.

Several lessons can be drawn from these three cases. First, an environment
of trust and confidence was not created in the second and third case. Second,
people must feel certain about land rights and tree tenure if they are to get
interested in the programme. Third, giving cent per cent subsidy may
sometimes be counter-productive, as not contributing labour by the allottees
may lead to indifference. Fourth, the role of innovation by local leaders is
crucial. In the first village, the school teacher's farm was used by the F.D. for
practical training to others.

As farmers increasingly turn to agroforestry, they would like to know the
relative degree of competition or complementarity between trees and crops.
As the USAID/World Bank Report (1988) admitted, at present none of the
State FDs know or can provide adequate guidance on agroforestry technology, environmental effects or silvicultural techniques required for income
maximisation.

A problem with government-induced programmes is that people's welfare
tends not to be the objective in itself. People and their participation are seen
rather as means to achieve a different end, which is to fulfil targets.

On the other hand, voluntary agencies often view development as
embracing all aspects of the life of a community. They have better contacts
with rural people and they take a process rather than an outcome approach to
projects, as the following examples illustrate.

The Dasholi Gram Swaraj Mandal, which pioneered the CHIPKO
movement, does not just plant trees. It organises protection committees,
ensures proper distribution, and promotes smokeless *chulhas*. It forced the
government to impose a 15-year ban on commercial green felling in the
Himalayan forests of Uttar Pradesh (Shiva and Bandhyopadhyay 1986:12).
And above all, it organises women at the village level, who are then the active
decision makers as regards choice of species and mode of protection.

Similarly, the Kashtkari Sangathana (Maharashtra) does not look at trees
as an income generating programme alone, but views forests as a life-support
system of the people, particularly tribals. Agencies like the Banwasi Sewa
Ashram, Mirzapur (U.P.) and Sewa Mandir (Rajasthan) organise the people
first, and benefits flow later. Experience of two such agencies working in the
most degraded region of Gujarat is described below (Mahiti 1987; Bhatt 1987;
Sohoni 1988).

The coastal villages of Dhandhuka taluka of district Ahmedabad, Gujarat
are very backward. More than 50 per cent of the land is saline. In some villages
such lands are up to 90 per cent of the total area. There is no underground
sweet water and the water table is very high. As a result of these conditions

most people are indebted and are forced to migrate in search of work. Mahiti, a voluntary organisation had been working in this area through village level organisations for women and youth. They found that women collected seeds of *salvadora*, a local shrub, which had a good market. It therefore, decided to take up plantation of *salvadora*. A local bank as well as the NWDB got interested in the project.

In the first year they raised two lakh saplings in nurseries, 40 per cent of which were raised by farmers themselves. Because of inexperience the average survival in the first year in the people's nursery was only 20 per cent, whereas it was 60 per cent in the central nursery run by Mahiti directly. Despite this setback, farmers felt confident that they would be able to raise these shrubs on their private lands which otherwise produced almost nothing. The problem of protection after planting was solved by stacking *Prosopis juliflora* branches around each individual *salvadora* plant. Most farmers in the area have now become interested in the project.

The Bharatiya Agro Industries Foundation (BAIF) is a large and reputed voluntary organisation active in work with poor farmers in several States. In Vansda Taluka of Valsad district in South Gujarat, 700 ha of forest land was leased out to tribals on the basis of usufruct. On each plot of land a tribal family worked to plant mango and other fast-growing forest trees such as subabul, eucalyptus, *casuarina* and bamboo. Other varieties were *amla*, *neem*, drumstick, *mahua* and jack fruit. Some of these trees support artisan-based activities such as bee-keeping.

By 1987 over 51,00,000 trees had been planted on tribals' private land as well as on the leased forest land. In 1987 the first crop of mango was harvested. Its marketing was also organised by BAIF in attractive packets of bamboo baskets, woven by another group of tribals. Fifteen tons of mangoes were sold in the town ensuring that the tribals got double the price offered by local merchants. By 1988 more than 5000 families from 40 villages had registered themselves under this scheme. Despite its best efforts, BAIF was not able to gain access to more degraded forest land, because of restrictions imposed by the Government of India via the Forest Conservation Act. The tribals were still keen to plant trees on their private land, so long as they got subsistence help during the first few years. This was arranged by the NWDB.

These two examples illustrate some of the advantages NGOs can have compared with most government organisations. NGOs tend to have better access to the poor, to make more realistic assessments of their needs, to involve them more in decision making, and to have more flexible programmes. Most important, their support is often sustained, starting with nurseries and planting, and carrying on through to marketing several years later. This continuity of support can engender confidence, especially among the poor.

On the other hand, for government officers, farm forestry in general, and for the poor in particular, is still not as high on the agenda as departmental works. An evaluation study (Om 1986) of the work of Tamil Nadu social forestry staff revealed that Range Officers devoted only 6 per cent of their time to extension, against a target of 40 per cent, the shortfall being attributed to preoccupation with administrative matters. Forestry being a new economic activity for poor farmers, investments are needed in extension, research and marketing. The substantial increases in Forest Department staff for social forestry have been largely occupied with the familiar work of departmental plantations, in the guise of community forestry, and these new activities of extension, research and marketing have been largely neglected.

In several States, however, separate extension motivators have been appointed. But the experience so far has not been very happy, except in West Bengal. In Tamil Nadu young people have been appointed as motivators, with a fixed honorarium. They are generally demoralised (Varadan 1987) because they do not have the security of government staff and no scope for further promotion. They are used for collecting monitoring information from the field. Because of their youth and inexperience, their advice does not carry much weight in the village and is anyway often inaccurate or badly focussed (CIDA 1988 and USAID 1985a). In Bihar, some women have been appointed as extension workers, but their area was too large, they had received little training, and being appointees of the F.Ds. they did not feel responsible to the villages (GOB 1987:7).

Instead of young people, West Bengal appointed old and retired people above the age of 50 years who were village residents and whose voice carried some weight in the village. They were community leaders and were often consulted by the villagers in other matters too. They worked as spokesmen of the community to the Forest Department, and not the other way round. Accountability to the people, and not to the Department is perhaps the single most important factor which determines the success of extension efforts.

The West Bengal Forest Department has also taken seriously the concept of decentralised Kisan nurseries; and in the process, it has enabled some of the poorest and assetless households to acquire a source of stable and decent income. Many of those who raised Kisan nurseries did not even have *patta* (leased) land, let alone *rayat* (inherited) land. They raised the nurseries (15,000 seedlings) in 20 × 20 feet plots in the courtyards of their homestead plots and earned about Rs 3,000 each. Decentralising seedling production to the poorest families may have major equity effects. In 1986, India produced 280 crore seedlings; at the current (1988) pace, the annual demand for seedlings may sharply increase to 500 crores (NWDB 1988b). At that level, and with 15,000 seedlings per nursery, decentralised nurseries would provide productive employment to some 3.3 lakh of the poorest rural families and benefit 15-20 lakh persons.

For Forest Department extension to be effective, its goals have to be properly defined (FAO 1986b). The normal tendency in any bureaucracy is to prefer simple and standardised programmes, and to reproduce familiar patterns. Farm forestry by resource-poor farmers presents a new set of priorities and demands a new set of patterns. These entail shifts from the promotion of single species and from fuelwood production, towards more diversity in species and in purposes. The species include fruit, fodder and other multipurpose trees. The purposes include more secure, sustainable and varied livelihoods for RPFs, meeting their needs for subsistence, savings, and income.

8.8 Various Hassles in Tree Patta Schemes

An important policy initiative by the Government of India in favour of the poor has been the Tree Patta Schemes. Some Indian States such as Uttar Pradesh and Andhra Pradesh had evolved schemes to lease out degraded revenue lands to poor people under land *patta* arrangements as early as the seventies (see table 8.4). A new impetus to such schemes was given by the Revenue Ministers' conference in mid-1985 after which a model tree *patta* scheme (hereinafter referred to as the model scheme) was drafted and recommended to the State governments as a means to involving poor people in raising trees on wastelands. Several States drafted or revised their own earlier schemes and brought them into force.

Andhra Pradesh, Bihar, Madhya Pradesh, Maharashtra, Tamil Nadu and Uttar Pradesh, introduced Tree Patta Schemes, mostly during 1986. By 1988 Rajasthan, West Bengal, Gujarat and Karnataka had land-leasing schemes for raising of trees by the rural poor. Some States like Assam and Haryana had expressed their unwillingness to introduce the scheme due to reasons like non-availability of land or peculiar tenurial conditions.

The physical achievements under the tree *patta* scheme reported by some of the States by March 1988 are shown in table 8.6.

Table 8.6: Progress of tree *patta* scheme in the States, as at March 1988

State	No of *pattas* beneficiaries	Area (hectares)
Andhra Pradesh	1,450	2,400
Bihar	9,912	6,799
Gujarat	771	6,746
Karnataka	41	25
Maharashtra	260	na
Rajasthan	na	62,456
Tamil Nadu	455,973	na
U.P.	59,410	19,276

(NWDB 1988'c)

Note: In Tamil Nadu, these are mainly *pattas* for fully grown tamarind trees on roadsides allocated to farmers of adjacent plots. Farmers are entitled to usufruct on the basis of protection.

These schemes have represented a big hope of enabling poor people to derive subsistence and livelihoods from tree cultivation (Chowdhry 1987:4). However, realising this hope faces two serious obstacles: various "catches" contained in the tree *patta* schemes; and problems of coordination between the departments involved in implementation.

THE "CATCHES" IN THE TREE PATTA SCHEMES

The tree *patta* schemes contain several clauses which would make them unpopular among the poor. The model scheme included some; and each State added others while drafting its own scheme to "suit the local situation". Table 8.7 lists some of these "catches" as they existed in 1988.

Table 8.7: The "catches" in the tree *patta* schemes

Provision	States
1. The beneficiary does not get a secure *patta* for the first two years, while he establishes the plantation with his labour. This adds to his uncertainty.	Model scheme, UP, Bihar, MP
2. Government decides what trees to plant, and when to harvest.	Orissa, Bihar, MP
3. The beneficiary is not free to sell his produce in the market. He can sell only to the Forest Department, which has not taken any steps to set up the vast machinery required to buy from dispersed producers.	Gujarat, Karnataka
4. The number of trees which can be planted by the beneficiary is restricted.	Tamil Nadu, Gujarat, MP
5. The beneficiary cannot fence his plot nor put up a temporary hut for protecting the trees.	Bihar
6. Forest lands are excluded from the purview of the scheme.	Model scheme, all States
7. The beneficiary is not free to do what he likes with the land, although in most cases it is so degraded that even trees would require investment and effort to grow.	UP, Bihar, MP
8. Several departments are involved in selection of land.	All States
9. Permission has to be obtained for felling trees and will be given only if new saplings are planted in place of each tree to be felled. This is impractical, as several trees regenerate on the principle of coppicing and not planting. Moreover, survival would be poor if saplings were planted in a densely forested area before the mature trees were cut.	Tamil Nadu, Gujarat, UP

The only uncurtailed right of *patta* holders is usufruct of the trees for subsistence, but this alone may not be a major attraction even for poor families where they have similar rights to collect dead branches, lop branches, and pick up wild fruits from trees on government lands and protected forests. In such circumstances, the incentives may not be strong enough for them to invest their labour and money in obtaining a *patta* and planting and protecting trees.

These catches raise several questions. The first is enforceability and the strain enforcement would cause to administration. The second is the opportunities for "rent seeking" that such catches create for village-level bureaucracies. Third, and the most important, these catches make the schemes unattractive and diminish their scale of impact. The main need is not to restrict and regulate the supply of wastelands to people and their rights to trees; it is to generate a demand among poor people for *patta* land on which to grow trees. The catches in the tree *patta* schemes do not encourage the poor; they deter. Unless the catches are removed, tree *patta* schemes are unlikely to become a mass movement, and the great potential they promise for livelihoods for the poor will not be realised.

PROBLEMS IN COORDINATION

Various departments have been involved in implementing these schemes in the States. Each department has conceived and planned the programme in different ways. Differences in target groups, lands planted, wage rates, regulations, and incentives have resulted in confusion and potential conflict both at the departmental level and among the people.

To illustrate, in Tamil Nadu the problem is two departments with different programmes for the same community lands: the Forest Department envisages plantations that will be taken over and managed for the collective benefit of the village and for generating revenue; the Rural Development Department envisages *pattas* being given to individual women from the landless section of the population. In Uttar Pradesh the problem is three departments involved in the same programme: the *patta* is to be given by the Revenue Department, funds are to flow from the Rural Development Department, and the Forest Department is to implement the scheme. If, as often occurs, either the list of beneficiaries or the funds do not reach the Forest Department before the rains, implementation of the scheme is delayed by a year.

Thus, giving a land or tree *patta*, in itself, does not lead to increased productivity. It must be backed by extension and sustained support. And above all, the conditions of the *patta* must be made hassle-free first.

8.9 Conclusions

There are many reasons why resource-poor farmers do and do not plant trees. Not all have been discussed in this chapter. Many aspects of agroforestry, of farming systems and of household economies have a bearing. But the finding of this chapter, again and again, has been that the acts and omissions of government play a major part; and especially that government restrictions and regulations, however well intended, in practice discriminate against the poorer and deter them from planting and protecting trees. Table 8.8 lists some major conclusions.

The message is clear. For resource-poor farmers to gain their full share of benefits from trees, their rights must be secure, their priorities must come first, and they must be free from restrictions.

Table 8.8: Why small farmers do not and do plant and protect trees

Factors	Do not plant and protect	Do plant and protect
Land tenure	Insecure	Secure
Rights to usufruct	Shared with government, or subject to taxation or control, or ambiguous	Vested entirely in the household, regularly exercised without restriction or rent
Choice of species	To meet officials' priorities	To meet farmers' priorities
Ownership of the trees	Owned by or shared with government or local authority, or ambiguous	Owned by the household in law and in practice
Protection	Hard to protect	Easy to protect
Rights to cut and fell	Restricted or believed to be restricted	Unrestricted and practiced at will by owners
Rights of transit to markets	Restricted or believed to be restricted	Unrestricted and practiced at will by owners and buyers
Marketing	Monopolistic	Competitive
Market prices	Not known, unastable or dropping	Known, stable or rising

CHAPTER NINE

A New Charter for the Poor

ABSTRACT

Forest policy since Independence presents three phases: the first, plantation phase, up to 1975, neglected village lands and promoted industrial plantations on forest lands; the second, social forestry phase, sought tree planting on village and private lands to draw pressure off the forest lands but could not meet social needs especially for fodder, MFPs and fuelwood, despite success in terms of trees reported planted on private land; the third, environment and people phase, was emerging in 1988.

In this new phase and policy, the objective of sustainable livelihoods for the poor integrates the interests of the environment and people. Forest lands are for livelihood forestry, with diverse and long gestation labour-intensive species planted for MFPs and livelihood goods, with increasingly shared management with communities and with competitive marketing. Revenue lands are for management by communities, with NGO support where suitable, and for tree *patta* schemes. Private lands are for agroforestry, especially for RPFs, and with high value, multiple purpose, market-oriented trees depending on farmers' preferences. Commercial and industrial needs are met increasingly from trees on private lands. On all three types of land, both the environment and people are served.

A poor-people-first policy requires participation in choice of species and in management, and special provision for the interests, needs and entitlements of women. Above all, poor people's rights, clearly defined, have primacy, together with information. In the plantation phase, mutual trust between the Forest Department and the people was difficult when the policy was keeping the people out but letting the contractors in. The new policy should lay the basis for better cooperation.

This chapter draws upon the analyses presented in chapters 7 and 8, and outlines policy and action to help the poor gain more from degraded lands and trees. We shall argue that altogether new policies and outlooks are needed towards forests and people. These can best be understood in a historical perspective. We shall therefore start by reviewing how forest policy has evolved during the last four decades.

9.1 The Three Phases in Forest Policy

Three distinct phases can be seen in the evolution of Indian forest policy since independence. Till 1975 man-made plantations of industrial species, called production forestry, were encouraged on forest lands. This could be called the "Plantation Phase". As it exacerbated "biotic" pressure, the National Commission on Agriculture in 1976 recommended fuelwood and fodder reserves on degraded village lands and government strips, and this was adopted as policy. From 1976 onwards production forestry on forest lands and social forestry on non-forest lands became the adopted policy, although fund availability during this phase was much better for non-forest than forest lands. We shall term this the "Social Forestry Phase". Social forestry projects started between 1977 and 1983 and were still continuing in 1988. But there were signs that a new policy framework might emerge. This we shall call the "Environment and People Phase".

1) THE PLANTATION PHASE

Policy statements in India on important issues like poverty eradication, health, water and women have generally been full of sympathy for the poor, at least on paper. That these policies do not get translated in action is another matter. But Forest Policy, even on paper, during the plantation phase, was different. The 1952 Forest Policy document, and various Five Year Plans, unequivocally blamed the poor for deforestation, and sought to use the public resources of forest lands for industry and commerce, rather than for meeting subsistence needs of the people.

The 1952 National Forest Policy in resolution No. 13/52-F dated 12th May, 1952, for instance, declared that village communities should in no event be permitted to use forests at the cost of "national interest" (para 7), which was identified with defence, communications and vital industries. It declared (para 13) that national forests should be used to produce valuable timber for industry and other national purposes.

During 1961-69 plantations of teak and other commercial species and of conifers were raised on an area of about 394,000 hectares of forest land, while a further area of about 246,000 hectares was planted with quick-growing species under a new centrally-sponsored scheme to meet the requirements of the pulp and paper industries (GOI 1970:206). Where reserve forests did not have blanks, fast growing and non-browsable exotics like eucalyptus were often planted on protected forests, and later these were converted into reserved forests. The area of reserved forests thus increased from 31.6 m ha in 1960-61 to 40.2 in 1986-87 (table 3.1). Out of the 67 crores rupees spent on afforestation during 1966-74, roughly 56 crores was on production forestry alone (GOI 1981a:45).

The National Commission on Agriculture (GOI 1976:32) put its stamp of approval on this approach in the following terms, "Production of industrial wood would have to be the *raison d'etre* for the existence of forests. It should be project-oriented and commercially feasible from the point of view of cost and return." Following its recommendations State Forest Corporations were established to which were transferred vast forest lands for raising industrial timber. Salim Ali, the famous ornithologist, called them Forest Destruction Corporations as they destroyed mixed forests vital for meeting people's needs.

Protected and village forests which were meant for meeting village needs continued to get degraded for several reasons. First, as they were close to village habitation the foresters did not believe that efforts to regenerate them would bear fruit because of biotic pressure, so little attention was paid to them beyond lip service. Second, central assistance as well as funds from the States which were in any case inadequate, were mostly concentrated on reserve forests for industrial plantations. Third, rights and privileges which village communities had in these areas were not compatible with their regeneration, unless concentrated efforts were made to work with the cooperation of the people. Before 1980 this approach was not generally tried and thus these lands as open access resources were victims to the "tragedy of the commons" phenomenon.

The policy of the government during the plantation phase, and its outcome with the three categories of public lands, are summarised in table 9.1.

Table 9.1: Government policy and its outcome in the plantation phase

	Community lands	Protected forests	Reserved forests
Control by F.D.	*Laissez faire*	Limited control as area "burdened" with peoples' rights	Full control
Management input from government	Nil	Limited	"Scientific" forestry to produce sustained yield of commercial timber
Fund support from government	Nil	Negligible except when exotics were planted	Limited, as forestry was given a low priority
Actual outcome	Degradation/ encroachment	Degradation & neglect, poor survival rate; where plantations succeeded, area was converted into reserved forests	Conversion of mixed forests into plantations
Benefit to people	A little grass after rains	Fuelwood and MFP, but productivity kept on declining	Mixed forests provided livelihood, plantations provided employment only

2) THE SOCIAL FORESTRY PHASE

The degradation of village lands and protected forests led to increased pressure on the reserved forests. In order to reduce this pressure, the National Commission of Agriculture (NCA) recommended growing trees on lands accessible to village people. To quote from its report:

> Free supply of forest produce to the rural population and their rights and privileges have brought destruction to the forest and so it is necessary to reverse the process. The rural people have not contributed much towards the maintenance or regeneration of the forests. Having over-exploited the resources, they cannot in all fairness expect that somebody else will take the trouble of providing them with forest produce free of charge. . . . . One of the principal objectives of social forestry is to make it possible to meet these needs in full from readily accessible areas and *thereby lighten the burden on production forestry*. Such needs should be met by farm forestry, extension forestry and by rehabilitating scrub forests and degraded forests. (GOI 1976:25) (our emphasis).

Thus social forestry was seen by the NCA as a programme which would release industrial forestry from social pressures. The core area was still reserved forest lands, and the core objective remained production of commercial timber. But in order to keep people out it was necessary to make them produce what they consumed free of charge using community lands to draw off some of the pressure on forest lands.

Social forestry projects in India are now more than a decade old. In terms of sheer production of trees the programme has been immensely successful. Between 1980 and 1987, the government claims to have raised 18,865 million trees. If the estimate of survival of 60 per cent is taken as correct (IIPO 1988), and taking the number of villages as around 5.8 lakhs, the average number of surviving new trees per village comes to nearly 19,500. This is by all means an impressive achievement.

There have, however, been marked divergencies between the stated objectives of social forestry and the actual outcomes. For example, the magnitude of tree planting on private lands has already made itself felt in the pole and pulp market (sec. 8.6), but in statements of objectives of the various social forestry projects, neither the production of poles nor increasing the supply of pulpwood is mentioned as part of the *raison d'etre*. The gaps between the objectives and outcomes of social forestry projects, many of which were admitted by the government (NWDB 1988c), are summarised in table 9.2.

The reasons for these distortions were analysed in chapters 7 and 8. A summary can help set the scene in the search for new policy.

First, as deforestation was perceived to be due to fuelwood and fodder demands of the people, it was assumed that given government help people would willingly invest their labour and capital in raising fuelwood and fodder trees. However, as fuel and fodder were often collected free, both farmers and panchayats preferred income-generating trees, and continued to collect branches, twigs, leaves and grasses from forests as before.

Table 9.2: Stated objectives and actual outcome in social forestry projects

Stated objective	Actual outcome
1. Produce fuelwood and fodder.	Market-oriented trees were planted which did little to improve consumption within the village. Fodder trees were generally ignored. Close spacing to accommodate more trees affected grass production.
2. Reduce pressure on reserved forest land.	As projects did little to meet the demand of the poor for fuelwood and fodder, pressure on forest land continued. Moreover, afforestation of reserved forests was given a low priority in this phase.
3. Regenerate wastelands, hills, barren slopes and eroded terrains.	Trees came up on farm lands, specially irrigated land, and strips belonging to government. Block plantation on degraded wasteland was given a low priority or survival rate remained poor. Wasteland Development was the slogan, tree farming the reality.
4. Involve community in management	Communities were generally not given government funds to raise trees. Instead, F.D. raised trees on common lands which were seen as government trees. The problem of handing over these plantations to panchayats remains unsolved.
5. Help the poor through improved access to forestry products, and higher incomes through asset creation.	Participation of small farmers in farm forestry has remained poor. Diversion of land from agriculture to forestry reduced employment opportunities, specially for women. Tribal areas where people's dependence on forests is more acute were generally ignored in social forestry projects. Producing MFP trees and strengthening the position of "gatherers" were not objectives of the projects. Social security schemes were implemented only on a small scale.

Second, there was a mistaken belief in the "trickle-down" theory that increasing over-all supplies through non-browsable exotics would reduce the demand-supply gap and help all concerned, including those who gather tree products (Shukla and Dalvi 1986:81-82). This led to saturation in poles and pulpwood, while the poor had to remain content with lops and tops only. While in the plantation phase industry got subsidised supplies directly from the State, in the social forestry phase the State played the role of facilitator subsidising the rich farmers who reached out to the pole market (Guha 1988). In both phases, the interest of the poor was bypassed.

Third, bureaucratic and departmental imperatives were more powerful than people's interests. Ever-increasing targets kept the Forest Department busy on departmental plantations, so that it had little time for extension or for seeking people's participation, which remained "an ideology without a methodology". Schemes like the social security plantations (sec. 7.3) were implemented half-heartedly keeping the poor at the level of wage-earners.

Fourth, as State funds got locked to meet the matching contributions required for external assistance for social forestry projects, forest lands got starved of funds, with several adverse effects. The neglect of forest lands hurt forest dwellers and tribals. It reduced timber supplies to the markets, resulting in price escalation. This increased smuggling which led State governments to clamp stricter laws on harvesting, movement and sale of trees even from private land. These regulations hit poor farmers worst, having dispersed production units and being late entrants to the markets.

Fifth, the nature of the dependence of poor people on forest lands for their livelihood needs was not clearly understood. Even a government report (GOI 1986b:3) admitted that forestry in the last thirty-five years had remained pre-occupied with plantations but not with how trees could serve the people. Several minor forest products were nationalised in the interest of revenue maximisation which seemed to have helped contractors and petty officials to the disadvantage of the people who depended upon them.

Sixth, social forestry was understood as planting trees for the nation or the next generation. For some, to see trees as economic assets was a moral sin. This was one reason for the neglect of marketing issues in farm forestry projects.

Seventh, species selection and spacing were considered technical questions, and hence left to foresters. Benefits which could flow to the poor from species yielding intermediate products were not properly appreciated. The value of a tree was linked in the minds of foresters with the final product obtained through felling. Thus production of grasses, legumes, fodder, fruit and MFPs was neglected.

Last but not the least, satisfactory arrangements for the distribution of benefits from trees were not worked out. Social forestry trees were, in the eyes of the people, government trees, and land on which these were planted had become an extension of forest land. This was because clear, firm and secure distribution mechanisms did not exist.

The confusion in 1988

In 1988, there was little evidence that these issues were being addressed with the seriousness they deserved. Government of India had been obsessed during the past three years with achieving the afforestation target of 5 million ha a year (equivalent to 10 billion trees, or planting of about 17,000 trees per village per annum!), and questions of quality, survival and people's welfare had generally been brushed under the carpet. As a consequence of this indifference and lack of perspective, forest policy in India seemed to be wavering. Different organisations were making different noises, and sometimes contradicting each other. The Forest Conservation Act, 1980 as amended in 1988 also added to the general confusion. For instance, on several occasions it had been stated that a peoples' movement would be launched in forestry, yet an amendment introduced in 1988 did not permit any assignment of forest lands to the people. Conventional solutions were still being advocated to check deforestation. The NWDB (6th Board Meeting, January

1988) advocated a large-scale programme of castration of scrub bulls to restrain the growth of animal population. Heavy grazing pressure, over-felling by the people to meet fuelwood needs and non-availability of suitable wastelands were identified by the Board as the main reasons for non-achievement of the afforestation target of 5 million hectares a year (NWDB 1988a). In other words, the problem lay with people, or their cattle, or land, and not with government policies. Interestingly an expert group appointed by government (GOI 1987c) concluded that contrary to popular belief sheep and goats did not pose a threat to the ecology.

Policy statements have often been contradictory and self-defeating. The new Forest Policy announced in December, 1988 and which replaced the 1952 Document, expressed several sentiments in favour of tribals, yet an amend-ment to the Forest Conservation Act introduced in 1988 restricted plantation of horticulture crops, palms, oil bearing and medicinal plants on forest lands, a provision which seems to show total insensitivity to the life style and the needs of the tribals. The Central Board of Forestry in its meeting of December 1987 decided to encourage farmers to grow commercial timber for the market, yet State after State had in the previous decade promulgated laws to put more restrictions on the free flow of forestry products. The National Land Use and Wastelands Development Council presided over by the Prime Minister in 1986 approved a paper which suggested "that laws relating to cutting of trees should be made more stringent", whereas a Committee appointed by the NWDB in 1987 pleaded for liberalisation of such laws. The new Forest Policy announced in 1988 recommended modifications of land laws to facilitate and motivate individuals and institutions to undertake tree farming, yet in the same paragraph it contradicted itself by stating that appropriate regulations should govern the felling of trees on private lands.

To match the confusion between various organs of government at the highest level there was little communication between the Government of India and the States. Despite a ban on leasing since 1982, the States of Orissa, Bihar and Karnataka subsequently leased out forest lands to contractors and industries (GOI 1985b:37). They extracted highly valued and easily market-able species from the forests, thus disturbing the sustainability of the remaining vegetation (Chetty 1988). Karnataka also gave forest land to rich farmers for arecanut plantations (Nadkarni et al. 1987), a commercial crop with few benefits to the poor. As so often, the coexistence of conflicting ideas and policies, and the debate surrounding them, were a sign of change, and of the need for a new and more consistent set of policies.

3) THE ENVIRONMENT AND PEOPLE PHASE

Despite this confusion, from 1985 onwards the Government of India has been gradually moving away from the model developed by the National Commi-ssion on Agriculture. A new phase in Forest Policy has been taking form. We shall call this the "environment and people" phase, to reflect its two main themes: a concern for the environment; and a concern for the livelihoods of the poor.

Some excellent elements of this new phase have been emerging piece-meal. For instance, the Seventh Plan Document recognised the importance of non-market and ecological benefits from forests. It did not explicitly mention producing timber for commercial purposes as one of the objectives of forest policy. It also stated that raw material for forest-based industries would be provided only after meeting the needs of the local people.

The Central Board of Forestry, in its December, 1987 (GOI 1987d) meeting presided over by the Prime Minister and attended by the Chief Ministers decided that forest lands would be used for preserving soil and water systems, and not for generating State incomes. All supplies to the market and industry would be met from farm forestry. Small and marginal farmers would be especially encouraged to use their degraded lands for meeting commercial requirements. This was followed by another announcement by the Forest Minister in May 1988 that 70 per cent of the total afforestation would be in the farm sector.

The new Forest Policy 1988, which replaces the 1952 Policy, also gives higher priority to environmental stability than to earning revenue. It discourages monocultures and prefers mixed forests. But it wishes to curtail the rights and concessions of forest dwellers by relating them to the carrying capacity of forests. It also looks down upon entry of forest dwellers into forests for gathering forest produce, as it declares that the domestic requirements of tribals should be made available through conveniently located depots at reasonable prices.

Reading the new Policy together with the amended Forest Conservation Act gives an impression that government wishes to have exclusive rights to management and ownership over forest lands, both reserve and non-reserve. This appears to revert to the State monopoly over forests, asserted in the plantation phase by denying the benefits of mixed forests to the people.

The monopoly, it may be noted, was diluted to some extent during the social forestry phase when some States tried to secure people's involvement on forest lands through social security schemes and others included degraded forest lands in social forestry projects, intending to transfer their management to village committees. On these lines, the social forestry projects of Bihar and Orissa have an important component on forest lands for meeting people's requirements. The mid-term evaluation of the A.P. social forestry project also recommended (CIDA 1988) strengthening the social security plantation scheme on forest lands through sharing of usufruct with the poor. Haryana F.D. transferred the responsibility of protection of some government forests to 50 village societies, *a la* Sukhomajri (sec. 7.3). In return the villages harvested the enhanced production of bhabbar and other grasses.

The future of these schemes is now in jeopardy, as the Forest Conservation Act frowns upon management sharing schemes. It is doubtful if the West Bengal government will be permitted to go ahead with the large-scale replication of Arabari model (sec. 7.3) for rehabilitation of degraded forests. Even where the programme is intended on road strips, (as in Uttar Pradesh where road strips have been declared as protected forests) or unclassed forests (Himachal Pradesh), the programme has been held back due to lack of permission from the GOI (USAID 1988). Environmental benefits cannot be realised by ignoring people's demands, nor is it possible to enforce exclusive property rights (Commander 1986), given the open and unguarded nature of forests in India. Working with the people and for them, howsoever desirable, is still a far cry, slogans notwithstanding (Kulkarni 1987).

The Central Board of Forestry has taken a courageous step in recommending a ban on commercial exploitation of forests. We hope that it will lead to planting trees which meet livelihood needs of the poor. However, forest policy would have truly become a "Poor-People-First" Policy had the Central Board of Forestry and the new Forest Policy explicitly recognised "meeting consumption and income needs of the poor through gathering" as one of the objectives. On the other hand, the new Policy relates rights and concessions of the people to carrying capacity of forests; and would like their requirements to be met from outside the reserved forests. Peoples' rights and access to forests have certainly been diluted in the new Policy by using the argument of restoration of ecological balance.

9.2 Policy Synthesis: Sustainable Livelihoods

Part of the difficulty in seeing what best to do arises from the conflict model in policy-makers' minds. People and the environment are seen, all too often, as antagonistic. The extreme bureaucratic view is then that people should be excluded from forests. The extreme humanist view is that the Forest Department should be excluded from forests. In our view, the conditons in which either is feasible and right are quite rare. Nor is the conflict model necessary or useful. To the contrary, ways can be sought in which the interests of people and of long-term sustainability are harmonised in a mutually supporting manner.

The key to this is the concept put forward by the Brundtland Commission (WCED 1987a and b) of sustainable livelihood security. It was given these meanings:

> Livelihood is defined as adequate stocks and flows of food and cash to meet basic needs. Security refers to secure ownership of, or access to, resources and income-earning activities, including reserves and assets to offset risk, ease shocks and meet contingencies. Sustainable refers to the maintenance or enhancement of resource productivity on a long-term basis. A household may be enabled to gain sustainable livelihood security in many ways —through ownership of land, livestock or trees; rights to grazing, fishing, hunting or gathering; through stable employment with adequate remuneration; or through varied repertoires of activities. (WCED 1987a:3)

The crucial point is that when people have secure and permanent rights, they wish to and can afford to take the long view, and to protect, conserve and enhance resources. Most of the behaviour which is interpreted as irresponsible and hand-to-mouth is the result of extreme poverty and insecurity.

Thus, so long as the F.D. auctioned grass in Sukhomajri and other villages fodder yield was as low as 0.2 tonnes per hectare (Chopra et al. 1988:11). Open grazing accentuated soil erosion problems. But after the F.D. decided to give the contract to the village societies for community protection for a period of five years, and norms of fodder harvesting by individual households were decided by the society and strictly enforced, forest productivity increased by a factor of 10 to 20 times (Mishra and Sarin 1987b). Once assured of secured rights, there was incentive for the families to resort to stall feeding. Villagers of Sukhomajri repeatedly announce now that forests belong to them. The same sense of identification and pride was noticed in the Orissa villages studied by the ORG (sec. 7.3).

When rights are secure, and poor people are not desperately poor, they often show extraordinary sacrifice and tenacity in holding onto assets. Where they own trees, they are often among the last things to be sold off in distress. The tragedy is that so many who depend upon forests are so insecure, or their rights are so uncertain, that it makes no sense for them to take the long view. The challenge and opportunity, is to establish and assure their rights and access, and to secure their livelihoods, so that it makes sense to them to take the long view, and to protect and enhance their environment. Through sustainable livelihoods, poor people cease to be the problem; they become the solution.

Linked with sustainable livelihoods, the policy we advocate is based upon three practical tenets:

i) *Poor people first.* The livelihood rights of poor people are paramount. Ethically, poor people should come first. Practically, their livelihoods are preconditions for sustainability.

ii) *Sustainability.* Policies should and can exploit many ways in which environmental objectives and the interests of the poor are mutually supporting in the long term.

iii) *Feasibility.* The main thrusts of policy should be based on the feasible rather than the ideal. This improves scale and effectiveness, bearing in mind the realities of politics and bureaucracy. It starts with organisations and people where they are, with what they control, and with their comparative advantages in access and capability.

The policy can be outlined for the three categories of land—forest, revenue, and private—used in chapters 7 and 8. In summary, the approach we advocate is mixed forests for livelihoods on forest lands, community trees, grasses and tree *patta* schemes on revenue lands, and agroforestry for resource-poor farmers on private lands. Pulpwood and other large-scale commercial demand from quick growing species would be met not from forest lands, but from private and *patta* lands, with livelihood benefits to villagers and farmers.

Forest lands

The plantation phase view that the proper use of forests was to meet industrial needs (see e.g. Shyam Sunder and Parameswarappa 1987a&b) should be abandoned. As these lands can satisfy a variety of needs of the forest dwellers and tribals, afforestation of degraded forests, both under the reserve and protected category, should be taken up as an integral part of social forestry schemes. "Scientific" forestry would now mean that wild fruits, nuts, MFPs, grasses, leaves and twigs become the main intended products from forest lands and timber a byproduct from large trees like tamarind, jack and Sal. Forest lands have a comparative advantage in growing long gestation trees which may be less attractive to panchayats and to some farmers. Fortunately, these are also the source of several MFPs. On forest lands, priority should be given to mixed forests and socially useful trees, like Sal, *mahua, arjun* and *neem*, in place of teak, pine, and eucalyptus. Rather than raise plantation crops these lands should be used for non-rotational trees and natural forests, the produce of which is gathered. Bamboo, fruit and oil-bearing trees like *karanj* and *kusum* which provide income to the poor as well as raw material for artisans, should get an equal priority as these too provide MFPs and subsistence products to support and sustain the livelihoods of the poor. These should be supplemented with shrubs, grasses and bushes to yield fibre, fuelwood and fodder in the shortest possible time. Thus the policy should be to encourage usufruct-based trees in place of trees which require clear-felling. To this end, social forestry projects should be extended to forest lands and tribal areas, and strengthening the position of gatherers should be an important objective of all social forestry.

For marketing MFPs, government should not have a monopoly. The solution is to set up promotional Marketing Boards, as distinct from commercial corporations (which are inefficient, and hence demand nationalisation), with responsibility for dissemination of information about markets and prices to the gatherers. The Boards would help in bridging the gap between what the consumers pay and what the tribals get. We would be quite happy if government organisations could compete in the open market, as in the wheat purchase scheme, but government should never acquire a monopoly. Nationalisation reduces the number of buyers and does not help gatherers in the long run. Setting up processing units within the tribal areas is also to be recommended.

Management on forest lands should be shared with the people in three ways. The first is to afforest degraded land wherever feasible, under the supervision of the NGOs by granting usufructuary rights to the poor, as in the BAIF project in Vansda described in chapter 8. This requires suitable changes in the Forest Conservation Act. The second is to remove constraints to the implementation of social security schemes. And the third is to extend to new areas the Sukhomajri and Arabari experiments of entrusting protection of forests to communities.

Revenue lands

The present practice of "taking over" common lands by the F.D. should be stopped, or drastically reduced to experimental projects. Funds for afforestation should either be transferred to the village community or to an NGO, if there is one, or the Tree *Patta* Scheme should be tried. As far as possible the catches and hassles in the design and implementation of the Tree *Patta* Scheme should be removed. People's wishes should be the guiding principle in species selection. There is a good case for non-rotational "low" market value trees and grasses in community plantations, so as to reduce problems in distribution, while Tree *Patta* and similar other individual-oriented schemes give priority to multiple use and income-oriented trees. This distinction needs to be kept in mind while planning location, species-mix and ownership of nurseries. Where panchayats represent several villages, single village organisations as in the Uttar Pradesh hills and Orissa should be created. Finally, distribution of produce is better done on the basis of one kitchen— one share, rather than alienating the rich by excluding them.

Private lands

Our recommendations which follow from the discussion in chapter 8 are as follows. First, to correct land records, especially on tribal and *patta* lands, and to involve NGOs in this task. Second, to abolish all harvesting, transport and sale restrictions for trees on private lands. Third, to recognise the role of markets, and to keep future farmers' incomes in mind while popularising a set of species. Government should not compete with the poor farmers in the marketing of poles and timber. Quick-growing trees should be reserved for the farm sector and excluded from government lands. Farmers' preferences for fruit and other income-generating trees should be kept in mind in seedling distribution programme. Fourth, to build up adequate infrastructure of extension and farmers' training. And last, to study traditional agro-forestry systems and new potentials in each region and to formulate extension programmes accordingly.

The important elements of the three phases in the Indian forest policy, as they affected or will affect the three categories of lands, are presented in a tabular form in table 9.3.

9.3 Tenurial Issues in Forestry

As we have seen (table 2.12), of the 84 m ha which need to be afforested, roughly 36 m ha is with the Forest Department, 35 m ha with farmers and the remaining 13 m ha is under the control or use of communities. With these very large areas involved, the sensible approach is to start with whatever scope there is for securing benefits to the poor through existing tenurial arrangements. This is not being practised currently in three respects: government or departmental forestry on revenue lands (sec. 7.6), the tree *patta* schemes, and the model being pursued of leasing forest and revenue wastelands to industries. However desirable it may be, community ownership of forest

Table 9.3: Three phases in forest policy

	I Plantation (1952-80)	II Social forestry (1975 -still continuing)	III Environment and people, becoming sustainable livelihood
Forest lands	Low priority to forestry for funds. Mixed forests replaced by plantations for industries	Generally ignored resulting in degradation, and high price of timber	Livelihood forestry on forest lands to be used for meeting livelihood needs of fodder, fuelwood, MFPs and low value fruits for people on a sustained basis.
Revenue lands	Area reduced due to allotment and encroachment. Degradation due to overuse and neglect	Departmental plantations raised with little participation from people. Long-term sustainability in doubt	Land to be regenerated by transferring funds direct to community, or NGOs or through Tree Patta Schemes.
Private lands	*Laissez faire,* farmers on their own practiced traditional agroforestry or planted horticultural trees	Monoculture plantation benefited large farmers and absentee owners generally. Little effective involvement of small farmers	Agroforestry to be a tool for strengthening the subsistence, income and security of the poor farmers through high value, multiple use and market oriented trees. All legal constraints to be removed.

lands demanded by environmentalists (e.g. Gadgil and Guha 1988) also involves a change of tenurial and management arrangements. The point we are making is not that any change is wrong: it is that for speed, scope and practicality, it makes sense to give priority to those actions which are more immediately feasible. This means first exploring and exploiting the possibilities of working within each existing class of tenure.

Since there are three forms of land—forest, community and private, and three patterns of organisation and tenure: the Forest Department, Village Panchayats, and individuals, there could theoretically be nine forms of management (Wiersum 1986) of land resources. Of these those tried so far, and those being advocated can be presented as a matrix in table 9.4.

In policy terms, we consider the top right hand corner models 2 and 3 to be undesirable and unnecessary. Model 3 is anyway not common, but model 2—departmental forestry on community (revenue) lands is a major element of current policy to be discouraged and abandoned. For reasons of immediate and short-term feasibility, we stress the diagonal of models 1, 5 and 9, while recognising the importance of developing and spreading the approaches of the lower left hand side, with models 4, 7 and 8. The rationale and requirements of these approaches will be outlined in the remainder of this chapter.

Table 9.4: Ownership and management of land for afforestation

Ownership of land → Managing Agency ↓	Forest	Community	Private
Forest Department	Practical to produce livelihood goods for the poor, with social security benefits (1)	Long-term viability of departmental forestry on common lands is in doubt, should be replaced by (5) and (8). (2)	Neither necessary nor desirable. Being tried on tribal lands in Dangs, Gujarat, and in H.P., but has not succeeded (3)
Panchayat	Sharing management and usufruct with co-mmunities as in Ara-bari and Sukhomajri should be tried (4)	To be tried on a large scale wherever village groups or NGOs are capable of manage-ment (5)	Not necessary, but ex-tension and marketing can be organised on a group basis (6)
Private	Large-scale commer-cial leasing of forest land is not desirable but smaller-scale leas-ing to the poor feasi-ble as in BAIF Vansda Project (7)	Being tried as a Tree Patta Scheme. Has good potential if catc-hes and hassles are removed (8)	Farm forestry has an excellent potential. To be extended to RPFs as agro-forestry (9)

9.4 Livelihood Forestry: From Clear-felling to Usufruct-based Trees

Donor agencies in India have so far fought shy of assisting in the rehabilitation of degraded forests. There is no State in which project funds were available on a large-scale for reserved lands. Only from 1988, a pilot project on reserved forest has been taken up in Tamil Nadu. In a few other States like Orissa and Bihar have protected forests been taken up on the condition that these are handed over to the village councils for management in due course. The World Bank assisted States have only a negligible component of social forestry on forest lands. Why this reluctance?

The implementation of social forestry programmes in India has been heavily influenced by the perspectives of foresters and of foreign experts who advise GOI and the donor agencies. Both of them, because of their training and experience, have looked upon trees as timber, to be obtained after clear felling. The charter given to the foreign experts has been that forestry should be for the benefit of the rural poor. They have then tended to see the problem as how to distribute benefits from timber of felled trees to the poor. They have suggested either ownership rights, or control in management, or share in final produce for the poor, implying that these are the only three ways of helping them. In all the three options, trees are raised for the final product to be obtained by felling. Since States and the GOI are reluctant to try either of these three models on forest lands, social forestry has not been extended to them.

The traditional Indian way of looking at trees has, however, been different. As opposed to trees for timber, Indian villagers for centuries have depended on trees for livelihood. There has been little felling. Instead, trees have been valued for the intermediate products they provide. To the extent that trees provided subsistence goods with little market value, and trees were abundant, questions of share or ownership hardly arose. Trees were valued for the diversity of their products and the many ways in which they helped to sustain and secure the livelihoods of the people.

To return to some supposed golden age of natural harmony of people and forests can only be a dream. The institutional and ecological mechanisms which existed till the 19th century for managing the commons and forests without State intervention are now fragmented beyond repair (Guha 1988), and therefore mere surrendering of control over forest lands by the State to local institutions, which are weak, may even hasten their degradation. Forests are now under the control of Forest Departments; people are interested not just in subsistence but also in marketable goods; and trees and tree products are in increasingly short supply. To harmonise these realities we argue for an approach which stresses planting on forest lands, with choice of species as the initial point of intervention, with a mix which will preserve and recreate diversity and strengthen and sustain livelihoods.

There are several arguments for this approach. Compared with departmental forestry on common lands, there are obvious advantages of scale and protection. The ambiguities of ownership which have plagued community forestry would not apply. Forest soils are generally better than the soils on revenue lands. Costs would be lower. The morale of the Forest Department would be high, since the trees would be planted within the territory they control.

9.5 Choice of Species

The major imponderable is whether the poor would really benefit. We consider below questions of environmental impact, participation, rights, information and organisation. At this point we can note that access would be strengthened by choosing species suitable for individual gathering by households; and that benefits would be directly appropriated by the poor through collecting and consuming or selling various MFPs, grasses, fruits and the like. Unlike commercial timber species, relatively low value non-rotational trees for intermediate products would not so much attract the attention of rich farmers and contractors. What people get out of trees can depend more on what is planted than on who manages.

Thus there would be a world of difference between plantation of eucalyptus and of *Prosopis juliflora* on roadsides. Eucalyptus benefits urban markets and industry, whereas *Prosopis* does not only solve the fuelwood problem of poor families, but also generate self-employment for the poor. What is significant about *Prosopis, ber, neem, mahua* or other trees which can be continuously harvested for fuelwood and other intermediate products is that they do not require decisions about market shares between rich and poor. Their usufruct is not of much interest to the rich, or is available to them only through gathering by the poor, so that by default the benefits are available for the poor.

Prosopis juliflora is a neglected tree in conventional forestry. Although the Forest Department ignores it in social forestry projects, it grows naturally on degraded soil. Field studies made by one of the authors in dry areas with low employment opportunities in the slack season like Anantpur in Andhra Pradesh (CIDA 1988), and Mathura in Uttar Pradesh (Saxena 1988) show that *Prosopis* has on its own solved the fuelwood crisis, besides providing employment to many who prune the branches and sell it in urban areas. A study shows that its yield on degraded soils in Bhavnagar was as high as 3 tonnes per ha per year (Patel 1987). *Prosopis* produces double the biomass on similar soils as compared to eucalyptus (Banerji 1986), and yet is considered by the Forest Department to be a "low" value tree. In the Central Board of Forestry Papers (GOI 1987d) it has unfortunately been described as a weed. One may recall that until the first two decades of this century bamboo was also described as a weed, till its use in the paper industry was discovered, which led to its plantation on a large scale.

Another way of looking at this issue of afforestation on public lands is to opt for species which have high proportions of branches and twigs relative to stem wood. Given the inefficiency of administration and "soft" character of the political system, one could generalise that out of a tree the stem goes to the rich and the towns, whereas branches and twigs belong to the poor. The proportions of stem wood and branches calculated for some trees are presented in table 9.5.

Table 9.5: Proportion of stem wood and branches in trees

Species	% in total biomass		Total biomass dry tonnes/ha
	Stem wood & bark	Branches & twigs %	
Eucalyptus	81	19	17.4
Subabul	77	23	23.0
Acacia nilotica	47	53	31.6
Prosopis juliflora	30	70	32.2

(Reddy 1987)

The table indicates the superiority of *Prosopis juliflora* to eucalyptus both on grounds of equity and potential biomass per ha. But despite GOI's clear instructions to discourage eucalyptus on public lands, its percentage in 1986-87 in Uttar Pradesh on non-private lands was still 21.2 per cent whereas *Prosopis* spp. accounted for only 1.8 per cent (IIPO 1988: xiv), although even on technical grounds *Prosopis juliflora* is a more suitable species for the saline/alkaline wastelands of Uttar Pradesh.

Fruit trees such as jack, mango, *jamun,* and tamarind have been important components of the indigenous form of forestry practised by the people. After a brief gestation period fruit trees yield annual harvests of edible biomass on a sustainable and renewable basis. Coconut, for example, besides providing fruit and oil, provides leaves used in thatching huts and supports the large coir industry in the country. More significantly, components of the crown biomass that are harvested from fruit and fodder trees leave the living tree standing to perform its essential ecological functions in soil and water conservation.

A further advantage of planting "trees of the poor" (which are essentially employment augmenting trees, as they require labour for gathering and collection, as opposed to trees which are clear-felled) on forest and revenue lands is the likelihood of improved cooperation. People are reluctant to protect trees which will be auctioned or felled, to the benefit of government, contractors and forest staff. They are much more likely to collaborate in protection of trees from which they, much more than others, are in a position to benefit.

Instead of the old division into production and social forestry, this implies a new unity in livelihood forestry. This reverses the recommendations of the NCA which favoured commercial plantations on forest land, and trees for consumption and subsistence on private land. With livelihood forestry, subsistence and consumption would be met more from forest land, and market demand would be met more from private land. Community and revenue land would have mixed uses, and farmers would also raise multiple-purpose trees for subsistence needs and for income. Many problems would remain, but social forestry on forest lands would be more sustainable than current uses and would serve both the environment and the poor. Using private lands for short rotation products will permit the large area of forest lands to be used for long gestation trees, which enrich the environment and provide a range of products to the poor. For quick benefits to the poor, long gestation trees would be supplemented with an understorey of grasses, bushes and shrubs so as to satisfy their immediate needs. In the absence of bushes and shrubs, large trees like tamarind, jack or *jamun* tend to be hacked for fuelwood, although these should remain to yield their usufructs (Shyam Sunder and Reddy 1986:17).

As we have shown in chapter 2, the likely scenario in 2000 A.D., if no corrective measures are taken, is that there would be wide and yawning gaps between the supply and demand for MFPs, fuelwood and fodder. The 35 mh of private degraded land would only indirectly produce fuelwood or fodder as a byproduct, as it is likely to be targeted to produce timber, pulpwood and other multiple use trees. Farmers are more concerned with their private consumption and incomes, and it is not fair to load upon them national concerns of demand from the poor. This places heavy responsibility on public lands which have to cater to the requirements of the poor.

The poor have suffered in social forestry programmes because they are not organised, and the bureaucracy has failed to deliver to them a share from timber and pulpwood trees. Usufruct-based trees overcome both these problems. Under the new policy suggested by us, technology produces an output which eliminates the need for both social and bureaucratic fine tuning.

9.6 Approach of Donor Agencies

The major donor agencies are gradually realising this, as is evident from the World Bank/USAID mid-term evaluation report (USAID 1988) for Rajasthan, Uttar Pradesh, Himachal Pradesh and Gujarat, and from the SIDA-assisted new Project Documents for Tamil Nadu and Orissa.

The World Bank Document admits that "neither private nor public plantations have been very effective in reducing local village pressure on nearby forest lands. This failure is due primarily to the commercial orientation of plantations on public lands and failure to plan social forestry operations in the context of local land use patterns."

The World Bank Report recognises that the objective of public forestry on community and degraded forests should be environmental and socio-economic concerns of the people. This would be achieved "by using wider spacing, increased sowing of trees and shrubs for low cost continuous fuelwood supply, contour furrow planting, and increased grass and legume production to provide fodder and increase soil and moisture conservation . . . . At present this is constrained by the widespread use of traditional timber-oriented models and management systems on all forms of public forestry which limit intermediate yields in order to maximise final harvests." The report goes on to say that benefit to the poor would flow from such species which yield a lot of twigs, branches, legumes, fodder leaves and MFPs. In this respect, thorn trees serve the poor much more effectively than short rotation commercial species.

The Tamil Nadu Social Forestry Project Phase-II (1988-89 to 1992-93) recognises (para 3.11) market orientation of the private tree growers, and aims at developing appropriate market information for them so that farmers' incomes and value of assests may improve. At the same time, for forest and community lands (para 3.14) the Project lays stress on greater fodder production, bushes and planting of fruit-bearing and MFP-yielding trees.

For the first time reserved forest lands would be taken up under a new programme called interface forestry for meeting (para 5.75) the employment and forest products needs of the adjacent communities. Catchments falling within the reserved forest areas would be treated to increase land productivity. Soil and water conservation, water harvesting, and agro-forestry will all be linked to provide increased benefit to the local people. Active participation of the villagers in planning, implementation and maintenance will be aimed at.

The draft Orissa Social Forestry Project Phase-2 (1988-1993) recommends planting of trees which would yield fruits, MFPs, fodder and fuelwood, on such degraded forest lands which are not to be handed over to village forest committees. Such plantation will not pose any management problem after initial establishment, as being of low value in money terms these will not attract the attention of contractors or the rich.

Thus both the World Bank and SIDA in their latest documents (1988) have favoured a shift towards the policy we advocate, of forestry for livelihoods. Unfortunately these proposals were still under discussion with the States and no change in the existing policy had been pronounced till December, 1988.

9.7 Trees, Livelihoods and the Environment

We shall now discuss the environmental impact of our recommendations separately for public and private lands.

For forest and revenue lands we have recommended livelihood forestry with usufruct-based people-oriented trees (which may sometimes be slow growing, like *mahua*, but may be fast growing like *Prosopis juliflora* or *arjun*) but supplemented by an understorey of quick-growing bushes, grasses and shrubs. This would mean that benefits in the form of fodder and fuel-wood would be quickly available to the poor and would continue for eight to 15 years or so (depending upon silvicultural maturity period of the tree), till the canopy of the main trees closed, preventing sunlight reaching the under-storey. At this time, benefits from the main trees in forms such as leaves, branches and fruit, would start flowing to the poor.

This would provide soils with a good cover of litter. The maintenance of life support systems is a function performed mainly by the crown biomass of trees. It is this component of trees that can contribute positively towards the maintenance of the hydrological and nutrient cycles (Shiva and Bandyopadhyay 1985:36). Trees which provide a lot of leaves, twigs, and branches enrich the soil much better than those which provide poles and timber alone.

The objective of soil and moisture conservation would be better achieved through grasses and shrubs, rather than with plantations (Maithani et al. 1988). In the latter case, there is progressive suppression of the grass growth by the closure of the tree crowns after the first few years of plantation. Leaf litter from plantations is collected by the villagers, and thus does not help in soil/moisture conservation. An understorey of shrubs, grasses and bushes is more suitable for site stabilization and reduction of run-off, given the practical conditions of acute shortage of fodder in India (USAID 1988).

Conventional forestry based on clear felling disrupts the annual circulation of nutrients, and increases soil erosion (Spurr and Barnes 1980:240). Monoculture plantation forestry is also prone to pest attack. Thus eucalyptus plantations in Kerala raised after clearfelling dense green and deciduous forests have been devastated by fungal diseases, and the consequent low productivity defeated the very purpose for which they had been raised (Nair 1985:15). Similar was the experience of teak plantations in north Bastar, Madhya Pradesh (Anderson and Huber 1988:63) and of pepper and carda-mom plantations in the Western Ghats (Gadgil 1985:316). On the other hand, mixed forests draw and give nutrients to the soil at different stages of their growth, and hence are ecologically far more beneficial than plantations (NWDB 1987b:6). As opposed to timber, which is a product of the dead tree, we have emphasized products of the living tree—fruits, nuts, flowers and twigs.

Sometimes land is too degraded and has little soil to support trees, spe-cially in arid and semi-arid areas. Tree growth is so slow that barely one tonne of wood gets added per hectare per year. This is then not sufficient to cover the cost of seedlings, planting and protection. But such lands can often support improved varieties of grasses (Nimbkar 1988). Even with scanty and irregular rains 4 to 5 tonnes of dry matter from stylosanthes and Cenchenn (Anjan) grasses can be produced from one hectare of such waste land. Besides, grass cover can reduce run-off of rain and soil loss. It also starts yielding income within two years. Despite suitability of grass plantation on degraded lands on technical grounds, an official paper from Maharashtra, presented in the seminar organised by BAIF at Pune in June 1988, admitted that trees were being planted indiscriminately even where soil was less than 30 cm in depth. Only 45 per cent of land taken up under social forestry in Maharashtra qualifies for tree plantation as a technical solution. The remaining 55 per cent required revegetation through grasses, legumes and soil bunding, yet only 3 per cent of sites were actually given this treatment. Rather, trees were being planted on such soils leading to further soil erosion. Such is the fascination of the F.D. for timber and non-browsable species that they ignore their own technical prescriptions.

In sum, non-rotational trees which provide permanent cover, and give recurrent annual yields in forms such as mulch, leaves and wild fruits com-bined with grasses, bushes and shrubs are environmentally superior to raising timber trees which have their value only in the stem.

Next we take up the impact on environment of afforestation on private lands.

Trees on farmbunds serve as a windbreak, and thus reduce soil loss. Likewise the soil binding effect of tree roots serves to reduce erosion from both wind and water action. Therefore strip and interplanting activity has a positive effect in reducing soil erosion.

When trees are planted along with annual crops, the net effect on produc-tion is complex, depending upon root competition, shading effects, and air circulation. These factors are not adequately understood in the field by foresters in India (USAID 1988), and therefore agroforestry has sometimes reduced crop yields. There is need for better research and extension in this direction.

Block plantations on previously barren lands have a favourable environ-mental effect, but are of questionable benefit where trees replace crops. In such cases site preparation often involves considerable earthwork and removal of competing vegetation. The soil surface is thus exposed to erosion. Grasses and shrubs could stabilise the sites, but close plantation kills grasses and understorey growth.

During the early stages of their growth, fast-growing trees draw more minerals and nutrients from the soil, than they replenish. After some years their rate of growth declines, and so does the drawal of nutrients. Thus even fast-growing trees may recycle minerals if allowed to continue beyond the silvicultural maturity period. But economic considerations demand felling at this stage, as their rate of physical growth starts declining. Thus there is a conflict between economic and environmental benefits from trees.

We discussed the success of Group Farm Forestry Programme in West Bengal (sec. 8.2) in which farmers planted eucalyptus on degraded allotted lands, to get cash income from the pole crop. The West Bengal Government later realised (GOWB 1988b:20) the shortcomings of the existing model of species selection. First, the steep fall in pole prices adversely affected small farmers. Second, as eucalyptus did not yield twigs and branches for fuelwood, the poor collected its leaf litter for burning, with the result that soil enrichment did not take place. Thus collection of leaf litter from private trees led to a conflict between short- and long-term interest of the poor tree owners. The West Bengal Government was considering (1988) another technical model of raising multi-tier crop of shrubs, bushes, fodder grasses and trees for multiple use, which besides providing cash would also provide immediate food, fuel and grasses, and at the same time prevent soil run-off and erosion.

A fundamental difference between afforestation on public and private lands is that whereas the latter lands are amenable to intensive care and management, public lands receive extensive management only. This means that soil enrichment on private lands can be not only through trees, but also through manure and water. Because such treatment is difficult for public lands for reasons of costs and staff time, the need to discourage plantation of timber trees is paramount for public lands, as value from these trees is realised only through felling.

9.8 Peoples' Participation

"Peoples' participation" has become a standard rhetoric in India today. Different actors interpret it differently. One view is that participation would be easy to achieve if secure private land rights are given (Chowdhry 1985:4; NWDB 1986b:15 & 20). Staff engaged on project implementation have a different approach. They understand participation as getting people to agree to and go along with a project which has already been designed for them, or to get support of a few leaders (Mahony 1987:13). "I manage, you participate", has been the dominant underlying principle behind government projects (Shingi et al. 1986). These have tended to try to make people aware of their responsibility towards environment and future generations by exhorting them not to cut trees, or to sell their goats. People's participation is then expressed not in a manner which would establish their rights over land or its produce. The important question is, participation for whose benefit, and on what terms?

The FAO (1982) defines peoples' participation as "the process by which the rural poor are able to organise themselves and, through their own organisation, are able to identify their own needs, share in the design, implementation and evaluation of the participatory action." Thus various elements of participation are decision making at various stages, control and management of funds, share in usufruct and final produce, and ownership.

While agreeing with the definition given by the FAO, we fear that transferring decision making, control and management on forest lands on a large scale to the people or panchayats may not be acceptable to governments. The capability of village organisations has to be improved first through joint management schemes, as in Sukhomajri and Arabari. What is easier to achieve, given the present policies of governments, is to enable people to have usufruct of intermediate and final products, rather than try to establish communal claims of ownership or full control over forest lands.

Moreover, the best organisation of management will depend on local conditions; and the balance of advantage to the poorer as between Forest Department management and panchayat management of trees will vary. It is by no means automatic that the poor will be better off with panchayat management, especially if it entails trees for commercial pulpwood, poles or urban fuelwood, as shown by the panchayat-run woodlots in Gujarat and Tamil Nadu. Where panchayats are dominated by the village elite, it may be safer to transfer the responsibility of afforestation to a NGO. In backward and tribal South Bihar a report could state that, "Concepts like representation, participation and decision making are completely alien to the rural women of the under-privileged communities" (GOB 1987:13). Whether this is so, or merely reflects an official view, might deserve deeper investigation. But what was crucial to rural women of Bihar was better access to forests for collection of fuelwood and minor forest products. Sharing management of forest lands with the people is an important goal, as we have argued (sections 7.3 and 9.2), but the process will proceed at different paces in different conditions. In the meantime, what is essential is to develop mixed forests on forest lands to meet their livelihood needs. Practical political economy considerations suggest that technology is easier to change than institutions.

Referring back to table 9.4, various elements of participation and disposal of produce in the models (1), (5) and (9), if our recommendations are accepted, would be as shown in table 9.6.

To sum up, the crucial elements are items 4 and 5—who gets the intermediate and final products. Item 3—control and management sharing schemes—would be facilitated and influenced by what is planned for items 4 and 5.

Thus, complete control by the people on decision making on public lands is an ideal which can be achieved in stages. The initial point of intervention is

Table 9.6: Elements of people's participation

Element	Type of land		
	Forest	Revenue under community management	Private
1. Ownership of produce	People	Community	Farmer
2. Main source of funds	Govt.	Govt.	Private/banks/Govt. support
3. Control/ management	Community/Govt.	Panchayat/village group/NGO	Farmer
4. Who gets intermediate products	People (These would be higher if socially useful trees, rather than timber oriented trees are planted)	People	Farmer
5. Disposal of final produce	Auction to be avoided if non-rotational or fruit, fodder, & fuelwood species, as opposed to eucalyptus & teak are planted		For income and consumption
6. Responsibility for maintenance	Govt./People	Panchayat/village group	Farmer

Note: Even usufruct based trees need disposal, albiet after they have for decades given ample benefits to the poor through gathering. Therefore clear orders are needed about the distribution of timber from trees on public lands, such as tamarind or jack. This has already been discussed in section 7.6.

labour-intensive trees and sharing schemes which strengthen peoples' organisations, and it would then be possible to transfer greater management responsibility to them.

9.9 Women

The problems of women have already been documented in sections 3.3, 7.1, 7.2, 7.4 and 8.4. We are concerned here with solutions. These can be listed:
— There should be strict enforcement of labour laws, especially as regards minimum wages, both when women work as wage employees on nursery and plantation sites, and when they are employed by contractors to collect tendu leaves and other MFPs. Government should take a lead in this respect and be a model employer for its own departmental works.
— Given the sex segregated and hierarchical nature of Indian society, separate women's organisations and staff are needed to work among women, to instil confidence in them, so that they will fight for their rights.
— Each social forestry project should specifically consider the role of women at the project design stage, and state in what way the project is going to help them, apart from exploiting their cheap labour. Projects should aim at giving new skills to women, like training them in operating nurseries.

— More women need to be recruited to executive positions in projects. Without this even existing orders may not get implemented. For instance, out of 57,546 *pattas* given in Uttar Pradesh only 2,949 (5 per cent) went to women, despite government instructions that 30 per cent of *pattas* should go to women (Tripathi 1988). In Bihar a woman was not even aware that she had been elected as a member of the Village Forest Committee (GOB 1987:13).
— Discriminatory land laws which prohibit women from owning land should be changed.
— A beginning can be made by making women owners of land, where new tenurial rights are being created, as on wastelands. Such a limited measure is likely to escape male hostility as the distribution of existing wealth is not involved. It may be pointed out here that section 3(c) of the Tree *Patta* guidelines of the Government of India, which states that "minors and persons who are not capable of planting and looking after the plants themselves may not be considered" is capable of being interpreted against the interests of women. One hopes this does not happen.
— Government should learn from the experience (Saxena 1987a) of NGOs, like Rural Development Agency (West Bengal), Manipur Adult Education Association (Manipur), Anand Niketan (Gujarat), Gram Bharti (Bihar), Myrada (Karnataka), Antyodaya Sangh (Tamil Nadu), and CROSS and BCT (Andhra Pradesh) who have achieved excellent results in helping women to become self-reliant through forestry. After all, Government cannot abdicate to the NGOs its basic responsibility of providing equality of rights and opportunity to women.

9.10 Primacy of Rights

Throughout our discussion in chapters 7 and 8 we have pointed out that people's rights of access and their rights to tree products are restricted, vague, or not known to them. We shall now pick up policy issues regarding rights separately for public and private lands.

PUBLIC LANDS

As regards forest lands, "rights" (now sometimes called "concessions" in official literature) of forest dwellers on forest lands, although well defined in the Forest Settlement Volumes are not publicised, nor is the help of the NGOs enlisted in their implementation. Sharing arrangements in social security plantations or community forestry schemes are ill-defined or not publicised, or poorly implemented. There appears to be general reluctance on the part of the field machinery to define clearly what people are to get, at what time, and at what price, in exchange for participation expected of them (ILO 1987:44). But participation of the poor is improbable unless their benefits are secure.

Therefore, we suggest that outside each forest coupe or social forestry plantation there should be a notice board publicising what rights people have as regards collection. The colonial tradition of secrecy or a wide gap between policy and implementation must be given up. A simple notice that, "these trees belong to the community, and not to government", may in itself, change peoples' attitude towards panchayat woodlots. Where rights are individualistic in nature, as in social security schemes, agreements must be entered in writing with the beneficiaries informing them about their entitlement. Traditional rights to forest lands must be brought into the framework of national legal system (Raintree 1987:345) by incorporating these rights within the Indian Forest Act. The reverse seems to be happening, as the new Forest Policy and the amendments to the Forest Conservation Act have considerably abridged these rights.

As we have seen (sections 7.2 and 8.5) people's rights to trees and markets have often been curtailed. Such restrictions, justified in the name of preventing tribal exploitation, create excellent opportunities for private traders and bureaucracy to extract "suitable" rents for "services rendered". Practical political economy considerations point out that government is incapable of effectively administer complete control. It is better for government to regulate private trade, and to act as a watchdog rather than try to eliminate it. Monopoly purchase by government requires sustained political support and excellent bureaucratic machinery. It is difficult to ensure these over a long period and hence nationalisation has often increased exploitation of the poor.

PRIVATE LANDS

Private forestry requires security of land and tree tenure, and secure access to markets. Improving marketing of wood and tree products is an important area of public policy initiative in its own right (sec. 8.6). However, a great source of market imperfections in tree product markets is the legal and procedural framework which makes cutting and selling privately owned trees so difficult, irksome and complicated, besides unremunerative. Therefore we suggest that, first of all these restrictive laws must be abolished.

Second, marketing should be recognised as an important aspect of tree cropping. The contrast between tree marketing and agricultural crop marketing is sharp: for marketing agricultural products, the State governments have set up vast infrastructure; remunerative procurement prices are announced several months in advance of the crop; generous subsidies are inbuilt into the system of government purchase which absorbs surplus and stabilises price; market yards have been set up to reduce exploitation; and middleman's commission has been fixed. None of these interventions have been made with tree marketing. To the contrary, markets for forest products are dominated by cartels, shrouded in secrecy, and impeded by legal bottlenecks.

Third, assessment of future demand, supply and prices, separately for each species, should be made by competent organisations, and given due publicity. This will help small and marginal farmers to decide what to plant.

For all its imponderables, given the long gestation periods of trees, long-term forecasting should be able to play a useful part.

Fourth, government interventions should be designed to safeguard the interests of small farmers. Five measures can be proposed:

1) Promoting marketing organisations to compete with but not eliminate private trade, as has been done for agriculture,

2) Informing tree farmers about the primary and secondary markets, prevalent prices, marketing practices and laws,

3) Linking farmers with industries, in ways similar to the linking of poplar growing farmers with a match factory in north Uttar Pradesh (Chatterjee 1987).

4) Stopping subsidies on government supply of wood to industries, thereby forcing industry to buy from the farmers at a remunerative price.

5) Reviewing the policy of liberal imports of pulpwood, as imports compete with farmers' production and depress its prices.

Finally, research, extension, and seedling supplies should be geared towards diversification, and meeting RPFs' own priorities, so that they can have a range of types of trees on their land, meeting various needs, and spreading the risk of the collapse of any one market. Research is needed to identify other short-rotation, high-value species besides eucalyptus.

The Forest Department would do well to give up its resistance to species which are already quite popular with the farmers, like fruits, palm and coconut. A visiting CIDA team in Andhra Pradesh was told (1988) that a district like Vishakhapatnam could easily absorb 10 million additional seedlings in a year if these and other grafted varieties could be supplied. To this a senior forester replied, "We are not a horticulture department; we can only promote woody species." On the other hand, F.D. in Rajasthan popularised grafted Ber (*Zizyphus mauritania*), a fruit variety, and it proved to be an instant success with the farmers. It had the advantage of high profitability, and returns to farmers' investment start flowing in from the second year of investment (USAID 1988). Diversification and adaptability in the Forest Department itself are required to enable RPFs to diversify and become more adaptable.

9.11 Administrative Structure

The debate "who loses and who gains" from an economic activity is often couched in conspiratorial terms; the neglect and the harm done to the poor is generally explained (Guha 1983:1945) in terms of compulsions of a capitalist State or the hold that the rich have over policy and delivery. While the explanatory power of social structure is not to be denied, other important factors are sometimes lost sight of. Administrative failures have their own autonomy and do not always stem from class bias. The reasons for slow progress of development projects are often unromantic and mundane. Where forestry has not helped the poor, part of the explanation can be sought in administrative structures and organisational weaknesses.

In 1985 policy formulation in social forestry was shifted from the Ministry of Environment and Forests to the National Wastelands Development Board (NWDB), whereas other traditional functions and control over the State Forest Departments continued to be exercised by the Ministry. This created confusion as clear division of responsibility between the two organisations did not exist. There were rumours in 1988 that the NWDB would be replaced by a Technology Mission which would evolve standardised solutions for different types of wastelands. Its formation had been delayed because another group of policy makers wanted to convert forest lands into national ecological parks with no responsibility towards peoples' needs. The failure to achieve the target of afforestation of 5 m ha a year was thus seen by the Government of India as an organisational failure; hence the desire to create a new structure. Not much effort has been made till late 1988 to re-examine the policy framework and redefine the terms of interaction between forests and the people.

At the same time, the influence of foresters on policy making and execution had been declining, causing widespread resentment and frustration in their ranks. This reduced their output. Some States have experimented by transferring afforestation funds to other departments, but it has not worked. Then, although implementation was again handed over to the F.D., control over release of funds was retained by several departments. The result has been that a forest official could, in 1988, receive funds from up to eight different departments, each having its own priorities and set of schemes. It has been quite common to have different prices for the same seedlings in the same area, or varying cost estimates for protection. Release of funds has also become *ad hoc* (ILO, 1988:10).

Half of the funds for the programme come from the Department of Rural Development. This is a part of the employment generation budget, which by its very nature is biased in favour of creating public assets in which the poor benefit through wage employment only. Although in 1986 the Ministry of Rural Development agreed to the utilisation of such funds for self-employment of the poor, yet successful implementation required a different degree of coordination between the Forest, Rural Development and Revenue Departments at the field level. Non-utilisation of the total budgeted amount and low survival rates for trees were direct results of such difficulties. During the two years 1985-87 only 16 per cent of NREP/RLEGP funds could be spent on social forestry despite clear instructions that a minimum of 25 per cent of NREP/RLEGP budgets should be spent on afforestation. This meant underspending of about Rs 200 crores on forestry. It would simplify matters if all forestry funds were pooled and amalgamated with each other with a common set of objectives.

In many States, following the recommendation of the NCA, most productive forest areas have been transferred to the Forest Development Corporations. In some others, the FDCs are not responsible for plantation, but for exploitation of the existing assets. In either case, it is in the interest of the corporations to promote commercial plantations. The imperatives of the new environment and livelihood oriented forest policy would require drastic changes in their charter. Our suggestion is to convert them into exclusive MFPs, Fodder and Fuelwood Development Corporations, and ban commercial plantations on forest lands.

Organisational questions such as these are important, but secondary to policy. Flirting with various forms of organisation, or control over funds, can divert attention from policy issues. Unfortunately, the new Forest Policy, which remained in the making for 15 years, has not given any clear direction, either to policy or to organisational matters.

9.12 Administration and Implementability

Policies which are unimplementable are bad policies. In this sense, many apparently good policies and programmes in India have been bad. The question has to be asked: how in practical political and administrative terms could policies for forests and trees which put poor people first realistically be implemented?

A start to answering this question can be sought in the interests and motivation of officials. Historically, the ethos of the Forest Department has been oriented towards estate management and territorial control. Laws have been framed to meet these objectives. People and their cattle have been perceived as a threat to the integrity of the forest "empire". The rationale for excluding and controlling people changes: in the plantation phase, it was to protect the forests in order to supply industrial raw material and raise State revenue; more recently, it has been to protect the environment.

At the same time, the integrity of the forests has been severely compromised through massive deforestation in which the culprits and beneficiaries have all too often been contractors and petty officials themselves. The natural reflex, though, has been to blame the people. That they have played a part in deforestation is not in dispute. But to blame them is a convenient diversion. Moreover, the prescription which follows is counterproductive. The prescription has not been, as we argue it should be, policies to meet people's needs for forest products such as fodder, MFPs, and fuelwood. It has been to demand and impose more stringent laws, with military style controls, compulsory castration of bulls, banning people from entering forests, and curtailing the rights and concessions of forest dwellers. These measures have their roots in the bureaucratic psyche which believes in the power of the stick and in rewards to those who wield it.

In this syndrome, power is all important. People are not trusted. Officials are conservative and hesitate to give secure benefits to people. They may even argue that alienating government resources would give rise to audit objections. Information is withheld from people as to what they are and are not legally permitted to do. Actual or supposed rules are invoked by low-level staff to assert their authority and to exact rents.

Nor are these attitudes confined to forest land or foresters. In private conversation, foresters admit that restrictions on felling and sale of trees from private lands affect farmers' interests; but they justify such laws help them to control theft from forest lands. Even where forest lands are not involved, secure land rights are deliberately not given because it is feared that the land would be used not for forestry but for agriculture. Imperfections in these rights have already been noted in tree *patta* and other similar schemes (sections 8.4 and 8.8). One of the authors visited a village in district Kurnool in Andhra Pradesh where tribals were settled on land obtained from surplus ceiling. When the project authorities were questioned about legal rights to land, it transpired that although government had issued orders for transfer of land to the tribals, this had been deliberately not implemented so that they would remain under the control of the Forest Department and accept forestry as the land use.

In practice, reflexes like these are often unenforceable and self-defeating as well as contrary to the interests of the poor. Strict regulations sometimes imply impossible burdens of work. To enforce the transit laws in District Meerut in Uttar Pradesh, one of the authors calculated that at least 300 permissions would need to be given every day by the department, if all wood movement took place as envisaged under the law. Nor have transit restrictions prevented continuing deforestation. But by far the most damaging effects of draconian rules are the disincentives which discourage the poor from planting trees. Advocated and justified in the name of protecting and promoting trees and the environment, these laws and regulations deter planting and provoke felling.

For new sustainable livelihood and poor-people-first-policies to be implemented requires two main preconditions. The first is awareness. Unless they see things differently, forest officials will, like their predecessors, continue to believe in the "tougher top-down" approach. Political leaders are also often not aware of critical elements in policy, and are liable to see foreign-aided projects as bringing jeeps, funds and new jobs for their unemployed friends and relatives, rather than helping the poor. How awareness, perceptions and behaviour can change will be taken up in chapter 10 (sec. 10.4). Suffice it here to say that there are grounds for hope.

The second precondition is countervailing power and pressure. Left to itself, bureaucracy in India cannot be relied on to promote reforms which effectively support the rural poor. But where there is organised political pressure from below, and direction from above, the bureaucratic machinery has sometimes responded well to the challenge. There are excellent examples of individuals who, having got clear political directions, have done exceedingly well in the implementation of, say, the Tenancy Reforms in West Bengal or subsidised rice distribution in Andhra Pradesh. The social forestry programmes of West Bengal, where there is strong political organisation on behalf of the poor at the local level, and where leadership has been sustained and determined, are another encouraging example. And young forestry officers take pride in their extension skill rather than their regulatory feats.

In promoting the interests of the poor, and applying pressures on forest departments, NGOs have shown themselves a potent force. They vary enormously in size, from one or two individuals to several hundred, and in orientation and effectiveness. But many have succeeded in promoting imaginative programmes, and also in mobilising action in support of the rights of forest dwellers.

For poor-people-first forestry, both preconditions are needed. Officials who want to change also need external pressures to enable them to do so, and to legitimate their new behaviour. NGOs and people need information about schemes and procedures. They also need to be able to document the bad effects of complicated laws and restrictive practices, and to bring these to the notice of senior officials, policy-makers, and political leaders. Those who wish to put poor people first can form alliances and together achieve much more than they could in isolation.

The policy needed is often described as "bottom-up", decentralised, differentiated according to local conditions, participatory in involving the people and especially the poor in deciding what should be done, and allowing people to define and realise their enlightened self-interest. Such an approach promotes self-reliance and fits better with people's self-respect and aspirations. The geographical dispersal of degraded lands too calls for decentralised planning and decision making structures. Working with people like this requires an open and responsive administration based on mutual trust.

It was difficult to achieve this in the past as the imperatives of industrial forestry meant "keeping people out but allowing contractors in" (Shepherd 1986:19). Under the new policy, foresters would have new roles, in extension, in providing choice of species, in marketing support, and in disseminating information. This new Charter should itself lead to a new form of cooperation between the people and the staff.

The existing ethos of the Forest Department has been to define forest-people interaction as a zero-sum game; forests can be protected only when people lose, and any gain to the people is at the cost of forest protection. In this scenario, both lose. The challenge is to convert this into a win-win game. This requires a new outlook and new strategies.

It is not utopianism, but realism, that makes us believe in this way forward: to work with the people, to satisfy their demands, to win their confidence, and thus to save land and forest from further denudation while enhancing their self-reliant livelihoods. Putting poor people first is not being romantic; it is the best way to secure both social and environmental objectives.

PART FOUR

Practical Strategy

CHAPTER TEN

Analysis and Action

ABSTRACT

Policies to put in the hands of the poor secure command over water and trees can be analysed in terms of practical political economy, of who gains who loses. For 17 of the 20 main measures advocated, there are gains to the rural rich and less poor as well as to the poorer, promising a solid rural interest group with political clout, and opportunities for politicians to gain popularity by supporting them.

Evaluated in terms of cost-effectiveness, political and administrative feasibility, scale, speed, sustainability and equity, the measures separate into four clusters: the beautiful and equitable but small and slow; those requiring continuing administration and maintenance; zipper programmes needing an intensive short-term local effort; and legal and administrative changes to rules and restrictions which apply over large areas.

The need for and potential of such widespread and fast changes are the most important single outcome of this book. Opportunities in lift irrigation include a progressive HP-linked flat power tariff, and abolition of licensing and spacing regulations in WA areas. With trees, they include the abolition of all restriction on harvesting trees on private land, and of transit and sale restrictions. One advantage of abolishing rules is reducing hassle by officials and the extraction of rents from the poorer.

Field officials often stand to lose. Conditions necessary for success are therefore clearly established rights, massive information campaigns about those rights, and organisation.

Finally, change depends on individual choice and action, and imagination, energy and courage. The reversals required to put water and trees in the hands of the poor are feasible; for them to occur soon requires insight and decision by those in positions of power.

The purpose of this book is practical. We have tried through analysis and evidence to generate policy. Chapter 1 argued that besides income, poor rural people have a hierarchy of three priorities—subsistence, security, and self-respect—and that lift irrigation and trees can often fit these priorities well. Chapter 2 showed how vast are the resource potentials of water from lift irrigation and of biomass from growing trees on wasteland, and that irrigation water, wood and various tree products have risen in value. Moreover, these resources and potentials are abundant in the same geographical areas as concentrations of rural poverty. In chapter 3 we showed that with normal development the benefits of these resources or potentials would be captured mainly by the rich and less poor. Considerations of practical political economy suggested that for more of the benefits to go to the poorer requires that those who are powerful and less poor are not made worse off, or are induced to accept their loss. In chapters 4 and 5 we then applied this approach to lift irrigation, and in chapters 7 and 8 to public and private lands and trees, concluding in chapters 6 and 9 respectively with practical implications for policy.

In this final chapter we review the feasibility first of current anti-poverty programmes, and then of our proposals, assessing their relative strengths, and identifying the importance for the poor of rights, information and organisation, and for professionals of awareness and commitment.

10.1 The Feasibility of Current Anti-Poverty Programmes

In chapter 1, we noted that administered anti-poverty programmes in the past and present include three types: land reforms; asset provision; and income and consumption support.

In the short term, the immediate needs of the desperate poor are best served by programmes of the third type, providing direct income and consumption, whether through employment remunerated in cash or kind, through subsidised food, or through social security. Those programmes which provide employment include the National Rural Employment Programme and the Rural Landless Employment Guarantee Programme. To the extent that these give employment and income at times of the year when the desperate poor lack work and are at their poorest, they meet some of their most basic needs. They reduce their suffering and help them to avoid becoming poorer— whether through indebtedness, sale or mortgage of assets, seasonal rural migration, or bonding their future labour—so that when better times come they can start again with their assets, however meagre, intact. Similarly, the programmes which subsidise consumption by the poor or which provide social security, for example pensions to widows, help to provide survival floors or safety nets. Whatever their defects, schemes such as these will always be needed for the desperate poor.

In themselves, though, these welfare support programmes do not provide for upward ratchet effects, that is, for stable and sustainable upward shifts in earning capacity, security and self-respect. For these, land reform and the IRDP have been the main thrusts, in each case with the objective of transferring an income-earning asset. As these have run into problems, so official responses have varied. Efforts at land reform continue, but tend to be played down. Efforts at non-land asset transfer, through the IRDP, have in contrast been redoubled. Much greater resources have been provided and used in "strengthening" the implementation machinery, and in attempting to manage and monitor the programme better. Costs have been high and benefits low: the Prime Minister himself publicly confessed in a workshop of district magistrates in Jaipur in June 1988 that 70 per cent of the resources earmarked for anti-poverty programmes are used up by the implementation machinery itself; and later, in November, that over 85 per cent of the funds allocated for development programmes never reach the people they are intended to assist (*TOI*, New Delhi, 2.11.1988). The cost-effectiveness of such programmes of asset transfer is, to say the least, questionable.

These shortcomings are less surprising when seen in the light of the development of the Indian political system since the late 1950s. The middle and large landholders all over the country, but especially in the northern belt, are better organised politically today than they were in the aftermath of Independence; and the present ruling elite is perhaps less politically strong and independent of local elites than was the Congress led by Nehru, and less committed to a major redistribution of land. Low-level government staff are less well paid and more dependent on the "rents" they can extract from their official positions.

In these conditions, it is futile, without countervailing power and pressure groups of the poor, to hope for massive, large-scale livelihood improvements from land reform, the IRDP, or other directly administered asset transfer. Such programmes can be marginally improved through administrative reforms, through better public information, and through the activities of NGOs. Some political commitment and administrative will can also fairly be hoped for, to target the anti-poverty programmes better, and to consolidate whatever has been gained from land reforms and the IRDP so far. In part this can be done by hooking in to measures outlined in chapters 6 and 9. In general, though, the main opportunities we see are in policies and programmes which are politically less vulnerable to subversion. These can, as we shall now argue, be sought in livelihood strategies aimed to put in the hands of the poor secure command over water and trees.

10.2 Gainer and Losers: Practical Political Economy

In chapter 3 (sec. 3.4) we argued for practical political economy, an approach which seeks feasibility either by choosing measures from which none would lose, or by ensuring countervailing power to persuade losers to accept their losses. The principal measures proposed in this book can, just like land reform and the IRDP, be analysed in terms of who in practice gains, or is likely to gain, and who in practice loses, or is likely to lose. Twenty main measures, cross-referenced to the relevant sections, are given in table 10.1.

There are many actors and many interest groups. A more detailed analysis might include senior officials, local politicians, and contractors. Their concerns vary and depend partly on local conditions, connections, and personalities. For purposes of generalisation, it is less difficult to consider the three other key groups: lower-level officials; the rural rich and less poor; and the rural poorer. Our assessment of the degree to which these are or would be gainers or losers from our main proposals is given in table 10.1.

Table 10.1: Proposed measures and some gainers and losers

	Section nos.	Proposed measures	Field-level officials	Rural rich and less poor	Rural poorer
L	6.3	Flat rate power tariff	– –	+	+ + +
I	6.3	Progressive flat rate power tariff	– –	–	+ + + +
F	6.4	Improved quality of power supply (some			
T		WS areas)	0	+ +	+ +
I	6.4	Restriction of power supply (some WS areas)	–/+	–/+	–/+
R	6.5	Saturation: Intensive Groundwater Deve-			
R		lopment Programme (some WA areas)	0	+ +	+ + +
I	6.7	Abolition of spacing and licensing norms			
G		(WA areas)	– –	+	+ + +
A	6.6	NGO-induced RPF groups (WS areas)	0	–	+ +
T	6.2	Improving pumping efficiencies	0	+ +	+
I	6.4	Rapid rural electrification	0	+ +	+ +
O	4.4	Landless LI groups (WA areas)	0	0	+ + +
N					
	9.4,9.5	Livelihood forestry on forest lands	– –	+	+ + +
	7.3	Social security schemes on forest lands	+	0	+ +
	7.3,9.2	Community protection schemes	– –	+	+ +
	7.4,7.6	NGOs and single village organisations in			
T		community forestry	–	+	+ +
R	8.5	Abolition of all cutting, transit and sale			
E		restrictions on private land	– –	+ +	+ + +
E	8.4	Clear land title to the poor	–	0	+ +
S	8.8	Tree *patta* schemes	+	–	+ +
	8.7	RPF farm and agro-forestry	+	0	+ + +
	7.2,9.10	Information on rights and marketing	– –	+	+ + +
	8.7	Landless and MF nurseries	0	+	+ + +
O	1.1	Land reforms (theory)	0	– –	+ + + +
T	1.1,10.1	(practice)	+	0/–	0/+
H	1.1	IRDP (theory)	0	0	+ + + +
E	1.1,10.1	(practice)	+	+	+/0/–
R					

+ = gain   – = loss   0 = neutral

Note: Since the purpose of the table is to assess feasibility, the ratings assume implementation. The +, 0 and – symbols indicate change relative to the present. Thus one + for the rural rich and less poor represents a bigger absolute gain than one + for the rural poor.

Table 10.1 indicates that in our judgement the rural poorer would gain in every case except that of restricted but high quality power supplies in WS areas. In that case, both short-term losses and long-term gains would be shared with the rich and less poor. Significantly, it is only with three measures —progressive flat rate power tariffs, groups in WS areas, and tree *patta* schemes—that the rural rich and less poor stand to lose, although not necessarily always. In the other 17 cases, both groups stand to gain. This promises a solid rural interest group of rich and poor with potential political clout. Political leaders might then find in these measures a basis for broad popularity and support.

The major losers are lower-level officials. Less hassle for the poorer means less power and less income for the hassler. The abolition of rules and regulations hurts petty officials. Abolition of pro-rata electricity tariffs removes the rents they exact for winking at pilferage. Relaxing spacing and licensing rules for wells removes another opportunity for securing payments for turning a blind eye. Giving clear land title to the poor would reduce the power and profit of those who gain from current uncertainties. Abolishing cutting and transit restrictions, and information about farmers' rights to harvest and move trees and tree products, would reduce the power and incomes of police and forest officials.

Higher up the scale, gainers and losers are harder to assess. Contractors profit from the illicit felling of trees. It is widely believed that politicians and forest officials at various levels profit both from felling and from the threatened enforcement of restrictions. To the extent that they exist, entrenched interests of this sort will be an obstacle.

A most hopeful aspect is that politicians stand to gain widespread support from their electorates if they espouse these reforms as their own, and promote their implementation. For instance, the 1987 change to a progressive flat power tariff in Gujarat generated massive good will for the government, especially amongst the poor. The same can be said about Mr. N.T. Ramarao's decision, early in his career as the Chief Minister of Andhra Pradesh, to switch from a pro-rata power tariff to low flat rates. In the case of trees too, the Left Front government of West Bengal has gained considerable political mileage from its early successes with farm forestry programmes on *patta* lands, as has the Gujarat government from its 5,000-odd village woodlots and social security forestry for the tribals.

Politicians sometimes stand to lose from more honest administration, but this can be at least partially offset by gains in goodwill, popularity and credibility with the electorate. In most cases, the rural rich and less poor stand to gain, and the gains of the poorer rural majority from the sum of these twenty measures are so large and so consistent that they should ensure support and votes to any leader who adopts, advocates and oversees their implementation. Although it will vary place by place, there is then nothing monolithic, and much that is hopeful, about the response and support of rural people and politicians. The main problem, to be taken up below (in section 10.4), is the lower-level staff who stand to lose.

10.3 Policies and Programmes Assessed

To gain sustainable livelihoods from the vast potentials of lift irrigation and of trees, the poor need secure access to water, trees and remunerative work, and full and free rights to trees as assets. The proposals that have emerged from our analysis have in common that they are designed to assure that access and those rights.

In many other respects, though, they differ. To highlight these differences, we will evaluate them according to six criteria, with benefits taken as sustainable and adequate livelihoods for the poorer, with access and assets to assure them of food, income, security and self-respect:

1) *Cost-effectiveness.* The cost side of cost-effectiveness includes administrative as well as financial costs. Administrative capacity is treated as a scarce resource. A highly cost-effective measure is therefore sparing in administration and in finance. Thus tariff changes and abolition of harvesting and transit restrictions for privately grown trees are highly cost-effective, in contrast with NGOs' groups for lift irrigation and creating new organisations in community forestry.

2) *Political and administrative feasibility.* This is the sum of an assessment in terms of practical political economy, related to who gains and who loses, and whether a measure will be supported and strengthened or hindered and subverted by parties affected other than the poorer. Political and administrative feasibility is high with flat tariffs and with landless and marginal farmers' nurseries, and low with landless LI groups and land reform.

3) *Scale.* This refers to the potential scale of implementation and impact, high with tariff and power supply changes and livelihood forestry on forest land, and low with landless groups and with social security forestry.

4) *Speed.* This is the speed of impact which varies from very high with changes to tariff systems, abolition of restrictions and community protection, to low with RPF groups in WS areas and NGOs and tree *patta* schemes.

5) *Sustainability.* This includes technical, social, administrative, and political sustainability, high with the Integrated Groundwater Development Programme and with livelihood forestry on forest lands once these have been established, and low with landless lift irrigation groups.

6) *Equity.* This indicates the degree to which the poorer who are affected benefit in absolute terms, very high with the progressive flat tariff and RPF farm and agro-forestry, and medium with pumping efficiencies.

It is at once evident from table 10.2 that the measures separate out into clusters.

One cluster of approaches is beautiful, but necessarily small in scale, slow to implement, and difficult to sustain unless well and patiently managed. There are typical trade-offs here between speed and scale on the one hand, and sustainability on the other. This cluster includes irrigation groups of the landless in WA areas, and of small and marginal farmers in WS areas. These require patience, participation, continuity of staff commitment, and management and maintenance support. They are unsuitable for government implementation but well suited to good NGOs. Community forestry on revenue lands is similar, posing problems for government and better undertaken by NGOs where capable ones are present. Highly desirable as these various schemes are, and important as their scaling up is, they are likely to be slow and relatively small-scale, at least at first, if they are to be sustainable.

A second cluster requires less intensive management, but sustained rou-

Table 10.2. Proposed measures assessed

	Cost-effectiveness	Political and admin feasibility	Scale	Speed	Sustainability	Equity
Flat rate power tariff	H	H	HH	HH	H	H
Progressive flat rate power tariff	H	H/M	HH	HH	H	HH
Improved quality of power supply (some WS areas)	H/M	H	H	H	M	M
Restriction of power supply (some WS areas)	H/M	L	H	H	M/L	M
Saturation: Intensive Groundwater Development Programme (some WA areas)	M	H	L	L	H	H
Abolition of spacing and licensing norms (WA areas)	H	H	H	H	M/L	H
NGO-induced RPF groups (WS areas)	L	M	L	L	M/L	H
Improving pumping efficiencies	M/L	H	L	L	M	M
Rapid rural electrification	M/L	H	H	L	H	M
Landless LI groups (WA areas)	L	L	L	L	L	HH
Livelihood forestry on forest lands	H	M	H	H	H	H
Social security schemes on forest lands	M	M	L	M	M	H/M
Community protection schemes	H	M	M	H	M	M
NGOs and single village organisations in community forestry	L	M	L	L	M	H/M
Abolition of all cutting, transit and sale restrictions on private land	H	H	H	H	H	H
Clear land title to the poor	H	M	H	L	H	H
Tree patta schemes	M	M	M	L	M	H
RPF farm and agroforestry	M	M	H/M	H/M	H	H
Information on rights and marketing	H	H	H	H	H	H
Landless and MF nurseries	M	H	L	M	M	H
Land reform (in practice)	L	L	M	L	M	L/M
IRDP (in practice)	L	M	M	L	L	L/M

HH = very high   H = high   M = medium   L = Low

In all cases high is desirable.

For definitions and explanations of the criteria please see the text.

tine support. With lift irrigation, this includes improving the quality of electricity supply to LISs. This may require reorientation of the electricity board managers in that 'quality' in this context implies supplying power predictably and when farmers need it most. With trees, this cluster includes social security schemes on forest lands, updating and maintaining land records, and landless and marginal farmer tree nurseries.

A third cluster is "zipper" programmes. These require intensive effort for a short period but can then be left "zipped up" in a stable state requiring less institutional maintenance. With lift irrigation this applies to the "saturation" of the Intensive Groundwater Development Programme proposed for WA areas. With trees, zipper programmes include group farm forestry, agroforestry for small and marginal farmers, and livelihood forestry on forest lands. All these can be implemented area by area.

Most important of all, though, is the fourth cluster, legal and administrative changes to rules and restrictions with immediate application over large areas. These vary in the specificity of their benefits to the poorer. Flat rate power tariffs benefit the poor through the sale of more water more cheaply; graduated rate power tariffs, in which owners of larger horsepower engines pay more per horsepower, benefit the poorer even more by making water relatively cheaper for those with smaller LISs. Similarly, the removal of tree transit restrictions and providing marketing support benefits smaller farmers more than larger since smaller farmers are more exploited and more helplessly dependent on contractor intermediaries. The removal of tree cutting restrictions probably benefits them even more since they are more likely than larger farmers to need to cut and sell one or a few trees for urgent purposes.

A mix of measures is needed. The danger of analysis of this sort is that those measures which appear to do badly because of their relative slowness and small scale, notably the NGO initiatives, may consequently be downgraded; but over the long haul they may prove very important indeed, and should be encouraged. All the same, taking account of all the criteria directs attention to those measures which score high across the board. Bearing that in mind, the main immediate priorities and linkages as we see them are:

Lift irrigation
* in all areas, a progressive HP-linked flat power tariff structure, preferably subsidised in water-logged areas of canal commands
* in WA areas, a saturation strategy through an Intensive Groundwater Development Programme.
* in WS areas, improved quality of power supply with judicious quantity restrictions to check over-exploitation, and support for NGO-induced groups

Other measures consistent with and supporting these three thrusts include: removal of siting and licensing norms for new LISs in WA areas and their rationalisation elsewhere; improvement in pumping efficiencies especially for diesel tubewells; subsidies on costs of underground pipelines to encourage their use by private LIS owners; increased pace of rural electrification, and ensuring that full advantage is taken by the RPFs once a village has been electrified; handing over State tubewells to farmer groups and local communities as in West Bengal; encouragement to landless groups owning LISs and selling water (as in Bangladesh); research and extension on low cost, small scale pumping technology.

Trees
* livelihood forestry on forest and revenue lands, with planting of usufruct and MFP based trees as the initial point of intervention, coupled with community protection schemes like Arabari, where feasible and appropriate
* making tree-based livelihood strategies attractive and safe for the poor by
  a. establishing full and secure ownership and use rights for privately grown trees
  b. minimising the hassle and "rents" involved in selling the produce of trees, and
  c. making markets for tree products efficient and accessible to the poor
* better designed and executed social security and tree *patta* schemes to enable the landless to adopt livelihood-intensive tree cultivation strategies

Other supportive measures include: encouraging village and community organisations such as the Forest Councils of the UP hills and the Chipko movement; supporting nurseries by the poor; intensive campaigns to educate the poor, especially those located in remote hinterlands, about their tree rights; updating land records to establish clear rights; and rationalisation -where possible, elimination - of the procedures used to regulate the marketing of tree products by private tree growers and gatherers of MFPs.

In both sets of proposals, scope can be seen for linkages with existing programmes. For all its shortcomings, the IRDP has the means to enable the resource poor to own LISs for own irrigation needs and for sale of water, which might generally provide for more sustainable livelihoods than, for example, milch buffaloes. The million tubewell programme announced in early 1988 by the Minister for Agriculture and Rural Development and the Jaldhara programme announced by the Finance Minister in his 1988 budget speech can very well be implemented on the lines of the Intensive Groundwater Development Programme discussed in chapter 6 to create conditions of saturation. Much land vested under the land ceiling laws in many States is not distributed to the landless as was originally intended; speeding up such distribution and involving village-level institutions in identifying potential "patta holders" could give a major fillip to the tree *patta* schemes without having to implement politically difficult land reform.

All that said, the most significant point, perhaps in this whole book, is that some legal and administrative changes are easy to make and can bring widespread early benefits to the poorer. The abolition of restrictions on harvesting trees on private land, and of rules to control transit, are an example where central deregulation can have an immense impact, to benefit both the poorer and the environment. The effects of the introduction of the progressive flat rate power tariff in Gujarat (sec. 5.12) dramatically demonstrate the scale and scope presented also by other instruments of public policy. As long as changes in rules and restrictions are known about and applied, as in this Gujarat example, they are likely to be quick acting, very wide in impact, and sustainable and stable in their long-term effects.

10.4 Rights, Information and Power

Providing poor people secure, clear rights over lift irrigation resources and trees and tree products are central to the scheme of things envisaged in this book. In many cases, these are rights to do what was previously prohibited or paid for — for instance, rights to sink a well on one's land; to receive credit for a pumpset and tubewell without paying "commissions" for the subsidy; to cut trees on private land; to move trees and tree products freely without permit; to enjoy the usufruct of trees allocated with tree *pattas* on revenue or forest land; to gather minor forest products without harassment or need for bribes; to receive fair access and an equal share of fodder and tree products from community forestry.

It is one thing to abolish a restriction or establish a right on paper, and quite another to enjoy the benefits. Those officials who stand to lose power and payments if the new freedoms are exercised may withhold information, pretend that old rules still apply, or make other threats to secure their customary tribute. Overcoming this resistance, where it occurs, requires two conditions.

The first is information. Ignorance of restrictions is widespread. Even district-level staff do not always know what is allowed and what is not. Not only must they know but more important, the rural people must themselves know, and know in detail and authoritatively. Many ways to achieve this are available. The television and video revolution in communications has already reached much of rural India, and can be expected to multiply in its impact in the 1990s. More traditional channels include the radio, posters outside offices of departments at block and tehsil level and nailed to trees in villages, speeches by politicians and officials, notices in newspapers, and especially widely distributed hand bills in local languages which people can grasp and present as evidence of their entitlements. The same message received through different channels gains in credibility, and weakens those who would deny it. NGOs can help, act as watchdogs, and support the poor in securing their rights.

The second condition is organisation and solidarity. When the issue may be one of loss of power by some—police, officials and others—who have previously gained illicitly, countervailing power is needed as well as information. Fortunately, in the abolition of restrictions, the less poor as well as the poor will usually gain, improving the chances of their forming a united front. Here again, political leaders and NGOs have a part to play in mobilisation and support.

In the case of removing tree cutting and transit restrictions, a massive and credible campaign of information with political support and with a well-focussed message is likely to work. It worked well in Haiti where a conscious decision to provide people with clear, secure and inalienable private rights to their own trees became the key to a highly successful programme which elicited massive involvement of small and marginal farmers in tree cultivation as a livelihood strategy. The message conveyed in all the announcements was: "You will be the owners of any trees that you plant" and "As far as we're concerned, you can cut the trees when you want". Researchers and officials marvelled at the speed with which poor families started planting trees on their land, and at their reluctance to harvest those they already had (Murray 1984, 1986; Conway 1987).

A note of caution is, however, in order. A half-hearted campaign can be self-defeating and do more harm than good. If people feared the policy might be reversed, the immediate effect of derestriction could, perversely, be more felling, to realise assets while the going was good. Moreover, as farmgate values of trees rose with derestriction, some farmers might temporarily harvest more to cash their gains. But most farmers are reluctant to cut their more valuable trees, like *mahua*, coconut, *neem*, *amla*, tamarind, and jack, and other trees which produce fodder, fruits or income seasonally or which appreciate fast as savings banks.

The obstacles to campaigns to provide information to the poorer about their rights, and to their claiming those rights, must not be minimised. At the same time, there are new opportunities for communication direct from senior political leaders and officials to the poor. Not only is there much greater public awareness than in earlier decades, but the means of communication are more varied and less corruptible. What is said in a local meeting may be distorted; but it is difficult to deny or subvert the evidence of video, television and handbills coming from high authority. The question then becomes whether those in authority will have the insight and will to use these powerful means.

10.5 Awareness, Commitment and Action

Many of the issues raised come back to individual choice and action. The policies advocated require that people, especially political leaders and officials, behave differently.

The keys to action are imagination, energy and courage. Erroneous beliefs about "the poor" are still part of the problem. As long as they are regarded as an amorphous mass—"the rural masses" in the common phrase—false stereotypes will persist. As long as programmes to provide them with capital assets are heavily subsidised, there is a danger that poor people will accept what they would not otherwise want so that they, or their patrons, can gain from the subsidy. As long as those responsible for laws, rules and regulations believe that the poor cannot be trusted to act in their own best interests, but must be cajoled and controlled, the poor will suffer from paying off petty bureaucrats and from insecurity and sanctions. As long as the poor do not have secure tenure and rights to use their assets as they wish, they will cash them while they can and not renew them, convincing officials and political leaders that they are feckless and unable to take the long view.

Much of the problem and opportunity, then, lie in new learning and changes of view among those who are senior and in authority. Changes in laws, rules and regulations depend on them. Yet they are often precisely those who have had least contact or have been longest out of touch with rural realities, who are treated with the most deference, who are least contradicted, and who find it hardest to make simple, unbiased rural visits. They thus suffer the professional disability of being hindered from learning. Policy is determined by political leaders, and by senior civil servants. Political leaders are more often younger and more in touch with popular opinion, while senior civil servants wield much of the technical and administrative power which prevents or promotes action. But both tend to be urban-based and urban-biased; and all professionals are vulnerable to easy acceptance of misleading stereotypes of the poor.

One solution is the rural research sabbatical in which mid-career officers examine first-hand the nature of poverty and rural conditions related to their work. Forest officers would thus study tribal life and economy, and the significance of, say, "minor" forest produce for livelihoods of the poor. Engineers would study how to match lift irrigation equipment supply with locally varying needs. Bank staff would study how poor people handle contingencies and their strategies for survival and staying out of debt. IAS officers would study the effects of restrictions on cutting and transit of trees (unless, as we hope, they will have all been abolished). Good methods of rapid rural appraisal are now known (KKU 1987) and are best used by senior researchers themselves, face-to-face with rural people, and especially the poor. For correcting misleading beliefs, keeping up-to-date with rapid change, and the excitement of discovery, direct personal investigation has no substitute.

Implementation of the measures identified in this book would not eliminate poverty in rural India. They are not a universal panacea. Their fit depends on local conditions. None fits everywhere. Although many poor people live alongside major potential, some live where the opportunities are constrained. Lift irrigation and trees cannot provide a programme to cover the whole country with a standard solution. But then such standard, universal programmes never work well anyway. Decentralised local initiatives, flexibly determined by local needs, resources and opportunities, are often required. The policies proposed can serve many areas, and many of the poorer, but not all.

The scope, though, is so immense, that even now we find it difficult to grasp. It is, to repeat, for a massive improvement in the livelihoods of crores of the poorest. Most of the measures are cheap and cost-effective. They correspond, we argue, closely with what poor people want, will welcome, and will sustain.

The change needed is not in the poor and weak and their aspirations; for they wish to become less poor and less weak. The change needed is in the perceptions and actions of those have power, and especially officials and political leaders.

Mahatma Gandhi's words are fitting here:

> I will give you a talisman. Whenever you are in doubt, or when the self becomes too much with you, apply the following test. Recall the face of the poorest and the weakest man whom you may have seen, and ask yourself, if the step you contemplate is going to be of any use to him. Will he gain anything by it? Will it restore him to a control over his own life and destiny? In other words, will it lead to Swaraj for the hungry and spiritually starving millions? Then you will find your doubts and your self melting away.

The question is—how often, and in what circumstances, with what learning and understanding, are the poor man, and more, the poor woman and child, met, listened to, and understood; and how often are the distant effects of decisions and actions, and of indecisions and non-actions, reflected upon.

In the past, many actions intended to help that poor child, woman, and man have harmed them, and many which could have helped them have remained unseen and undone. In this book we have explored new actions which, though largely commonsense, have been less obvious. The priority now is to recognise such actions and to learn to recognise more. This means re-examining beliefs, reversing views, and seeing things as poor rural people see them. Many professionals—political leaders, officials, voluntary workers, and others — already have the vision to make those reversals and to put those who are last first. Many already have the conviction and courage to act. May this book support them, and encourage others to join them. If it does only that, it will have been worth writing. For there is much that is new and good to be done, and many good people to do it. And there is no need to wait.

Bibliography

Abbie, H., J.Q. Leslie and J.W. Wall. 1982. *Economic Return to Investment in Irrigation in India*, World Bank Staff Working Paper 536, The World Bank, Washington DC.

ADB 1987. A review of forestry and forest industries in the Asia Pacific Region. Asian Development Bank, Manila.

Agarwal, Anil and Sunita Narain. 1985. Strategies for the involvement of the landless and women in afforestation. Centre for Science and Environment, New Delhi. (mimeo).

Agarwal, Anil. 1987. Between need and greed — the wasting of India; the greening of India, in: Anil Agarwal, Darryl D'Monte and Ujwala Samarth (eds.) *The Fight for Survival;* Centre for Science and Environment, New Delhi.

Agrawal, A.N. et al. 1986. India, *Basic Economic Information*, National Publishing House, New Delhi.

Ahluwalia, Montek, S. 1986. Rural poverty, agricultural production and prices: A re-examination, in: Mellor and Desai (eds.), *Agricultural Change and Rural Poverty*, pp. 59-75.

Alam, M. et al. 1985. *Fuelwood in Urban Markets: A Case Study of Hyderabad*, Concept Publishing House, New Ii ....

Andersen, Kirsten, E. 1988. Models of popular participation in social forestry projects in India, DANIDA, New Delhi. (mimeo).

Anderson, Robert and Walter, Huber. 1988. *The Hour of the Fox: Tropical Forests, the World Bank and Indigenous People in Central India*, Vistaar Publications. New Delhi.

Appadurai, Arjun. 1985. Small-scale techniques and large-scale objectives *MMW*

Appu, P.S. 1974. The bamboo tubewell, *Economic and Political Weekly*, June.

Arnold, J.E.M. 1987. Economic considerations in agroforestry, in: H.A. Steppler and P.K.R. Nair (eds.), *Agroforestry: A Decade of Development*, ICRAF, Nairobi.

Attwood, D.W. 1988. Social and political pre-conditions for successful cooperatives: The cooperatives sugar factories of western india, in: D.W. Attwood and B.S. Baviskar (eds.), *Who Shares? Cooperatives and Rural Development*, Oxford University Press.

Ballabh, Vishwa and Katar Singh. 1988. Managing forests through people's institutions: A case study of van panchayats in Uttar Pradesh hills, *Indian Journal of Agricultural Economics.* July-Sept., Bombay.

Bandyopadhyay, J. et al. 1983. The challenge of social forestry, in: Walter Fernandes and Sharad Kulkarni (eds.), *Towards a New Policy*, Indian Social Institute, New Delhi.

Banerjee, A.K. 1986. Community woodlot. World Bank, New Delhi. (mimeo).

Bell, C., P. Hazell and R. Slade. 1982. *Project Evaluation in Regional Perspective*, Johns Hopkins University Press, Baltimore.

Bentley, William R. 1984. The Uncultivated Half of India: Problems and Possible Solution. DP No. 12, Ford Foundation, New Delhi. (mimeo).

Bhatt, Anil. 1987. Rehabilitation Approach to Poverty Alleviation: A Study of BAIF's Tribal Development Project in Vansda. Indian Institute of Management. Ahmedabad. (mimeo)

Bhatt, Ela. 1988. Shramshakti: *National Commission on Self Employed Women and Women in the Informal Sector.* Department of Women & Child Development, Government of India.

Bhattacharjee, Asit. 1987. *Towards a Conscious New Society.* Peoples Institute for Development and Training (PIDT). New Delhi.

Bhattacharjee, Abhijit. 1988a. Gramdan villages, *National Herald* June 22 and 23, 1988.

Bhattacharjee, Abhijit. 1988b. Eucalyptus: A distress study, *Hindustan Times*, Sept. 25, 1988, New Delhi.

Blaikie, Piers M., John Harriss and Adam Pain. 1986. The management and use of common property resources in Tamil Nadu, in: *Common Property Resource Management*, National Academy Press, Washington. D.C.

Blair, H.W. 1986. Social forestry: Time to modify goals? *Economic and Political Weekly*, 21 (30).

Brahmbhatt, D.M. 1986. Socio-economic profile of action research programme area in Mahi-Kadana irrigation project, Economic Research Centre, Sadar Patel University, Vallabh Vidyanagar, Gujarat. (monograph).

Breman, Jan. 1985. *Of Peasants, Migrants and Paupers: Rural Labour Circulation and Capitalist Production in West India,* Oxford University Press, Delhi, Bombay, Calcutta, Madras.

Brokensha, David. 1988. Village-level management of common property resources, especially fuelwood and fodder resources, in Karnataka, India. A Report Prepared for the World Bank. (mimeo).

Burman, B.K. Roy. 1987. Historical ecology of land survey and settlement in tribal areas and challenges of development. Council for Social Development. New Delhi. (mimeo).

Campbell, Jeffrey, Y. 1987. Tropical forestry and biological diversity in india and the role of USAID. USAID, New Delhi.

CENDIT. 1985a. Social forestry in Madhya Pradesh: Case study of Salvai & Lohgarh gram panchayat. Cel Technology, New Delhi.

CENDIT 1985b. The Maharashtra social forestry project in Bhandara district: Case studies of three gram panchayats. Centre for Development and Instructional Technology, New Delhi. (mimeo).

Chambers, Robert. 1981. Gram gourav pratishthan, Naigaon, Purandhar tehsil, Pune district: Notes and reflections on a field visit 28-30 April 1981 Ford Foundation, 55 Lodi Estate, New Delhi 110 003. (typescript).

Chambers, Robert and Deep Joshi. 1982. A note on groundwater in Chotanagpur, Ford Foundation, New Delhi. (mimeo).

Chambers, Robert. 1983. *Rural Development: Putting the Last First*, Longman, Harlow.

Chambers, Robert and Deep Joshi. 1983. Notes, reflections and proposals on groundwater development following a visit to Gonda District, Eastern UP, Ford Foundation, New Delhi. (mimeo).

Chambers, Robert. 1986. Irrigation against rural poverty, presented at INSA National Seminar on Water Management held at New Delhi.

Chambers, Robert and Richart Longhurst. 1986. Trees, seasons and the poor, in: Richard Longhurst (ed.), Seasonality and Poverty, *IDS Bulletin Vol. 17 No. 3*, Sussex.

Chambers, Robert and Melissa, Leach. 1987. Trees to meet contingencies: savings and security for the rural poor. *IDS Discussion Paper 228*. Institute of Development Studies, Sussex.

Chambers, Robert 1988, *Managing Canal Irrigation: Practical Analysis from South Asia*, Oxford and IBH Publishing Co. Pvt. Ltd., 66 Janpath, New Delhi 110001

Chatterjee, N. 1987. Marketing and pricing of Social forestry produce: An overview. Presented in the Workshop on Role of Incentives in Social Forestry. August 1-3, 1987. ISO/Swedforest. New Delhi. (mimeo).

Chetty, N.V. Ramachandra. 1988. Forestry for provision of raw materials for industries. Paper presented at the SIDA/GOI Workshop on Forestry Sector Administrative Development. November. (typescript).

Chopra, Kanchan, et al. 1988. Sukhomajri and Dhamala watersheds in Haryana: Participatory approach to management. Institute of Economic Growth New Delhi. (mimeo).

Chowdhry, Kamla, et al. 1984. Hill resource development and community management: Lessons learnt on micro-watershed management from cases of Sukhomajri and Dasholi Gram Swaraj Mandal, Society for Promotion of Wastelands Development, New Delhi, August.

Chowdhry, Kamla. 1985. Wastelands and the rural poor. Paper presented at the FAO Symposium on Forestry for Rural Development, October 2, 1985 and included in (FAO 1986a).

Chowdhry, Kamla. 1986. Institution building: role and constraints of intermediate agencies, in: M.L. Dantwala, Ranjit Guha and Keith D'Souza (eds.) *Asian Seminar on Rural Development*, Oxford and IBH Publishing Co. Pvt. Ltd., New Delhi.

Chowdhry, Kamla. 1987. Wastelands and the rural poor: Essentials of a policy framework. National Wasteland Development Board, New Delhi. (mimeo).

Chowla, A.S., L.S. Ranghuvanshi and Anil Kumar. 1987. Access of small and marginal farmers to groundwater: A field study, presented at the "Workshop on Common Property Resources: Groundwater", organised at Roorkee University, Roorkee, 23-25 February, 1987.

CIDA. 1986. Interim evaluation of Andhra Pradesh social forestry project, CIDA, New Delhi.

CIDA. 1988. Andhra Pradesh social forestry project: Mid-term review, March. Canadian International Development Agency, New Delhi.

Commander, Simon. 1986. Managing Indian forests: A case for the reform of property rights, *Development Policy Review.* Vol. 4, London.

Conway, Frederick, J. 1987. Case study: The agroforestry outreach project in Haiti. Conference on Sustainable Development, February, 1987, International Institute for Environment and Development, London. (mimeo).

Copestake, James, G. 1986. Finance for wells in a hard rock area of southern Tamil Nadu, unpublished, ODA-NABARD research project on "Credit for Rural Development in Southern Tamil Nadu" Department of Agricultural Economics, Agricultural College and Research Institute, Aladurai 625 104.

Copestake, James, G. 1987. Loans for livelihoods? An assessment of Government sponsored schemes designed to promote rural development in India based on field work undertaken in the Madurai region of Tamil Nadu, between September 1984 and August 1986, Final Report Number Two submitted to the Overseas Development Administration of the United Kingdom under ESCOR Project Number R3905, February.

CSE.1985. *The State of India's Environment 1984-85: The Second Citizen's Report.* Centre for Science and Environment, 1985.

Dandekar, V.M. and Nilakantha Rath. 1971. Poverty in India, *Economic and Political Weekly,* Bombay.

Das, Bhagwan. 1988. Gloomy prospects for eucalyptus growers, *Patriot.* 13th April, 1988.

Dasgupta, Biblab. 1975. A typology of village socio-economic systems from Indian Village Studies, *Economic and Political Weekly,* special number August, pp. 1395-1414.

Dasgupta, Biplab. 1984. Deep tubewell irrigation, water rates and social benefit: A case study of West Bengal, University of Calcutta, Calcutta. (typescript).

Dasgupta, Subhachari. 1986. *Forest, Ecology and the Oppressed.* People's Institute for Development & Training (PIDT), New Delhi.

Dasgupta, Supriya. 1988. *Understanding the Tribal Dilemma: Tribal Women and Forest Dweller Economy,* Media Centre, Bangalore.

Datye, K.R. and R.K. Patil. 1987. *Farmer Managed Irrigation Systems: Indian Experience,* Centre for Applied Systems Analysis in Development, Bombay.

DDRI. 1981. Gonda Gramodaya Project: An Evaluation, Deen Dayal Research Institute, New Delhi 110 055.

Deshpande, V.D. n.d. Pani Panchayat: A movement to secure irrigation facility to the poor farmers, Indian Institute of Education, Pune. (typescript).

Dhawan, B.D. 1982. *Development of Tubewell Irrigation in India,* Agricole Publishing Academy, New Delhi.

Dhawan, B.D. Improving economic returns from well irrigation in hard rock areas: the Maharashtra case. Institute of Economic Growth, Delhi University, Delhi. (mimeo).

Dhawan, B.D. 1987. Management of groundwater resource in India: Direct versus indirect regulatory mechanisms, presented at the "Workshop on Common Property Resources: Groundwater" organised at Roorkee University, Roorkee, 23-25 February 1987.

DN. 1988. Factors in the Jharkhand movement, *Economic and Political Weekly,* 30th January.

Dogra, Bharat. 1987. Forest people: Victims of ever changing yet unchanging official policy, included in: *The India Papers: Aspects of NGO Participation in Social Forestry Bangalore, India. September 1986,* International Tree Project Clearinghouse, NGLS/ New York.

Dreze, Jean. 1988. Social insecurity in India: A core study, paper for the Workshop on Social Security in Developing Countries, London School of Economics, July.

Dreze, Jean. 1989. Beyond the IRDP delusion, London School of Economics. (mimeo).

Eckholm, Eric. 1979. *Planting for the Future: Forestry for Human Needs.* Worldwatch Institute. Washington.

FAO. 1982. As reported in participation in forestry. Paper by Siteke Kuperus presented at a workshop October, 1987. Department of Forest Management. Agriculture University. Wageningen.

FAO. 1984. *Intensive Multiple-use Forest Management in Kerala*, FAO Forestry Paper 53. Rome.

FAO. 1985. *Evaluation of the Gujarat Social Forestry Programme*, FAO, Rome.

FAO. 1986a. *Five Perspectives on Forestry for Rural Development in the Asia—Pacific Region*, RAPA Monograph: 1986/1, FAO. Bangkok.

FAO. 1986b. *Forestry Extension Organisation*, FAO Forestry Paper No. 66, Rome.

FAO. 1988. Case studies of farm forestry and wasteland development in Gujarat, FAO, Bangkok. (mimeo).

Feinerman, Eli. 1988. Groundwater management: Efficiency and equity consideration, *Agricultural Economics* No. 2, pp. 1-18.

Fernandes, Walter and Geeta Menon. 1988. *Deforestation, Forest Dweller Economy and Women*, Indian Social Institute, New Delhi.

Fernandes, Walter et al. 1985. Forests environment and forest tribal economy in Chattisgarh, Indian Social Institute. (mimeo).

Fernandes, et al. 1988. *Forests, Environment and Tribal Economy: Deforestation, Impoverishment and Marginalisation in Orissa*, Indian Social Institute, New Delhi.

FRI. 1984. *India's Forests*, Forest Research Institute. Dehradun.

FSI. 1988. *State of India's Forests*, Forest Survey of India. Dehradun.

Etienne, Gilbert. 1985. *Rural Development in Asia: Meetings with Peasants*, revised edition, Sage Publications, New Delhi, Beverley Hills, London.

Furer-Haimendorf, C. von. 1985. *Tribes of India: The Struggle for Survival*, Oxford University Press, New Delhi.

Gadgil, Madhav et al. 1982. Forest management and forest policy in India: a critical review, in: Walter Fernandes (ed.), *Forests, Environment and People*, Indian Social Institute, New Delhi.

Gadgil, Madhav, 1985. The Western Ghats of India: An ecodevelopment approach, in: Tejvir Singh and Jagdish Kaur (eds.), *Integrated Mountain Development*, Himalayan Books, New Delhi.

Gadgil Madhav. 1987. Depleting renewable resources: a case study from Karnataka Western Ghats, *Indian Journal of Agricultural Economics*, July-Sept., Bombay.

Gadgil, Madhav. 1988. Greening the commons in Karnataka, *Deccan Herald*, 12.6.1988.

Gadgil, Madhav and Ramchandra Guha. 1988. The Law and Our Forests, *Statesman*, 24.2.1988.

Gaikwad, V. 1981. Community development in India, in: R. Dore and Z. Mars (eds.) *Community Development: Comparative Case Studies in India, the Republic of Korea, Mexico and Tanzania*, Croom Helm, London.

GEB. 1985. *Annual Report: 1985*, Gujarat Electricity Board, Race Course Road, Baroda.

Ghosh, M.G. 1984. Impact of irrigation on income and employment—a case study in a Bengal village, *Indian Journal of Agricultural Economics*, July-August, p. 549.

Ghosh, M.G. 1985. Impact of new technology on income and employment study—a case study in a Bengal village, typescript, Agro-Economic Research Centre, Viswa-Bharti, Santiniketan.

GGP. 1983. *Pani Panchayat (Dividing line between poverty and prosperity)*, The Gram Gurav Pratishthan, Taluka Purandhar, District Pune, Maharashtra, November.

GOB. 1987. Study on the participation of women in the social forestry project, March 87, Forest Department, Government of Bihar, Patna. (mimeo).

GOI. 1962. Timber trends and prospects in India, Ministry of Food and Agriculture, Government of India, New Delhi. (mimeo).

GOI. 1970. *Fourth Five Year Plan: 1969-74*, Planning Commission, Government of India, New Delhi.

GOI. 1976. *Report of the National Commission on Agriculture, Part IX. Forestry*, Ministry of Agriculture and Cooperation, Government of India, New Delhi.

GOI. 1979. *Report of the Working Group on Energy Policy,* Planning Commission, New Delhi.

GOI. 1981a. Development of forestry and forest products; country profile India, Ministry of Agriculture, Government of India, July 1981, New Delhi. (mimeo).

GOI. 1981b. *Report on Development of Tribal Areas,* National Committee on the Development of Backward Areas, Planning Commission, Government of India, New Delhi.

GOI. 1982. *Report of Committee on Forest and Tribals in India,* Ministry of Home Affairs, Government of India, New Delhi.

GOI. 1984. *Report of the Working Group on Development of Scheduled Tribes During Seventh Five-Year Plan* 1985-90, Ministry of Home Affairs, Government of India, New Delhi.

GOI. 1985a. Basic rural statistics. Department of Rural Development, Government of India, New Delhi. (mimeo).

GOI. 1985b. *The Seventh Five Year Plan, Vol. 1,* Planning Commission, Government of India, New Delhi.

GOI. 1985c. Agenda papers for Conference of Revenue Secretaries and Revenue Ministers, 17th and 18th May, 1985. Department of Rural Development, Government of India. New Delhi.

GOI. 1985d. Report of the working group on paper industry, Ministry of Industrial Development, Government of India, New Delhi. (mimeo).

GOI, 1985e. *The Seventh Five Year Plan, Vol II,* Planning Commission, Government of India, New Delhi.

GOI. 1986a. Agenda papers for Conference of Revenue Secretaries and Revenue Ministers, 24th and 25th November, 1986, Department of Rural Development, Government of India. New Delhi.

GOI. 1986b. Report of the inter-ministerial group on wood substitution, Ministry of Environment and Forests, Government of India, New Delhi. (mimeo).

GOI. 1986c. *NREP & RLEGP Manual.* Department of Rural Development, Govt. of India, New Delhi.

GOI. 1986d. *Indian Agriculture in Brief.* 21st Edition, Directorate of Economics & Statistics, Department of Agriculture & Cooperation, New Delhi.

GOI. 1987a. Evaluation report on integrated tribal development projects programme evaluation organisation, Planning Commission, Government of India. (mimeo).

GOI. 1987b. Background note prepared for the seminar on welfare and development of tribals, Ministry of Tribals, Government of India. (typescript).

GOI. 1987c. *Report of the Task Force to Evaluate the Impact of Sheep and Goat Rearing in Ecologically Fragile Zone,* Ministry of Agriculture & Cooperation, New Delhi.

GOI. 1987d. Proceedings of the meeting of Central Board of Forestry held on 7th and 8th December, 1987. Ministry of Environment and Forests, Government of India, New Delhi. (mimeo).

GOI. 1988a. Allotment of government wasteland in some states. Department of Rural Development. Government of India. (typescript).

GOI. 1988b. Land utilisation statistics for the years 1950-51 to 1984-85 (as on 15.2.88). Directorate of Economics & Statistics, Ministry of Agriculture and Cooperation. Government of India. (mimeo).

GOI. 1988c. Commodity studies. (in six Volumes) by Progressive Agro-Industrial Consultants. Ministry of Welfare, Government of India.

GOI. 1988d. Integrated rural development programme: A review of the performance during 1987-88, Department of Rural Development, New Delhi. (mimeo).

GOI, 1988e. National seminar on poverty alleviation, Department of Rural Development, Government of India, February. (mimeo).

GOK. 1986. Annual administration Report for 1984-85, Forest Department, Government of Karnataka, December 1986. (mimeo).

GOMP. 1986. Annual plan for the year 1987-88, Forest Department, Government of Madhya Pradesh, December 1986, Bhopal. (mimeo).

GOMP. 1987. Forestry project of rehabilitation of degraded forests and afforestation in M.P., Madhya Pradesh Forest Department, July 1987. (mimeo).

GOO. 1987. Evaluation of Orissa social forestry project, phase I, Government of Orissa, Bhuba-neswar. (mimeo).

GOO. 1988. Social forestry project document, Phase-II (1988-93), Department of Forests, Government of Orissa, Bhubaneswar. (typescript).

GOTN. 1988. Sample survey on tree cultivation extension programme during the years 1984-85, 1985-86 and 1986-87, Social Forestry Wing, Tamil Nadu Forest Department, Madras. (mimeo).

GOUP. 1983a. *Forest Statistics, Uttar Pradesh,* Forest Department, Uttar Pradesh, Lucknow.

GOUP. 1983b. Report of the high level committee to enquire into problems of land records in South Mirzapur, December 1983, Government of U.P. (in Hindi), (mimeo).

GOUP. 1984. Preliminary evaluation report, social forestry project, U.P. Forest Department, Government of Uttar Pradesh, Lucknow. (mimeo).

GOWB. 1988a. Project report on resuscitation of Sal Forests of south-west Bengal through people's participation. Department of Forests, Government of West Bengal. (mimeo).

GOWB. 1988b. Technology manual for forest management with people's participation. Social Forestry Wing, Forest Directorate, Government of West Bengal. (mimeo).

Griffin, Keith. 1974. *The Political Economy of Agrarian Change: An Essay on the Green Revolution,* Harvard University Press, Cambridge, Mass.

Guha, Ramachandra. 1983. Forestry in British and Post-British India, *Economic and Political Weekly,* October 29.

Guha, Ramachandra. 1988. Towards the sociology of forest decay: The Indian case, Paper presented at the Forestry Sector Administrative Development Workshop, November 1988, ISO/Swedforest, New Delhi. (typescript).

Guhan, S. and G. Mencher. 1983. Iruvelpattu revisited, *Economic & Political Weekly* June.

Gulati, Leela. 1981. *Profiles in Female Poverty: A Study of Five Poor Working Women in Kerala,* Hindustan Publishing Corporation (India), Delhi.

Gupta, Anil K. 1984. Socio-ecology of land use planning in semi-arid regions, Working Paper No. 525, Indian Institute of Management, August 1984. (mimeo).

Gupta, Anil K. 1985. Socio-ecology of grazing land management, in: *Rangelands: A Resource Under Seige,* Proceedings of the Second International Rangeland Congress, CSIRO, Australia.

Gupta, A.K., J.K. Vergese, J. Ganguly, G. Krishna, T. Sreekrishna. 1986. Cost-benefit analysis of groundwater irrigation using underground pipelines, unpublished term paper submitted to the Institute of Rural Management, Anand.

Gupta, Tirath and Amar Guleria. 1982a. *Non-wood Forest Products in India,* Oxford and IBH Publishing Co. Pvt. Ltd., New Delhi.

Gupta, Tirath and Amar Guleria. 1982b. *Some Economic and Management Aspects of a Non-Wood Forest Product in India: Tendu Leaves,* Oxford & IBH Publishing Co. Pvt. Ltd., New Delhi.

Gupta, Tirath, 1986. Farm forestry, Indian Institute of Management, Ahmedabad. (mimeo).

Gupta, Tirath and Nitin Shah. 1987. *Paper and Paperboards in India: Demand Forecasts and Policy Implications,* Oxford and IBH Publishing Co. Pvt. Ltd., New Delhi.

Hardin, G. 1968. The tragedy of the commons, *Science* 162.

Hardin, Garrett and John Baden. 1971. *Managing the Commons,* Freeman and Co.

Harrison, Abbie, Leslie, James Q. and John W. Wall. 1982. *Economic Return to Investment in Irrigation in India,* World Bank staff working paper number 536, The World Bank, Washington, DC, USA.

Hartmann, Betsy and James Boyce. 1983. *A Quiet Violence: View from a Bangladesh Village,* Zed Press, London.

Hazell, Peter B.R. and C. Ramasamy. 1988. Green revolution reconsidered: The impact of the high-yielding rice varieties in South India, International Food Policy Research Institute, Washington D.C.

Hill, Polly. 1982. *Dry Grain Farming Families: Hausaland (Nigeria) and Karnataka (India) Compared,* Cambridge University Press.

Hiralal, Mohan Hirabhai. 1986. Wasteland development scheme, Paper presented at the SPWD Seminar, April 1986, Society for Promotion of Wasteland Development, New Delhi. (mimeo).

Hirway, Indira. 1986a. Garibi Hatao: Can IRDP do it? *Economic and Political Weekly*, March 30.

Hirway, Indira. 1986b. *Abolition of Poverty in India with Special Reference to Target Group Approach in Gujarat*, Vikas Publishing House, New Delhi.

Howes, Michael. 1984. The social organisation of deep tubewell irrigation in Bangladesh: A case study, paper for the Conference on Community Responses to Irrigation, Bangalore, 7 January.

Howes, Michael. 1985. *Whose Water? An Investigation of the Consequences of Alternative Approaches to Small Scale Irrigation in Bangladesh,* Bangkok Institute of Development Studies, Dhaka, Bangladesh.

IDS. 1980. Who gains from the last resource? The potential and challenge of lift irrigation for the rural poor, ODI *Irrigation Management Network paper 1,* April, Overseas Development Institute, London.

IEG. 1988. Participatory development: An approach to the management of common property resources, Institute of Economic Growth, New Delhi. (mimeo).

IFAD. 1984. *Mid-term Evaluation Report: Bhima Command Area Development Project,* India, International Fund for Agricultural Development, Rome.

IFMR. 1984. *An Economic Assessment of Poverty Eradication and Rural Unemployment Alleviation Programmes and Their Prospects,* 3 Vols, Institute for Financial Management and Research, 30 Kothari Road, Nungambakkam, Madras 600 034, April.

IIM. 1985. Impact of social forestry project on locals. A case study in Badaun District, U.P. Centre for Management in Agriculture. Indian Institute of Management, Ahmedabad. (mimeo).

ISST, 1987. Small scale forest enterprises in India, with special reference to role of women: National Review Paper. Institute of Social Studies Trust, New Delhi. (mimeo).

IIPO. 1988. *Survival Rate of Trees: 1983-84 to 1987-88.,* Indian Institute of Opinion Poll, New Delhi.

ILO. 1986. *The Rural Energy Crisis, Poverty and Women's Roles in Five Indian Villages,* Subhachari Dasgupta and Ashok Kumar Maiti, International Labour Organisation, Geneva.

ILO. 1987. *Employment and Income Generation in Social Forestry: A Case Study from Orissa,* Gunilla Olsson, International Labour Office, Geneva.

ILO. 1988. *Employment and Income Generation through Social Forestry in India: Review of Issues and Evidence,* ILO. Asian Employment Programme (ARTEP), New Delhi.

Jagawat, Harnath. 1988. A story of massive forestry programme. Paper for the Edinburgh Conference on Agroforestry, June 1989. Sadguru Water and Development Foundation, Dahod. (typescript).

Jairath, Jasvin. 1984. Private tubewell utilisation in Punjab: A study of costs and efficiency, *Economic and Political Weekly*, No. 40.

Jambulingam, R. and E.C.M. Fernandes. 1986. Multipurpose trees and shrubs in Tamil Nadu State (India), *Agroforestry Systems,* 4: 17-32, Netherlands.

Jayaraman, T.K., M.K. Lowdermilk, L.J. Nelson, W.C. Lyma, J.M. Reddy and M.I. Hyder. 1983. *Diagnostic Analysis of Farm Irrigation in the Mahi-Kadana Irrigation Project, Gujarat, India,* WMS Report No 18, Colorado State University, Fort Collins, Colorado.

Jetley, Surinder. 1987. Impact of male migration on rural females, *EPW,* 22 no 33, October 31, pp WS 47-53.

Jodha, N.S. 1985. Social science research and rural change: Some gaps, Paper for the Workshop on Measuring Economic Change in South Asia, Bangalore, 5-8 August 1985.

Jodha, N.S. 1986. Common property resources and rural poor in dry regions of India, *Economic and Political Weekly,* July 5.

Jodha, N.S. 1987. A note on contribution of CPRs to PPR-based farming systems in dry tropical regions of India, Paper presented at the Ford Foundation Workshop on Common Property Resources, Sariska. India. May 1987. (mimeo).

Jodha, N.S. et al. 1987. The effects of climatic variations on agriculture in dry tropical regions of India, in: M.L. Parry, T.R. Carter and N.T. Konijin (eds)., *The Impact of Climatic Variations on Agriculture, Volume 2. Assessments in Semi-Arid Regions.* Reidel, Dordrecht, The Netherlands.

Khan, Irshad. 1987. *Wastelands Afforestation,* Oxford & IBH Publishing Co. Pvt. Ltd., New Delhi.

KKU. 1987. Proceedings of the International Conference on *Rapid Rural Appraisal, Rural Systems Research and Farming Systems Research Projects,* Khon Kaen University, Khon Kaen, Thailand.

Kolavalli, Shashi. 1986. Economic analysis of conjunctive use of water: The case of Mahi-Kadana Irrigation Project in Gujarat, India, Unpublished Ph.D thesis, Urbana IL: University of Illinois.

Kolavalli, Shashi and D.L. Chicoine 1987. Groundwater markets in Gujarat, India, Indian Institute of Management, Ahmedabad. (mimeo).

Kolavalli, S., V.N. Asopa and A. Kalro. 1988. Issues in the development and management of groundwater resources in eastern Uttar Pradesh, Indian Institute of Management, Ahmedabad. (mimeo).

Kolhe, A.K. et al. 1986. *Pani Panchayat: An Overview,* Development Group, "Yashodan" 2071 Vijayanagar, Pune 411 030, Maharashtra, December 6.

Kulkarni, Sharad. 1987. Forest legislation and tribals: Comments on forest policy resolution, *Economic and Political Weekly,* December 12, 1987.

Kumar, Praveer. 1987. Marketing of trees in Moradabad. Office of the Chief Development Officer, Moradabad. (U.P.). (typescript).

Kurien, N.J. 1987. IRDP: How relevant is it? *Economic and Political Weekly,* Review of Agriculture, December 26.

Lapierre, Dominique. 1986. *City of Joy,* Arrow Books, London.

Leach, Gerald, 1987. *Household Energy in South Asia,* International Institute for Environment and Development, London.

Maheshwari, S.R. 1985. *Rural Development in India,* Sage Publications India, New Delhi.

Mahiti, 1987. Mahiti's Experience in Promoting *Salvadora persica* among the poor: Lessons for extension, Mahiti, Ahmedabad. (mimeo).

Mahoni, Des. 1987. Forestry extension training in Somalia, *ODI Social Forestry Network Paper* 4b. June, London.

Maithani, P. et al. 1988. Survey of shrubs for hastening the process of reclamation of ecologically vulnerable areas of Central Himalayas, *Indian Forester,* May. Dehradun.

Malmer, Pernilla. 1987. Socio-economic change in social forestry. A case study of Kovilur village, Tamil Nadu, India. The Swedish University of Agriculture Sciences, Department of Economics & Statistics, Uppsala.

Mandal, M.A.S. and R.W. Palmer-Jones. 1987. Access of the poor to groundwater irrigation in Bangladesh, presented at the Workshop on Common Property Resources: Groundwater organised at Roorkee University, Roorkee, 23-25, February 1987.

Mehra, S. 1976. Some aspects of labour use in Indian agriculture, *Indian Journal of Agricultural Economics.*

Mellor, John W. and Gunvant, M. Desai (eds). 1986. *Agricultural Change and Rural Poverty: Variations on a Theme by Dharam Narain,* Oxford University Press, Delhi.

Mellor, John and T.V. Moorti. 1971. Dilemma of state tubewells, *Economic and Political Weekly,* No. 4.

Menon, Ramesh. 1986. Saurashtra: The tears of salt, *India Today,* Bombay.

Mishra, P.R. and Madhu Sarin. 1987a. Social security through social fencing—Sukhomajri and Nada's road to self-sustaining development, paper for Only One Earth; Conference on Sustainable Development, International Institute for Environment and Development, London, 28-30 April 1987.

Mishra, P.R. and Madhu Sarin. 1987b. Sukhomajri-Nada: A new model of eco-development, *Business India,* November 16 to 29, 1987.

MMW. 1985. Paper for the Workshop on Measuring Economic Change in South Asia: Differences in Approach and in Results between Large-scale Surveys and Intensive Micro-studies, Bangalore, 5-8 August 1985, known as the "Macro-Micro Workshop". The papers of the workshop are being edited for publications by Pranab Bardhan as a book entitled, *Measurement Problems of Socio-economic Change.*

Morehouse, Ward. 1987. Levitation revisited: Small-scale lift irrigation technology and poverty alleviation, *Development Forum,* June, pp. 8-9.

Murray, Gerald F. 1986. Seeing the forest while planting the trees: An anthropological approach to agroforestry in rural Haiti, in: D.W. Brinkerhoff and J.C. Garcia Zamor (eds.), *Politics, Projects, and People: Institutional Development in Haiti,* Praeger, 1986.

NABARD, 1987. *Minor Irrigation in Muzaffar Nagar District, U.P., An ex-post Evaluation Study,* Evaluation Study series No. 27, National Bank for Agriculture and Rural Development, Economics Analysis and Publications Department.

Nadkarni, M.V. et al. 1987. Political economy of forest use and management in the context of integration of a forest region into the larger economy. Institute for Social and Economic Change, Bangalore. (mimeo).

Nagabrahmam, D. and K. Vengama Raju. 1987. Poor and groundwater: Some institutional alternatives, in: Workshop on Common Property Resources: Groundwater, held at University of Roorkee, 23-25 February, 1987.

Nagabrahmam, D. and S. Sambrani. 1983. Women's drudgery in firewood collection, *Economic & Political Weekly,* Jan. 1-14.

Nair, C.T.S. 1985. Crisis in forest resource management, in: J. Bandyopadhyay et al. (eds.), *India's Environment: Crises and Responses,* Natraj Publishers, Dehradun.

Nair, M. Achuthan and C. Sreedharan. 1986. Farming systems in the homestead of Kerala, *Agro-Forestry Systems,* Vol. 4, No. 4, U.K.

Narain, Pratap et al. 1985. Agroforestry programme in watershed management. Paper presented at the National Seminar on Soil Conservation and Watershed Management, September 17-18, 1985. New Delhi.

NCAER. 1987. Haryana wood balance study, National Council of Applied Economic Research, New Delhi. (mimeo).

NCAER. 1988. Evaluation study of rural fuel wood plantations, November, New Delhi. (mimeo).

NCHSE. 1987. Documentation on forest and rights. Volume One. National Centre for Human Settlements and Environment, New Delhi. (mimeo).

Nimbkar. B.V. 1988. The greening of Maharashtra, *Economic and Political Weekly,* 20th February.

Ninan, Sewanti. 1981. Women in community forestry, included in the Report of the Seminar on Role of Women in Community Forestry, Ministry of Agriculture & Cooperation. Govt. of India, Dehradun. (mimeo).

NIRD. 1985. *Rural Development Statistics,* National Institute of Rural Development, Hyderabad.

NISWASS. 1986. Forest farming for rural poor (FFRP). Report of a case study. National Institute of Social Work and Social Sciences. (NISWASS). Bhubaneswar. (mimeo).

NRSA. 1985. Mapping of wastelands in India from satellite imagery 1980-82, National Remote Sensing Agency. Department of Space, Government of India, Hyderabad. (mimeo).

NWDB. 1985. Wasteland development, National Wasteland Development Board, Government of India. (mimeo).

NWDB. 1986a, Report of the committee on fuelwood, Govt. of India, New Delhi. (typescript).

NWDB. 1986b. Discussion papers, Minutes and Decisions: First Meeting of the National Landuse and Wastelands Development Council, New Delhi.

NWDB. 1987a. Description and classification of wastelands, National Wastelands Development Board, New Delhi.

NWDB. 1987b. Microplanning, a tool for social forestry implementation, National Wasteland Development Board, New Delhi.

NWDB. 1987c. Report of the committee on fodder and grasses, National Wastelands Development Board, New Delhi. (mimeo).

NWDB. 1988a. Note for the meeting of the consultative committee of parliament: afforestation, February 19, 1988. (mimeo).

NWDB. 1988b. Agenda papers for the 7th Meeting of the NWDB, dated 9th May, 1988, National Wasteland Development Board, New Delhi. (mimeo).

NWDB. 1988c. A critical appraisal of performance and programme, July 1988, National Wastelands Development Board, New Delhi. (typescript).

ODA. 1986. Karnataka social forestry project, mid-term review, ODA, London.

ODA, 1988. Mid-term evaluation of the Karnataka social forestry project, ODA, London.

Odell, Malcolm, J. 1982. Local institutions and management of communal resources: Lessons from Africa and Asia, *ODI Pastoral Network Paper 14e,* London.

Om. 1986. SIDA-aided Tamil Nadu social forestry project: management study, Om Consultants (India) Pvt. Ltd., Bangalore. (mimeo).

ORG. 1985. Case studies on rehabilitation of degraded forests, sponsored by Directorate of Social Forestry Project. Orissa. Operations Research Group, Bhubaneshwar. (mimeo).

Padmanabhan, B.S. 1988. Groundwater irrigation; delayed recognition of the role, *The Hindu Survey of Indian Agriculture* 1988.

Palanisami, K. 1981. Organisation, management and economics of cooperative lift irrigation schemes in and around Namakkal Taluk, Salem District, Tamil Nadu, India, Department of Agricultural Economics, Tamil Nadu, Agricultural University, Coimbatore, July. (typescript).

Pandit, S.K. 1983. Operation and water management of state deep tubewells in Haryana, in: CBIP, *Symposium on Water Management,* pp. 113-162.

Pant, M.M. 1980. Employment of women in forestry, Paper presented at the Seminar on Role of Women in Community Forestry, Ministry of Agriculture and Cooperation, Government of India. Dehradun. (mimeo).

Pant, Niranjan. 1984. *Organisation, Technology and Performance of Irrigation Systems in Uttar Pradesh,* Giri Institute of Development Studies, B 42, Nirala Nagar, Lucknow.

Parulkar, Vijay. 1982. Pani panchayat can save Bombay, *Imprint,* April 1982, pp. 7-16.

Patel, S.M. and K.V. Patel. 1971. Economics of tubewell irrigation, Indian Institute of Management, Vastrapur, Ahmedabad. (mimeo).

Patel, S.M. and C.B. Gupta. 1979. *Study on Conservation of Light Diesel Oil used in Pumpsets for Lift Irrigation in Gujarat State,* Institute of Co-operative Management, Ellisbridge, Ahmedabad.

Patel, Himmat. 1987. Agro-forestry programmes, *Economic Times.* 11th November, 1987.

PEO. 1968. *Report on the Evaluation of Rural Electrification Programme,* Project Evaluation Organisation, Planning Commission, Government of India, New Delhi, cited in Patel and Patel 1971.

PEO, 1988. Evaluation of the social forestry projects in India, Programme Evaluation Organisation, Planning Commission, New Delhi.

Planning Commission. 1982. Report of the fuelwood study committee, Planning Commission, Government of India.

Prahladachar, M. 1987. Factors promoting and inhibiting the access of small farmers to lift irrigation in Karnataka, in: Workshop of Common Property Resources: Groundwater, organised at Roorkee University, Roorkee 23-25 February, 1987.

Prasad, Durga, et al. 1984. Resource poverty and technology enterprise choices by small farmers in Indian agriculture: An analysis based on seven village reports, Institute of Rural Management, Anand 388 001, India. (mimeo).

PRIA. 1984. *Deforestation in Himachal Pradesh,* Society for Participatory Research in India, New Delhi.

Raintree, John B. (ed.). 1987. *Land Tree and Tenure,* ICRAF and the Land Tenure Center Nairobi and Madison.

Rath, Nilakantha. 1985. Garibi hatao: Can IRDP do it? *Economic and Political Weekly*, 20, 6, February 9, pp. 238-246.

Ray, Siddhartha. 1988. The dying forests of North Bengal, *Amrit Bazar Patrika*, 31st January.

REC, 1980. *Summary: Comparative Study of Flat Rate Tariff and Metered Tariff in Agricultural Sector*, Research and Evaluation Division, Rural Electrification Corporation Ltd., DDA Building, Nehru Place, New Delhi 110 019.

Reddy, Amulya K.N. 1987. On the loss and degradation of tropical forests, Department of Management Studies, Indian Institute of Science, Bangalore. (mimeo).

Repetto, Robert. 1986. *Skimming the Water: Rent Seeking and the Performance of Public Irrigation Systems*, Research Paper 4, World Resource Institute, Washington.

Riddell, James C. 1987. Land tenure and agroforestry: A regional overview, in: John B. Raintree (ed.), *Land Tree and Tenure*, ICRAF and the Land Tenure Center Nairobi and Madison.

Romm, Jeff. 1981. The uncultivated half of India. Centre for Monitoring Indian Economy, Bombay. (mimeo).

Roy, S.N. 1988. Depleting sandalwood production, *Economic Times*, 12th January, 1988.

Sangal, S.P. 1980. Groundwater resources and development. Agricultural Refinance and Development Corporation, Bombay. (mimeo).

Sangal, S.P. 1987a. Economics of irrigation by groundwater sources in alluvial formation with special reference to Uttar Pradesh, in: *Proceedings: Seminar on Groundwater Development —A Perspective for Year 2000 AD*, Indian Water Resources Society, Roorkee, U.P., India.

Sangal, S.P. 1987b. Minor irrigation and groundwater resource, paper for the *First National Water Convention (Proceedings), Vol. II* (Themes 1, 2 and 3) sponsored by Ministry of Water Resources, GOI, organised by CBIP, New Delhi, October.

Satya Sai. 1987. Performance of irrigation farming based on water purchased from fellow farmers, paper presented at the Workshop on Common Property Resources—Groundwater held at Roorkee University, Roorkee, February 23-25.

Saxena, N.C. 1987a. Women in forestry. *Social Action*. Vol. 37. April-June. New Delhi.

Saxena, N.C. 1987b. Commons, trees and the poor in the Uttar Pradesh hills. *ODI Social Forestry Network Paper* 5f. London.

Saxena, N.C. 1988. Participatory planning for wastelands development. FAO. Bangkok.

Seckler, David and Deep Joshi. 1980. Sukhomajri: a rural development programme in India, Ford Foundation, New Delhi. (mimeo).

Sen, Amartya. 1983. How is India doing? *Mainstream*, Republic day. New Delhi.

Sen, D. et al. 1985. Peoples participation in farm forestry. A case study in West Bengal. *Journal of Rural Development*, Hyderabad, 4 (4).

Sen, D. and P.K. Das. 1987. Problems of water management and its socio-economic implications in the command areas of minor irrigation sources. *Journal of Rural Development*. Vol. 6, No. 6, November.

Sen, D. and P.K. Das. 1988. Poverty alleviation through group farm forestry—A case study. *Journal of Rural Development*, November. Hyderabad.

Shah, Anil C. 1987. Whither common property resources. *Wasteland News*. August-October. Society for Promotion of Wastelands Development, New Delhi.

Shah, Tushaar. 1984. Externality and equity implications of groundwater markets in Gujarat, UP and the Punjab, Institute of Rural Management Anand, 388 001, India. (mimeo).

Shah, Tushaar. 1985. Transforming groundwater markets into powerful instruments of small farmer development: Lessons from the Punjab, Uttar Pradesh and Gujarat", *ODI Irrigation Management Network Paper* 11d.

Shah, Tushaar. 1986a. Externality and equity implications of private exploitation of groundwater presented in "National Workshop on Common Property Resources: Groundwater" held at Roorkee University, 23-25 February 1987. Also forthcoming in *Agricultural Systems*.

Shah, Tushaar. 1986b. Transforming groundwater markets into powerful instruments of small farmer development: Field notes from Karimnagar District, Andhra Pradesh, Institute of Rural Management, Anand, 388 001 (mimeo).

Shah, Tushaar and K. Vengama Raju. 1986. Working of groundwater markets in Andhra Pradesh and Gujarat: Results of two village studies, prepared for "Workshop on Common Property Resources: Groundwater" held at Roorkee University, 23-25 February 1987. Also published in *Economic and Political Weekly* no. A-23-28, March 26, 1988.

Shah, Tushaar. 1987a. *Gains from Social Forestry: Lessons from West Bengal,* presented in IDS-ODI Workshop on "Commons, Wastelands, Trees and the Poor: Finding the Right Fi:" at the Institute of Development Studies, University of Sussex, UK, 8-9 June 1987. Published as *ODI Social Forestry Network Paper* October 1987.

Shah, Tushaar. 1987b. Groundwater grids in the villages of Gujarat: Evolution, structure, working and impacts, Institute of Rural Management, Anand. (mimeo).

Shah, Tushaar. 1987c. Profiles of collective action on common property: Community fodder farms in Kheda district. Institute of Rural Management. Anand (mimeo).

Shankar, Kripa. 1981. *Working of Tubewells in Phulpur Block,* Project report no. 3, G. B. Pant Social Science Institute, Allahabad.

Shankar, Kripa. 1987a. Working of private tubewells in Phulpur Tehsil of Allahabad District in UP, paper for the Workshop on Common Property Resources—Groundwater, held at the Water Resource Development Training Centre, University of Roorkee, February.

Shankar, Kripa. 1987b. Sale of trees in South Allahabad. Pant Institute of Social Sciences, Allahabad. (typescript).

Shankar, Kripa. 1988. Private tubewells in Eastern UP, paper presented at the Workshop on Groundwater Development in Eastern UP held at the University of Agricultural Science, Faizabad.

Sharma, I. 1984. Some aspects of shallow tubewells and groundwater development in the Gangetic Basin, ANS Institute of Social Studies, Patna. (mimeo).

Sharma, Indradeo. 1988. Groundwater management in Eastern Uttar Pradesh: A study in under-development, paper presented at the "Workshop on Groundwater Development in Eastern Uttar Pradesh", University of Agricultural Science, Faizabad, 5-6 April.

Shepherd, Gill. 1986. **Forest policies, Forest politics.** *ODI Social Forestry Network Paper 3a.* London.

Shepherd, Gill. 1987. Conflicts and contradictions in social forestry programme. Paper presented at the ODI/IDS seminar, June 1987. Sussex. (mimeo).

Shingi, P.M. et al. 1986. *Development of Social Forestry in India.* Oxford and IBH, New Delhi.

Shiva, V. and J. Bandyopadhyay. 1985. *Ecological Audit of Eucalyptus Cultivation.* English Book Depot. Dehradun.

Shiva, V. and J. Bandyopadhyay. 1986. CHIPKO: *India's Civilisational Response to the Forest Crisis.* The Indian National Trust for Art and Cultural Heritage, New Delhi.

Shukla, Rohit and M.K. Dalvi. 1986. *Evaluation of Gujarat Social Forestry Programme.* Sardar Patel Institute of Economic and Social Research, Ahmedabad.

Shukla, Sanat. 1985. Salinity ingress in coastal areas of Kutch and Saurashtra (Gujarat) No. 8, Vol. 26, June 21-27; Gandhinagar.

Shyam Sunder, S. and A.N. Yellappa Reddy. 1986. **Pressure on our forests.** Included in *Karnataka: State of Environment Report,* edited by Cecil J. Saldanha, Centre for Taxonomic Studies, Bangalore.

Shyam Sunder, S. and S. Parameswarappa. 1987a. Forestry in India. The forester's view. *AMBIO,* Vol. XVI, No. 6.

Shyam Sunder, S. and S. Parameswarappa. 1987b. Social Forestry in Karnataka. *Economic and Political Weekly.* November 21.

SIDA. 1987. Evaluation of the SIDA supported social forestry project in Orissa. SIDA. New Delhi. (mimeo).

SIDA. 1988. *Forestry for the Poor: An Evaluation of the SIDA Supported Social Forestry Project in Tamil Nadu, India.* SIDA. Stockholm, Sweden.

Silliman, Jael and Roberto Lenton. 1987. Irrigation and the land-poor, in Wayne R. Jordan (ed.) *Water and Water Policy in World Food Supplies,* Taxas A and M University Press, College Station, Texas, pp. 161-172.

Singh, Chhatrapati. 1986. *Common Property and Common Poverty: India's Forests. Forest Dwellers and the Law.* Oxford University Press. New Delhi.

Singh, G.B. 1987. Agroforestry in the Indian subcontinent: past, present and future, in H.A. Steppler and P.K.R. Nair (eds.) *Agroforestry: A Decade of Development,* ICRAF, Nairobi.

Singh, Hukum et al. 1982. Stabilisation and Reclamation of Eroded Areas and Wastelands. AR, CSWCRTI, Dehradun.

Singh Jagdesh. 1988a. Impact of lift irrigation on village community: A study of five models, paper presented in the Workshop on the Development and Management of Groundwater Resources in Eastern UP, NDUAT, Faizabad, April 5-6.

Singh, K. K. and S. Satish. 1988. Public tubewells in Uttar Pradesh: Performance and management, paper presented in the Workshop on the Development and Management of Groundwater Resources in Eastern Uttar Pradesh, Narendra Dev University of Agriculture and Technology, Faizabad, April 5-6.

Singh, K.S. 1980. Tribal unrest. Seminar on Development Aspects of Tribal Areas. November 1980. Tribal and Harijan Welfare Department. Government of Orissa. Bhubaneswar.

Singh, R.P. and Mohd. Usman. 1986. Agro-forestry systems for small holdings, in (eds.), R.P. Khosla, Sunil Puri and D.K. Khurana, *Agro-forestry Systems—A New Challenge,* Indian Society of Tree Scientists.

Singh, R.V. 1988b. Forestry and food security in India. Indian Council of Forestry Research and Education. Dehradun. (mimeo).

Singhal M.K. 1988. Conjuctive use of surface and groundwater in Eastern UP, paper for the "Workshop on Groundwater Development in Eastern Uttar Pradesh" held at the University of Agricultural Sciences, Faizabad.

Skutsch, Margaret M. 1986. The not-so-social forestry in Gujarat, India, VOK Working Paper No. 29. University of Twente, The Netherlands. (mimeo).

Slater, Gilbert. 1918. *Economic Studies Volume 1: Some South Indian Villages,* Humphrey Milford, Oxford University Press.

Sohoni, Girish G. 1988. Social forestry: A new perspective. Bharatiya Agro-Industries Foundation, Pune. (mimeo).

Spurr, Stephen H. and Burton V. Barnes. 1980. *Forest Ecology,* 3rd edition, John Wiley and Sons, New York.

SPWD. 1984. Estimates of wastelands in India. Bhumbla, D.R. and Arvind Khare. Society for Promotion of Wastelands Development. New Delhi. (mimeo).

SPWD. 1986. Case Studies of Sukhomajri and Jawaja, Paper presented at International Conference on the Economics of Dryland Degradation, Canberra.

Subbarao, K. 1985. Regional variations in impact of anti-poverty programmes: A review of evidence, *Economic and Political Weekly,* 20, 43 October 26 1985, pp. 1829-1834.

Swaminathan, L.P. 1987. A study on the over-exploitation of groundwater in Coimbatore District, Tamil Nadu, presented at the "Workshop on Common Property Resources: Groundwater", organised at Roorkee University, Roorkee, 23-25 February 1987.

Thakur, D.S. 1985. A survey of literature on rural poverty in India, *Margin,* April, pp. 32-49.

Tiwari, G.C. 1986. Social forestry in Eastern U.P. and Bundelkhand region, G.B. Pant Social Science Institute, Allahabad. (mimeo).

Toulmin, C. and M. Tiffen. 1987. Groundwater management equity, feasibility and efficiency, *ODI-IIMI Irrigation Management Network paper 87/e* Overseas Development Institute, London.

Tripathi, Kamlesh Chandra. 1987. Local Institutions involved in forest management: Panchayat case studies, in: Richard Morse et al. (eds.). *Peoples' Institutions for Forest and Fuelwood Development.* East West Centre.

Tripathi, S.L. 1988. Wastelands management in U.P.—Problems and prospects. Paper presented at the BAIF Workshop on Wasteland Development. Poone. April 1988. (typescript).

TSL. 1986. *Statistical Outline of India 1986-87,* Tatal Services Limited, Department of Economics and Statistics, Bombay House, Bombay 400 001.

UNDP. 1986. India: *Meeting Basic Energy Needs of the Poor.* Rishi Sharma and Ramesh Bhatia. UNDP and ESCAP. New Delhi.

UNICEF. 1987. *The State of the World's Children,* UNICEF, New York.

USAID. 1983. Madhya Pradesh social forestry project. Mid-term evaluation report. USAID. New Delhi. (mimeo).

USAID. 1985a. Maharashtra social forestry project. Mid-term evaluation report. USAID. New Delhi. (mimeo).

USAID. 1985b. Second mid-term evaluation report: Madhya Pradesh. USAID, New Delhi. (mimeo).

USAID. 1988. *National Social Forestry Project. Mid-term Review.* USAID. New Delhi.

Varadan, M.S.S. 1987. Cash and kind incentives. Paper presented in the Workshop on Role of Incentives in Social Forestry, August 1-3, 1987. ISO/Swedforest. New Delhi. (mimeo).

Vidhyarthi, Varun. 1984. Energy and the poor in an Indian village. *World Development,* Vol. 12, no. 8. August, pp. 821-36.

Vohra, B.B. 1985. The greening of India, in J. Bandyopadhyay et al. (eds.) *India's Environment, Crises and Responses.* Natraj, Dehradun.

Vohra, Gautam S.G. 1986. Voluntary action for wastelands development: Case studies of NGOs involved in social forestry. NWDB, New Delhi. (typescript).

Wade, Robert. 1985. Common property resource management in south Indian villages. IBRD. Washington. (mimeo).

Wade, Robert. 1987. The management of common property resources: Collective action as an alternative to privatisation or state regulation. *Cambridge Journal of Economics.* 11.

Wade, Robert. 1988. Why Some Indian Villages Cooperate. *Economic and Political Weekly.* April 16, 1988.

Walker, Thomas S. 1987. Economic prospects for agro-forestry interventions in India's SAT: Implications for research resource allocation at ICRISAT, Hyderabad. (mimeo).

Warner, F. 1982. Background Document on Indo-Swedish Forestry Programme II, Swedish International Development Agency, New Delhi. (mimeo).

WCED. 1987a. *Food 2000: Global Policies for Sustainable Agriculture,* Report of the Advisory Panel on Food Security, Agriculture, Forestry and Environment to the World Commission on Environment and Development, Zed Books. London.

WCED. 1987b. *Our Common Future,* Report of the World Commission on Environment and Development, Oxford University Press, Oxford and New York.

WDR 1984, *World Development Report 1984,* Oxford University Press for the World Bank.

WDR 1986, *World Development Report 1986,* Oxford University Press for the World Bank.

Weirsum, K.F. 1986. Social forestry and agroforestry in India. Report No. 456. Department of Forest Management. Wageningen. The Netherlands. (mimeo).

Westoby, Jack. 1985. Public Lecture at the University of California, Berkley, November 22. USA.

Wilson, J. 1986. Management of community forests in Tamil Nadu. *Indian Forester.* April 1986. pp. 305-313. Dehradun.

Wilson, Patrick H. and Dipak Trivedi. 1988. Eucalyptus—The five-year wonder. VIKSAT. Ahmedabad. (mimeo).

Wood, Geoffrey D. 1982. The socialisation of minor irrigation in Bangladesh, a review and financial analysis of the 81-82 season for 83 groups supported by PROSHIKA as part of the irrigation assets for the rural landless Action Research Programme, Dhaka, October.

Wood, Geoffrey D. 1983. The socialisation of minor irrigation in Bangladesh, PROSHIKA, Dhaka. (mimeo).

Wood, G.D. and R. Palmer-Jones with Q..F. Ahmed, M.A.S. Mandal and S.C. Dutta. 1988. *Social Entrepreneurialism in Rural Bangladesh: Water Selling by the Landless,* PROSHIKA, Dhaka, August.

World Bank. 1987. World Bank Report on forestry in India. Lennart Ljungman, Douglas McGuire and Augusta Molnar. (mimeo).

World Bank. 1988. *India: Wasteland Development Review.* World Bank, Washington.

Abbreviations

AP	=	Andhra Pradesh
CCF	=	Chief Conservator of Forests
CIDA	=	Canadian International Development Agency
CPR	=	common property resource
DDRI	=	Deen Dayal Research Institute
DFO	=	District Forest Officer
FD	=	Forest Department
FR	=	flat (power tariff) rates
FSI	=	Forest Survey of India
GOI	=	Government of India
ha	=	hectare (s)
HP	=	Himachal Pradesh
hp	=	horse power
IAS	=	Indian Administrative Service
IMR	=	infant mortality rate
IRDP	=	Integrated Rural Development Programme
LIS	=	lift irrigation system
MFP	=	minor forest produce
m ha	=	million hectares
m ha m	=	million hectare metres (the volume of water that would cover a million hectares to a depth of one metre)
MP	=	Madhya Pradesh
NABARD	=	National Bank for Agriculture and Rural Development
NCA	=	National Commission on Agriculture 1976
NDDB	=	National Dairy Development Board
NGO	=	non-government organisation
NREP	=	National Rural Employment Programme
NSS	=	National Sample Survey
NWDB	=	National Wastelands Development Board
pc	=	personal communication
PL	=	poverty line
PR	=	pro-rata (power tariff) rate
RLEGP	=	Rural Landless Employment Guarantee Programme
RPF	=	resource-poor farmer or farm family
Rs	=	Rupees, 1 US Dollar = 15 Rs in 1988
SIDA	=	Swedish International Development Agency

SPWD	= Society for Promotion of Wastelands Development
TN	= Tamil Nadu
TOI	= Times of India
UP	= Uttar Pradesh
USAID	= United States Agency for International Development
VIKSAT	= Vikram Sarabhai Centre for Science and Technology, Ahmedabad
WA	= water abundant
WS	= water scarce

Glossary

agroforestry	a collective word for all land-use practices and systems in which woody perennials are deliberately grown on the same land management unit as annual crops and for animals.
achar	*Buchanania lanzan* Spreng
amla	*Emblica officinalis*, yields fruit, tannin and fodder
aquifer	the underground formation of water deposits tapped by wells
arjun	*Terminalia arjuna*; host for tasar silk-worm, an excellent shade tree, bark used in native medicine
babul	*Acacia nilotica*; a small evergreen tree, can stand periodical flooding, hence ideal for tank foreshore afforestation
bamboo	*Bambusa arundinacea* and *Dendrocalamus strictus* are the two most common species; wanted by both paper industry and the poor
ber	*Zizyphus mauritania*; a fruit-yielding tree which is both cultivated and found wild
bhabbar	*Eulaliopsis binata*; grass which can be used for pulp and also ropes
bhoodan	voluntary surrender of land in favour of government or the poor, often such land is infertile
bidi	local cigarette which uses leaves in place of paper
bouldery lands	lands subject to fluvial action in recent past resulting in the presence of gravel boulders at the surface or in sub-soil
cashew	*Anacardium occidentale*
casuarina	*Casuarina equisetifolia*; widely grown in coastal areas for poles and fuelwood.
chiranji	*Buchanania latifolia*.

coconut	*Cocos nucifera*; widely grown on private lands in coastal India. Every part of the tree is used.
competitive market	market conditions which oblige sellers to sell at a price close to average cost
community forestry	growing and protecting of trees on non-private and often non-forest lands, which are known as revenue lands
coppice	re-sprouting of trees after felling
core poverty	deprivation of poor people in the cores or economic heartlands, which are generally more economically developed and accessible to urban centres.
crore	10,000,000
cropping intensity	ratio of gross area cropped during a year to net cropped area
crown cover	area covered by leaves and living branches of a tree
culturable wastes	land suitable for cultivation, but not taken up for cultivation at least in the last five years.
desi	local or indigenous
fallows	land suitable for cultivation, but out of cultivation for a period not exceeding five years.
farm forestry	practice of growing trees by farmers on private lands
flat tariff	electricity cost charged on the basis of the hp rating rather than on actual use
fixed costs	costs such as interest and depreciation which do not vary directly with the level of the use of an equipment
forest dwellers	living inside or in the close vicinity of forests
forest villages	villages set up by the Forest Department inside forests to ensure timely supply of labour for forest operations
gaon sabha	village council
gross irrigated area	area of land irrigated in a year (two irrigation seasons on the same land counting as two)
groves	land, generally private, used for growing fruit trees
gujjar	a nomadic tribe subsisting on cattle rearing, who have now taken to farming in Haryana and northwest U.P.

harijan	Scheduled castes, those who were considered untouchable in the past
incremental pumping cost	direct cost per additional hour of operation of a lift irrigation system
induced groups	groups of water users formed by the effort of an external agent such as an NGO on a government agency
jack	*Artocarpus integrifolia*; a large evergreen tree with dense crown, yields large fruit weighing 5-15 kg
jamun	*Syzygium cumini*; a large evergreen fruit yielding tree bark and seeds are used medicinally
jat	a farming caste of Haryana and western U.P., known for its industriousness and hard work
karanj	*Pongamia pinnata*; a multi-purpose tree used for fuel, fodder and medicines. Seed contains high percentage of oil
khair	*Acacia catechu*; its wood yields commercial catechu which is used for dyeing and tanning
kharif	the summer southwest monsoon season with onset of rain mainly in May and June, and withdrawal of rain mainly in September.
kundis	outlets of a piped, underground water distribution system
kuth	produced from the heartwood of khair (*Acacia catechu*) trees, used in betel-leaf.
kusum	*Schleichera trijuga*; used as a host for the lac insect, seeds yield medicinal and hair oil
lakh	100,000
mahalwari	a system of revenue settlement in which village was the unit for assessment. Mostly prevalent in Punjab and Haryana
mahua	*Madhuca indica*; occurs most commonly near tribal habitations in Central India, flowers and seeds and rich in oil, and are eaten
major irrigation	irrigation systems with command areas of over 10,000 ha
malguzari	land revenue levied by the state on cropped lands
medium irrigation	irrigation systems with command areas of between 2,000 and 10,000 ha

minor irrigation	irrigation systems, whether lift or surface gravity, with command areas of up to 2,000 hectares
mixed forests	forests raised for preserving biological diversity and ecological stability which provide a variety of livelihood goods to the gatherers
monopoly power	power to raise the price without losing a substantial chunk of one's market
moonj	coarse grass used for thatching, and weaving baskets and cots; controls sand dunes
mulberry	*Morus alba*; leaves are used as food for silkworms, fruit is eaten, and its wood is used for sport goods
net irrigated area	area of land surface that receives irrigation water in a year, two irrigation seasons counting as one
non-rotational trees	trees which are used for recurrent benefits of fruits, leaves etc. There is no organised felling of such trees. This type of management is also known as physical rotation.
neem	*Azadirachta indica*; considered a sacred and health-giving tree because of its insecticidal and medicinal properties
oak	*Quercus spp.*, multiple use trees, used for fodder and making agricultural implements
palmyrah	*Borassus flabellifer*, used mainly for extraction of toddy. Leaves are used for thatching and for carrying water
panchayat	village council. lowest form of local government, consists of elected members headed by a chairman
panchayat lands	non-private lands under the control of village councils
pani panchayat	water council
pastures	open access lands meant for grazing; often highly degraded
patta	literal meaning is contract, refers to leasing of government land on specific terms, also means title deed to land
peripheral poverty	deprivation of poor people in the peripheries, which are generally less economically developed and less accessible to urban centres

poles	wood of diameter less than 20-25 cm, which is generally used for scaffolding and as posts
poplar	an agroforestry tree, has grown well in Haryana, Punjab and western U.P., timber used for matchwood, veneer and sport goods
production forestry	growing of trees of commercial value on forest lands
pro-rata tariff	electricity cost charged on actual metered consumption of power
rabi	the winter cropping season
resource-poor	applied to farms, farmers and farm families, means that the farm resources do not currently permit a decent and secure family livelihood. Such families include many, tough not all, of those with marginal (0-1 ha) and small (1-2 ha) farm holdings, and many others with more than 2 ha but whose land is infertile, vulnerable to floods or erosion, or subject to low and unreliable rainfall
revenue lands	lands under the control of revenue department, these are non-forest and non-private lands, often highly degraded
rotation	time interval between regeneration of a tree and its felling
ryotwari	a system of land settlement in which cultivators pay land revenue directly to government
sabai grass	*Eulaliopsis binata*
sal	*Shorea robusta*; a common but slow growing large tree in Indian forests. Yields both timber and important MFPs like seeds and leaves
saline ingress	intrusion of sea water into coastal aquifers
salvadora	*Salvadora persica* and *Salvadora oleoides*
santhal	name of a tribe of south Bihar and West Bengal
sapota	*Parkia roxburgii* gives fuel, fruit and medicines
sarpanch	chairman of panchayat
sarpagandha	*Rauwolfia serpentina*
sheesham	*Dalbergia sissoo*; a favourite road-side tree in north India, wood used for wheels, boats and furniture
sisal	*Agave* spp., yields fibre and binds soil

social forestry	programme of growing trees to satisfy rural needs of fuelwood, small timber and fodder, and to enhance farmers' incomes
spontaneous groups	groups of water users formed and sustained by their own initiative
stylosanthes	a cultivated grass of high nutritive value
subabul	*Leucaena leucocephala*, a fast-growing nitrogen-fixing tree, yields both fodder leaves and fuelwood
tamarind	*Tamarindus indica*; an evergreen multipurpose tree, yields edible sour fruits, fodder and timber
tasar	silk tasar, a product of insects which are cultivated on the leaves of arjun and sal trees
teak	*Tectona grandis*; highly valued for quality timber used in furniture, house building and cabinets
tendu	*Diospyros melanoxylon*; used as wrappers of tobacco to produce *bidi*, Indian cigarettes
timber	tree logs of more than 25 cm diameter, used for making sawn planks
tribals	nomadic people who till recently lived by hunting and gathering of forest products
unculturable wastelands	covers all barren and unculturable land like steep mountains, snows, deserts etc.
water intensive	crop enterprises using large quantities of water
zamindari	system of land ownership by non-cultivators, which has now been legally abolished

Author Index

Subject Index